Breaking
the
SILENCE

Breaking the SILENCE

Overcoming
the
Problem
of
Principal
Mistreatment
of
Teachers

Joseph Blase

Jo Blase

CORWIN PRESS, INC.
A Sage Publications Company
Thousand Oaks, California

For information:

Corwin Press, Inc.
A Sage Publications Company
2455 Teller Road
Thousand Oaks, California 91320
www.corwinpress.com

Sage Publications Ltd.
6 Bonhill Street
London EC2A 4PU
United Kingdom

Sage Publications India Pvt. Ltd.
M-32 Market
Greater Kailash I
New Delhi 110 048 India

Printed in the United States of America

Library of Congress Cataloging-in-Publication Data

Blase, Joseph.
  Breaking the silence: Overcoming the problem of principal mistreatment of teachers / Joseph Blase, Jo Blase.
      p. cm.
Includes bibliographical references and index.
  ISBN 0-7619-7771-6 (cloth) — ISBN 0-7619-7772-4 (pbk.)
  1. Teachers—Job stress. 2. School principals. 3. Psychological abuse. 4. Bullying in the workplace—Prevention. 5.
Work—Psychological aspects. I. Blase, Jo Roberts. II. Title.
  LB2840.2 .B53 2002
    371.2′012—dc21   20020051777

This book is printed on acid-free paper.

03 04 05 06 10 9 8 7 6 5 4 3 2 1

Acquisitions Editor:	Robb Clouse
Editorial Assistant:	Erin Clow
Developmental Editor:	Ann West
Copy Editor:	Toni Williams
Typesetter:	C&M Digitals (P) Ltd., Chennai, India
Proofreader:	Teresa Herlinger
Indexer:	Teri Greenberg
Cover Designer:	Michael Dubowe
Production Artist:	Michelle Lee

Contents

Foreword

From a district leadership perspective, it's important to recognize the importance of this book in the context of our contemporary political and philosophical climate as it pertains to public education. The authors accurately note the "existential insecurity, instability, and lowered self-esteem" which characterize American teachers' experience during a time when politicians and critics diligently work to manipulate and control the direction and spirit of education in the United States.

Leaders who attempt to work with teachers and principals to promote systemic change within this environment realize district efforts to create a positive atmosphere and common purpose leading to improved student achievement and well-being are hindered by behaviors which create a loss of trust among school professionals. Funding difficulties, curricular narrowing, high-stakes testing of debatable utility, special interest advocacy, and other factors already conspire to evoke a feeling of powerlessness and frustration among staff. When these elements are combined with a teacher's perception that "I will probably never truly trust an administrator again," it's hard to imagine how the organizational *gestalt* essential for reform and improvement can be generated and sustained in a district or school. In this vein, the authors aptly quote Bok, whose statement that "Trust and integrity are precious resources, easily squandered, hard to regain" illustrates what we all know about administrative-staff relations.

For all these reasons, this book should come with a warning. The challenges implicit in these findings reflect issues affecting the gamut of school performance and the success of related initiatives to guide and improve teaching and learning: abuse and denigration of staff members is seldom dealt with easily or without creative, dedicated effort and courage. The research and the findings presented in this book must not be brushed aside as a natural outcome of human interaction in the form of so-called personality conflicts or as grousing from poorly performing staff members. On the contrary, the complexity and depth of change required to ensure consistent progress in education demands that the problem of mistreatment of teachers be taken very seriously and that appropriate preventative and corrective action serve as one of the keystones of growth and productivity in district and school cultures.

Over the past two decades, Joseph and Jo Blase have shown a clear, prolific, and reliable dedication to describing behaviors and organizational practice consistent with the cultural and individual growth necessary to support a productive instructional climate and positive student-teacher interaction. Their work and writing reflects my belief that school-based, collaborative, shared decision making, and genuine inclusion, in concert with parallel district leadership-level activities, constitute a major tactical tenet of school improvement. Not surprisingly, I've found that boards of education and superintendents, regardless of their degree of dedication and effort, will fail in their efforts to improve school performance without the guidance of principals and teachers working together and with an energy based on trust and belief in a commonly accepted vision. Staff leadership, systematically encouraged and facilitated, lies at the heart of true reform, if we want to use that term. In preceding books by Blase and Blase, that has been the message. Now, these researchers turn their attention to what they refer to as a "dark side" of administrative behavior which intrudes on and obstructs the ideals of organizational development they have promoted so convincingly in their earlier work. The result of their courage is truly a groundbreaking effort and one that deserves serious attention.

In the course of this book, the authors draw on a growing background of research describing workplace mistreatment and abuse throughout American industry and across a broad range of organizations and occupations. They employ this background of research to help characterize different levels and types of damaging supervisory behavior. Experienced administrators will see parallels and familiar examples as they follow escalating examples of mistreatment and principals' bullying of teachers through the early chapters. Although the spirit and impact of the anecdotal records vary somewhat, a characteristic of this sort of qualitative research, it's clear that a teacher's effectiveness and energy must dissipate after months and years of the kind of negativity and ambivalence described herein. Further, the authors convincingly describe the continuing emotional and somatic impact of a frightening range of belittling, isolating, and condemning behaviors on teachers' personal lives and relationships.

Blase and Blase's findings leave us to struggle not only with the notion of barriers to organizational growth but with violation of standards of decency and humanity which fly in the face of our beliefs and values as educators. These are tough issues to face and fathom, indeed. However, if the referenced literature regarding mistreatment of employees in the American workplace accurately reflects the frequency and pervasive nature of these behaviors, the imperatives are clear. Both central office and building-level educational leaders must commit themselves to support and assist each other and our teaching staffs to minimize interpersonal strife and the resulting anxiety and fear which detract from the growth and success of individuals, schools, and districts. If we doubt for a moment the importance of dealing with the problem of teacher mistreatment, we need only read articulate and truth-ringing statements from apparently outstanding classroom teachers who have lost their zest for teaching or been reduced to the practice of "defensive teaching." These attitudes are inconsistent with the work we're all trying to do.

Given today's scrutiny of public education and the attendant advance of varying qualities and quantities of accountability measures with their resulting initiatives, the task seems daunting. Principals are faced with a raft of requirements and increased expectations from all levels. The art of balancing a demanding sense of responsibility for data-based results and a need to foster positive and collaborative relationships with staff can be vexing and difficult. Statutory and policy-based constraints often ensure the difficulty of pursuing the perfect equilibrium of fairness to the individual and high quality instruction for students. In this climate, school and district leadership requires even greater extension of consistent and positive interchange between players. Blase and Blase make it clear that "overtly or covertly authoritarian" leadership styles are incompatible with these demands and that those styles can be regularly identified as leading to the dysfunction they've identified in this study.

Those of us on the job in central administration usually don't have to look far to find evidence of staff mistreatment in our own organizations. In my work, I've been faced with the need to replace school leaders whose intimidating and insulting styles placed entire schools and district-wide relations at risk. As we examine the possible effects, well described in this book, of these and similar conditions on our schools and students, we may find ourselves discouraged and on the horns of a veritable administrative dilemma. How can we best use policy, evaluation, coaching, and other tools to construct an institutional spirit designed to improve relationships and minimize the destructive impact they may bring to our organizations? Is this possible and can we sustain a positive political climate among our leadership staff as we do so? These are hard questions to answer. In that regard, we should be thankful that the authors promise us further work designed to sniff out the most successful practices for accomplishing those ends. We should read this work with an open mind and a vision of what we seek together in the future of American education. Beyond that, we can look forward to the assistance and support we're assured of gaining from their ongoing research. In order to help us to not become discouraged or dismayed by this component of the many tasks before us, Jo and Joseph provide at one point a remarkably telling quote from J. R. R. Tolkien. His inspiring observation is worth looking for. On the way to discovering it, I predict that most of us will find ourselves on an exceptionally important road toward further growth in our capability to sense and respond to the needs of our schools and districts.

— Don Saul
AASA American Superintendent of the Year, 2000
Deputy Superintendent, International School Bangkok
Former Superintendent, Loveland-Thompson School District, Colorado

Foreword

The relatively recent attention in educational research to the *micropolitics* of schools—to which the authors have made a major contribution—has opened up new possibilities for exploring what Hoyle (1986) refers to as "the dark side of organizational life" in schools and school districts (p. 87). Rational approaches to organizational life tend to overlook micropolitics altogether or treat it as an inevitable but minor aspect of school life. In this book, Blase and Blase take up a dimension of the underside of organizational life that is not only ignored, but, as they convincingly argue, is often responsible for poor schools. Just as abusive teachers cannot preside over a caring and rigorous classroom, abusive principals cannot foster the kind of caring learning communities schools require to be successful. Furthermore, as the authors point out, an abusive principal is more likely to foster abusive teachers. Principals' abuse has a ripple effect that impacts not only teachers, but their colleagues and students as well as their relationships with friends and family.

However, as important as the implications of this book are for school improvement and student achievement, its most powerful contribution is its thick description of the behaviors abusive principals engage in and the multiple ways abuse affects individual teachers. Anyone who has experienced an abusive organizational environment will find this book cathartic. While many of us have learned to recognize the signs of abuse in marriages and families, with the exception of sexual abuse, workplace abuse has gone largely unexamined. This book will help teachers identify those behaviors that they may have come to tolerate because they have failed to view them as abusive, and this book will help school administrators recognize their own potentially destructive behaviors.

Perhaps more disturbing to some of these teachers than the abuse they received from their principals was the silence or lack of support by their colleagues and in some cases their families. Moreover, some abused teachers felt like scapegoats who were being blamed for larger problems the principal was either incapable of or unwilling to address. This problem of teacher scapegoating has interesting implications for current school reform. Some have half-jokingly referred to current teacher accountability systems that rely on high-stakes testing, scripted curricula, and increased surveillance and work intensification as "teacher abuse." They point to the tendency to make teachers scapegoats for poor student performance in low-income areas.

The current reform discourse of "no excuses" not only implies that teachers are not doing their jobs, but also shuts down needed discussion of the neglect of our inner cities which have been gutted of jobs and the economic and social capital needed for communities and families to prosper. Thus, teachers and public schools are blamed for social and economic policies that have left our society more divided by race and class than at any time since the Gilded Age of the 1920s. One cannot help but wonder if this climate of blame and finger pointing will not embolden these abusive principals to justify their abuse as "tough love" defense of disenfranchised students.

While we would all agree that consistently bad teaching should not be tolerated by administrators, the data Blase and Blase present suggest that it is most often the good teachers that incur the wrath of abusive principals. Press reports bear out the fact that it is not uncommon for particularly creative and dynamic teachers and principals to end up the target of irate administrators and school boards. According to Argyris and Schön (1974), organizations have a way of protecting mediocrity and being threatened by professionals who rock the boat by standing out. They characterize organizations as displaying *dynamic conservatism*, a tendency to maintain a stable state which defends them against change. Whether the cause is conservative organizations, professional jealousy, or something else, Blase and Blase have done a major service in calling attention to a phenomenon that is robbing education of many of its brightest and most competent teachers.

The implications of this book for research are significant. Blase and Blase have opened a door to a plethora of new questions about the causes and manifestations of mistreatment and possible ways to break the cycle. But the implications for both administrator and teacher preparation are even more exciting: How do we better prepare teachers for this dark side of the micropolitics of school life? How do we help them identify the various gradations of principal mistreatment and the forms it can take? How can teachers, both as individuals and in group solidarity, fight back when confronted with the kinds of mistreatment the authors document? How do we identify the characteristics of principals with a tendency toward abuse before we credential them? How do we raise the consciousness of principals about what constitutes abuse and mistreatment of teachers? How do leaders foster school cultures in which abusive behavior is not tolerated?

Unfortunately, many teachers will identify with the abused teachers in this book. The first step to eliminating teacher abuse is to get folks talking about it and show abused teachers they are not alone. This book represents the beginning of a much needed conversation about teacher abuse. The result will be that the dark side of organizational life will be opened up to scrutiny, making it harder for abusive administrators to take cover there.

—Gary L. Anderson
Professor of Educational Administration
California State University, Los Angeles

REFERENCES

Argyris, C., & Schön, D. (1974). *Organizational learning*. Reading, MA: Addison-Wesley.

Hoyle, E. (1986). *The politics of school management*. London: Hodder and Stroughton.

**CORWIN
PRESS**

The Corwin Press logo—a raven striding across an open book—represents the happy union of courage and learning. We are a professional-level publisher of books and journals for K-12 educators, and we are committed to creating and providing resources that embody these qualities. Corwin's motto is "Success for All Learners."

Acknowledgments

We appreciate the enthusiastic support for this book from our fellow academics: Gary Anderson, Colleen Capper, Bill Greenfield, Catherine Marshall, Mike Martin, and Charol Shakeshaft.

This book is better than it might have been, due to the feedback we received from teachers, administrators, state department officials, and colleagues who conscientiously critiqued drafts of our manuscript: Lea Arnau, Lisa DeGironimo, Debra Gallagher, Mike McGonigle, Vicky Husby, Ellen Sabatini, and John Smith. We are especially grateful to Brenda Beatty for her thoughtful comments and criticism and to Gary Anderson and Don Saul for their splendid forewords.

We wish to express our thanks to Robb Clouse, our editor at Corwin Press, who has encouraged us and provided guidance throughout this endeavor. For her interest, patience, kindness, and expertise over the past decade, we are profoundly grateful to our dear friend Gracia Alkema, founder and President Emerita of Corwin Press.

We are indebted to the tireless and accurate work of our technical assistants, transcriptionists, research assistants, typists, and editors: Angie Callaway, Amanda Fisher, Donna Bell, Teresa Wood, Ann West, and Toni Williams.

We are also indebted to others who have previously studied the phenomenon of workplace abuse. We hope our work enhances the rapidly expanding body of research on this problem.

We acknowledge the mistreated teachers whose stories we are able to tell only because they braved the perils of exposing the dark and frightening phenomenon that damages those who work and learn in our schools.

Finally, we acknowledge American teachers and principals, our national treasure.

To the courageous and honorable teachers who shared a profoundly
traumatic part of their lives so that others might be helped.

About the Authors

 **Joseph Blase** is a Professor of Educational Leadership and Codirector of ATLAS, the Alliance for Teaching, Leadership, and School Improvement, in the College of Education at the University of Georgia. Since receiving his Ph.D. in 1980 from Syracuse University, his research has focused on understanding the work lives of teachers. He has published many studies in the areas of teacher stress, relationships between teachers' personal and professional lives, teacher socialization, and principal-teacher relationships. His work concentrating on school-level micropolitics received the 1988 Davis Memorial Award given by the University Council for Educational Administration, and his coauthored article published in the *Journal of Educational Administration* won the W. G. Walker 2000 Award for Excellence. He edited *The Politics of Life in Schools: Power, Conflict, and Cooperation* (winner of the 1994 Critic's Choice Award sponsored by the American Education Studies Association, Sage, 1991); coauthored, with Peggy Kirby, *Bringing Out the Best in Teachers* (Corwin, 1994, 2000); coauthored, with Jo Blase, Gary Anderson, and Sherry Dungan, *Democratic Principals in Action: Eight Pioneers* (Corwin, 1995); coauthored, with Gary Anderson, *The Micropolitics of Educational Leadership* (Teachers College Press, 1995); and coauthored, with Jo Blase, *Empowering Teachers* (Corwin, 1994, 2000), *The Fire Is Back: Principals Sharing School Governance* (Corwin, 1997), and *Handbook of Instructional Leadership* (Corwin, 1998). His numerous articles appear in journals such as the *American Education Research Journal* and *Educational Administration Quarterly*.

 **Jo Blase** is Professor of Educational Leadership and Codirector of ATLAS, the Alliance for Teaching, Leadership, and School Improvement, at the University of Georgia, and a former public school teacher, high school and middle school principal, and director of staff development. She received a Ph.D. in educational administration, curriculum, and supervision in 1983 from the University of Colorado at Boulder. Through work with the Beginning Principal Study National Research Team, the Georgia League of Professional Schools, and public and private school educators with whom she consults throughout the United States, she has pursued her interest in preparation for and entry to educational and instructional leadership as it relates to supervisory discourse. Winner of the W. G. Walker 2000 Award for Excellence for her coauthored article published in the *Journal of Educational Administration*, the 1997 University of Georgia College of Education Teacher Educator Award, and the 1983 American Association of School Administrators Outstanding Research Award, her recent publications include articles in the *Journal of Staff Development*, the *Journal of Curriculum and Supervision*, *Educational Administration Quarterly*, and *The Alberta Journal of Educational Research*; and four books, *Empowering Teachers: What Successful Principals Do* (with Joseph Blase, Corwin, 1994, 2000), *Democratic Principals in Action: Eight Pioneers* (with Joseph Blase, Gary Anderson, and Sherry Dungan, Corwin, 1995), *The Fire Is Back: Principals Sharing School Governance* (with Joseph Blase, Corwin, 1997), and *Handbook of Instructional Leadership* (with Joseph Blase, Corwin, 1998). She has authored chapters on becoming a principal, school renewal, supervision, and organizational development. She also conducts research on supervisory discourse among physicians as medical educators.

1 The Problem of Principal Mistreatment of Teachers

Truth is not only violated by falsehood; it may be equally outraged by silence.

— Henri Frédéric Amiel (*Webster's Book of Quotations*, 1992)

PROLOGUE: A PERSONAL NOTE

This book is written for all concerned with the improvement of public education in the United States, especially public educators themselves, prospective and practicing school principals and teachers, superintendents, district office supervisors, staff developers, boards of education, and state department officials as well as professors of educational leadership and teacher education. *Breaking the Silence* addresses a problem that has heretofore been neglected in the scholarly and professional literature in the areas of both educational leadership and teacher education. It deals with a situation that has not been exposed to light, whose silence has been without challenge, and for which public and professional awareness, scrutiny, and improvement efforts have not been forthcoming. This information exposes what may be a surprisingly common problem that has alarmingly destructive effects on teachers as professionals and as people, one that reaches directly into classrooms to drastically undermine and even destroy opportunities for effective instruction and student learning. The powerholders who create this problem and those who collude by permitting it to continue are participating in a phenomenon that has the potential to devastate an entire school, even an entire school system, by relentlessly and unconscionably crushing its spirit and destroying educators' morale, commitment, trust, caring, hope, and basic human rights, including the right to respectful and dignified treatment.

Breaking the Silence is about long-term patterns of principal mistreatment of public school teachers.

As public school teachers, school administrators, and for the past two decades as professors of educational leadership, both of us have career-long commitments to the improvement of public school education. Throughout our careers, we have heard heartbreaking stories from exemplary teachers, stories about principals who bully teachers, and we have listened in disbelief and shock to descriptions of the profoundly devastating consequences such mistreatment has for teachers professionally and personally, psychologically, and physically. Principal mistreatment of teachers is surely a dark topic, one that has undoubtedly been a part of the legacy of public education in the United States for some time; it is also a problem for which there exists literally no research base. Three years ago we commenced the study that yielded the findings we reveal to you throughout this book. As strange as it may sound, *Breaking the Silence* has been our labor of love. In many respects, the study was the most difficult we ever conducted. However, as we examined each painful experience encountered in our database, we became convinced of the incredible significance of our topic.

We believe that this is the right time to break the silence, as it were, that has surrounded and concealed the reality of principal mistreatment of teachers from professional and public scrutiny. We also believe that all of us, especially educators, must recognize our own role, directly and indirectly, in keeping this behavior from view. Principal mistreatment of teachers is an insidious and elusive problem. Even if confronted by people of integrity and courage, the issue is potentially explosive, requiring special attention. We are taking the first step to break the silence by providing the opportunity for people to speak of these awful secrets. It is our hope that our work will help in creating the awareness and compassionate understanding required to design and implement preventative and corrective programs and policies; by doing so, we hope to begin to overcome this problem constructively and systemically. We expect this will include, among other things, serious reconsideration of administrator hiring practices, evaluation procedures, and professional development opportunities as well as development of sound mediation and grievance processes for victims of mistreatment. Put differently, these chapters are more than an exposé; they were written to encourage those responsible for public education at all levels as they provide practical support structures for both the victims of mistreatment and the purveyors of such mistreatment.

Our study of teacher mistreatment is based on a qualitative research protocol designed specifically to describe and conceptualize the mistreatment problem under investigation. This is the first study of its kind. However, a study of this nature does not produce statistical generalizations; therefore, we offer no conclusions about the pervasiveness of the mistreatment problem. Our next study will attempt to answer that question. Having said this, it is important to note that other researchers who have used survey protocols to study large samples of the general population estimate that between 10 and 20% of all American employees work for an abusive boss. Perhaps more important, these same researchers have found that victims of boss abuse seldom have viable sources of help available to ameliorate their situations. Given this, we suggest that there may be significant numbers of school principals who routinely mistreat teachers and much larger numbers of teachers who, if the estimates are correct, find they have little or no recourse available to redress their dreadful fates.

As professors of educational leadership, we have spent decades researching and teaching about school leadership. We are aware that school principals are confronted with what seem to be insurmountable challenges and pressures: their work is characterized by long hours and inadequate compensation (Olson, 1999), and they now face an explosion of demands and pressures related to school safety and violence, drugs, diversity, inclusion, site budgeting, aging teaching staffs, and unresponsive bureaucracies (Rusch, 1999) as well as new responsibilities linked to school reform, including new power arrangements, collaborative planning, evaluation, and accountability (Murphy & Louis, 1994a). We are also aware that principals are confronted with unique challenges associated with the retention of quality teachers, inadequate facilities and instructional materials, and discouraged, disillusioned faculties (Steinberg, 1999). Moreover, we recognize that such challenges can result in dramatic emotional experiences for principals (Ginsberg & Davies, 2001); feelings of anxiety, loss of control, disempowerment, insecurity, anger, and frustration are not uncommon (Beatty, 2000; Evans, 1996). *Indeed, we cannot adequately express our appreciation and respect for the women and men who meet such challenges with professional integrity, courage, and ingenuity.*

More than ever before, school reform efforts require that principals and teachers at the school level work together collaboratively to solve educational problems. Such collaboration is successful when school principals build trust in their schools. Trust, in turn, serves as a foundation for open, honest, and reflective professional dialogue; problem solving; innovative initiatives; and, more directly, the development of the school as a powerful community of learners willing to take responsibility for success and are capable of achieving it. All principals need to work toward such ends, and all educational scholars need to willingly confront the kinds of administrative mistreatment that, most assuredly, undermine such possibilities.

We wish to offer a cautionary note. Feedback from teachers, administrators, and researchers who reviewed an earlier draft of this manuscript recommended we advise readers that this book may be upsetting: Some reviewers experienced strong feelings of sadness, anger, and anxiety about the many forms of principal mistreatment reported by teachers and the life-altering effects of such treatment.

INTRODUCTION

The "Bright Side" of School Leadership

In 1916, John Dewey eloquently explicated the notion of democracy with respect to educational leadership:

A democracy is more than a form of government; it is primarily a mode of associated living, of conjoint communicated experience. The extension in space of the number of individuals who participate in an interest so that each has to refer his own action to that of others, and to consider the actions of others to give point and direction to his own, is equivalent to the breaking down of those barriers of class, race, and national territory which kept men from perceiving the full impact of their activity. (p. 87)

Three decades later, Tyler (1949) advised educational leaders to use teachers' perspectives and experiences when developing curriculum, instruction, and educational policy. Indeed, for the past half a century, effective educational leadership, having been repeatedly examined with respect to functions, roles, personal attributes, and culture (Ogawa & Bossert, 1995), and with respect to principles, behaviors, and organizational outcomes (Davis, 1998), remains significantly contingent upon notions such as democracy, empowerment, the creation of learning communities, and supportive school culture (Blase & Blase, 1996; Leithwood, Thomlinson, & Genge, 1996; Murphy & Louis, 1994b). For example, Foster (1986) stated,

Leadership is not manipulating a group in order to achieve a preset goal; rather it is empowering individuals in order to evaluate what goals are important and what conditions are helpful. The educative use of leadership results in the empowerment of followers. The leader here is truly concerned with the development of followers, with the realization of followers' potential to become leaders themselves. (pp. 185-186)

More dramatically, Albrecht (1988) wrote the following:

[Effective educational leaders] believe teachers are their professional allies and colleagues. . . . Encourage teachers to spend time in thoughtful reflection about what we are doing in this educational business . . . [and] seize every opportunity to help teachers broaden and elevate their vision about the nature of education, the mission of schools, the obligation of public education to every student and the importance of helping kids be successful. . . . The obstacles to overcome are the siren songs of the traditional rewards system. . . . Real leaders know that educational leadership begins and ends with proper regard for the integrity and professionalism of teachers. . . . (p. 30)

In essence, principals' work involves "getting things done through people" via participation, communication, team building, and motivation (Friedkin & Slater, 1994; Krug, Ahadi, & Scott, 1991, p. 242; Leithwood, Jantzi, Ryan, & Steinbach, 1997). Further, school principals' influence on instruction, effected through support of teachers' efforts to improve instruction, is critical to students' academic performance (Heck & Hallinger, 1999). Leithwood et al. (1996) found that such transformational leadership is positively related to student participation in school, to student learning, and to teachers' professional commitment, job satisfaction, collective professional learning, and productive school culture.

Blase and Blase (2001) found that exemplary transformational principals significantly affected teachers' behavior, thinking, and attitudes; a principal's encouragement of autonomy and innovation, for example, enhances teachers' self-esteem, confidence, professional satisfaction, creativity, sense of classroom efficacy, and ability to reflect on instructional issues. Generally, the leadership approaches used by effective transformational principals positively influence all major aspects of teachers' work:

- The *affective* dimension: teachers' satisfaction, motivation, esteem, confidence, security, sense of inclusion, identification with the group and its work
- The *classroom* dimension: teachers' innovation, creativity, reflection, autonomy, individualization of instruction, professional growth, classroom efficacy
- The *schoolwide* dimension: teachers' expression, ownership, commitment, and schoolwide efficacy

The following comments from teachers illustrate the significant positive outcomes of exemplary transformational leadership:

Our principal involves every faculty member in educational decisions and believes that we are capable of making intelligent decisions. Shared decision making makes me feel empowered. I am more involved in school matters and feel the need to keep abreast of current educational issues. I communicate more with my colleagues and find myself eager to attend meetings because I know I will be actively participating rather than passively listening. (Blase & Blase, 2001, pp. 42-43)

The principal is very receptive to new ideas and ways of doing things. She values the opinions of all her staff members. She realizes that our school and our students are unique and welcomes suggestions and ideas for improving instruction. We have an instructional task force that continually teaches new methods of instruction and we are encouraged to try new techniques. (Blase & Blase, 2001, p. 90)

Anybody who knows our principal can sense her love for what she does; she loves people, and kids especially. And her enthusiasm is contagious. She can make me feel that I'm capable of accomplishing almost anything that I tackle. I feel motivated and I keep working, planning, and trying to be better. (Blase & Blase, 2001, p. 96)

Specifically, Blase and Blase (2001) found that exemplary transformational principals contribute to teachers' growth and development by

- Modeling, building, and persistently supporting an environment of trust and openness among teachers, whom they consider professionals and experts
- Systematically structuring schools to encourage authentic collaboration by establishing readiness and common goals and by responding to the school's unique characteristics

- Supporting shared decision-making efforts by providing basic resources for teachers' professional development
- Maintaining the school's focus on teaching and learning
- Supporting teacher experimentation and innovation, granting professional autonomy, and viewing failure as an opportunity to learn
- Modeling professional behavior, especially by exhibiting a sense of caring, optimism, honesty, friendliness, and enthusiasm
- Encouraging risk taking and minimizing threat (or constraints on teacher discretion and growth)
- Praising teachers and using other symbolic rewards (e.g., valuing and respecting teachers)
- Setting the stage for confronting the metaproblems of the school through effective communication, action research, and exemplary procedural methods for solving problems

To be sure, a strong stream of "bright side" empirical research focuses on the considerable contribution of exemplary school principals to schools in general and to teacher development and student learning in particular. In stark contrast, no empirical studies have systematically examined the "dark side" of school leadership and the resulting harmful consequences. *Breaking the Silence* describes types of principal behavior that teachers define as "abuse" or "mistreatment" (teachers who participated in our study used both terms synonymously) and how such behavior undermines teachers, classroom instruction, and student learning.

Why This Book?

It is widely acknowledged that power is a fundamental dimension of all human relationships (Muth, 1989; Russell, 1938) and is central to understanding relationships between administrators and subordinates in organizational settings (Burns, 1978; Gardner, 1990; Gibb, 1954; Kets de Vries, 1989). Likewise, administrators, in general, exercise power in both constructive and destructive ways; in both cases, the exercise of power has considerable effects on individuals and organizations (Kreisberg, 1992; Muth, 1989; Pfeffer, 1992). In fact, prominent power theorists have demonstrated that power itself may have a corrupting effect on a powerholder and even those over whom power is exercised (e.g., Kets de Vries, 1989; Kipnis, 1972; Nyberg, 1981). Kipnis, for example, has described the potential *metamorphic* (or corrupting) effects of power on powerholders. Lord Acton's (1948) famous aphorism, "Power tends to corrupt and absolute power corrupts absolutely," speaks directly to the problematic nature of power; it also describes in a nutshell one aspect of the findings from our study, as the reader shall see.

To date, two long-standing avenues of research in education (teacher stress studies and micropolitical studies of the school principal-teacher relationship) have produced only glimpses of how principals misuse power and, specifically, how principals mistreat (abuse) teachers. For example, a number of stress studies have linked elements of principals' leadership style and behavior (e.g., non-support, assertiveness) to significant stress and burnout in teachers (Adams, 1988;

Barnette, 1990; Blase, Strathe, & Dedrick, 1986; Diehl, 1993; Dunham, 1984; Dworkin, Haney, Dworkin, & Telschow, 1990). Micropolitical studies have yielded richer descriptions of some aspects of principal mistreatment; these studies describe, among other things, principal favoritism with regard to appointments, promotions, enforcement of rules, evaluations, and recognition and rewards (Blase, 1988a). Other micropolitical studies have examined principal behaviors including sanctions, harassment, lack of accessibility, and manipulation as well as teachers' response to such behaviors (Ball, 1987, Blase, 1990, 1991a; Blase & Anderson, 1995).

Taken together, these two research directions provide provocative clues to the principal mistreatment problem and its destructive outcomes for teachers; however, such studies are few in number and have generated only limited understandings of, for example, the range of abusive principal behaviors; how such behaviors interact to form a pattern of abuse in a given situation; and their damaging effects on teachers, teaching, and schools.

It should be mentioned that, in education, some empirical work has been published on sexual harassment of students by teachers and other professional staff (Shakeshaft & Cohan, 1995). A more substantial collection of studies on peer harassment among schoolchildren focuses on verbal bullying—threatening, degrading, teasing, humiliating, name calling, sarcasm, put downs, and silent treatment—and its devastating effects on victims (Clarke & Kiselica, 1997; Ma, 2001; Olweus, 1993; Shakeshaft, Mandel, Johnson, Sawyer, Hergenrother, & Barber, 1997). The Dylan Klebold and Eric Harris murders of 13 people at Columbine High School in Colorado in 1999 raised the nation's consciousness about peer mistreatment among students. Responses to such events include the following:

- The National Educational Service published *The Bullying Prevention Handbook* (1996) and produced a video to help educators and families understand and prevent bullying.
- The Bully Doctors of Benicia, California, designed an online blueprint for students and adults dealing with the dilemma of school bullying (see www.bullybusters.org).
- The Conflict Resolution Education Network (CREnet) provided information on states' programs to teach K-12 students conflict management skills, including how to deal with a bully and how to refrain from engaging in bullying behaviors (see www.crenet.org).

Undoubtedly, our failure to study this dimension of the dark side of school leadership, to apply the same rigorous research protocols we use to investigate other educational problems, has resulted in incomplete, naïve, and even false understandings of how some, perhaps a noteworthy percentage of, school leaders and teachers experience their work (Hodgkinson, 1991). Moreover, this failure allows the problem of mistreatment to continue without challenge and without hope of improvement (Keashly, Trott, & MacLean, 1994; Robinson & Bennett, 1995).

This book is a first attempt to bring to light a problem that has heretofore been ignored by both the academic and the professional educational community in the United States. As a first step it provides a knowledge base and understanding essential to developing a constructive approach to a deeply disturbing problem in American public education:

> When his novels were criticized for their portrayal of darkness and immorality in human relations—in today's parlance they would be called "negative"—Thomas Hardy replied that "to know the best, we must first regard the worst." It is that unwillingness to look at the dark side of the human condition that prevents administrative science from dealing with the heart of administrative problems and also from ascending to the height of human possibility and accomplishment. (Thomas Greenfield, in Hodgkinson, 1991, Foreword, p. 7)

WORKPLACE ABUSE: A REVIEW OF RESEARCH

> From the beginning, he singled me out for criticism. He criticized me publicly and loudly. He criticized my dress as too casual and told me that I couldn't wear Birkenstocks [shoes] because they were gang related. He would mock me in front of other teachers in his "in" group, with whom he ate lunch. After a fellow teacher and I pointed out a possible solution to a duty problem, he called me into his office and berated me for over an hour on the proper way to show respect to a principal. He called me a trouble-maker and told me that I needed to stop changing things and stop being so smart. He ridiculed me in a faculty meeting as someone who was "too smart for your own good." He said that he would never believe a word that I said; he would always take the word of a parent or student against me anytime. (Victim of principal mistreatment)

Internationally, systematic research on the problem of workplace abuse, notably nonphysical forms of abuse, has increased significantly during the past two decades in countries such as Sweden, Norway, Germany, Austria, Australia, and Britain. Several of these countries have also enacted legislation against work-place abuse, and private organizations have been created to help victims of abuse (Björkvist, Österman, & Hjelt-Bäck, 1994; Davenport, Distler-Schwartz, & Pursell-Elliott, 1999; Keashly, 1998; Namie & Namie, 2000b). For most of this same period, organizational scholars in the United States have largely ignored the problem of work abuse. In recent years, however, scholars have begun to address the problem; indeed, the emerging national literature suggests that workplace abuse may be a pervasive problem with serious deleterious consequences for both employees and organizations (Baron & Neumann, 1996; Davenport et al., 1999; Hornstein, 1996; Keashly, 1998; Keashly et al., 1994).

In addition, a number of popular books focusing on workplace abuse (e.g., *Work Abuse: How to Recognize and Survive It* by J. Wyatt & C. Hare, 1997) and articles in the popular media on workplace abuse (e.g., Judith Newman, "The Worst Boss I Ever Had," *Mademoiselle*, July 1999) have already been published. Television programs have begun to address the topic as well. On November 24,

1998, for instance, the hugely popular show *Oprah* was devoted to the topic of "Bully Bosses." Several websites have been established (e.g., Campaign Against Workplace Bullying[1] [CAWB] [http://www.bullybusters.org] run by Namie & Namie, 2001) that are devoted to stopping workplace abuse and providing assistance to victims of abuse. This website also includes related newspaper, television, radio, magazine, and newsletter coverage such as

- "When Your Boss Is a Bully" (*Harvard Management Newsletter*, July 2001)
- "Do You Work for a Bully Boss?" (*Industry Standard*, March 7, 2001)
- "Bullybusters Help in the Battle Against Workplace Browbeaters" (*Pittsburgh Post-Gazette*, November 26, 2000)
- "Boss or Coworker Downright Cruel?" (*Observer-Reporter,* Washington, PA, August 19, 2000)
- "Tyrant at the Top" (*Dallas Morning News,* June 13, 2000)
- "Working With Wolves" (*HR Executive Magazine*, August 1999)
- "When a Boss Turns Abusive" (*New York Times*, November 29, 1998)

Nevertheless, response by governmental agencies in the United States has been slow in coming. In February 2001, the Oregon Department of Environmental Quality was the first government agency, and among the first organizations in the United States, to adopt an antimobbing policy. Other government agencies in Oregon are considering similar policies (National Public Radio, Marketplace, February 2001)—wise decisions given the psychosocial and financial costs associated with workplace abuse.[2]

A variety of terms have been used in the theoretical and empirical literature to describe the workplace abuse phenomenon, including the following: bullying (Einarsen & Skogstad, 1996; Namie & Namie, 2000a), mobbing (Davenport et al., 1999; Leymann, 1990), incivility (Anderson & Pearson, 1999), petty tyranny (Ashforth, 1994), mistreatment (Folger, 1993; Price Spratlen, 1995), abuse (Bassman, 1992), harassment (Björkvist et al., 1994), aggression (Baron & Neumann, 1998), deviance (Robinson & Bennett, 1995), abusive disrespect (Hornstein, 1996), emotional abuse (Keashly, 1998), and victimization (Swedish National Board of Occupational Safety and Health, 1993).

Scholars have also defined workplace abuse in a variety of ways. *Mobbing* (or psychical terror), the most common term used in Europe, refers to "hostile and unethical communication that is directed in a systematic way by one or a number of persons mainly toward one individual" (Leymann, 1990, p. 120). Einarsen and Skogstad (1996) define *bullying,* a term commonly used in the United States and Europe as

harassment, badgering, niggling, freezing out, offending someone . . . repeatedly over a period of time, and the person confronted . . . [has] difficulties defending him/herself. It is not bullying if two parties of approximately equal "strength" are in conflict or the incident is an isolated event. (p. 191)

Ashforth (1994) uses the term "petty tyrant" to discuss boss abuse, defining this as "an individual who lords his or her power over others . . . acts in an arbitrary and self-aggrandizing manner, belittles subordinates, evidences lack of consideration, forces conflict resolution, discourages initiative, and utilizes noncontingent punishment" (p. 772). "Abusive disrespect," a concept developed by Hornstein (1996), refers to "transgressions" by bosses that include deceit, constraint, coercion, selfishness, inequity, cruelty, disregard, and deification.

From a comprehensive review of the workplace abuse literature, Keashly (1998) developed the concept of "emotional abuse" to emphasize "hostile verbal and nonverbal behaviors . . . directed at gaining compliance from others" (p. 85). Keashly identified emotional abuse with a *pattern* of abuse (not a single event), behaviors that are *unwanted* by the target, behaviors that *violate norms for appropriate conduct* or an individual's rights, behaviors that result in harm to the target, behaviors that *intend to harm* the target, and *power differences* between the abuser and the target of abuse.

Studies disclose a wide range of nonverbal and verbal-behavioral forms of workplace abuse. To illustrate, nonverbal behaviors include aggressive eye contact (e.g., staring, dirty looks), snubbing or ignoring, the silent treatment, and physical gestures such as violations of physical space, finger pointing, slamming objects, and throwing objects. Some examples of verbal-behavioral abuse discussed in the research literature are sexual harassment, angry outbursts, yelling and screaming, put downs, lying, public humiliation, threats of job loss, physical harm, name calling, excessive or unfounded criticism of work abilities or personal life, unreasonable job demands, stealing credit for another's work, blaming, exclusion or isolation, initiating malicious rumors or gossip, withholding resources or obstructing opportunities, favoritism, dismissing an individual's feelings or thoughts, unfriendly behavior, not returning phone calls, and behavior that implies a master–servant relationship (Björkvist et al., 1994; Davenport et al., 1999; Hornstein, 1996; Keashly et al., 1994; Leymann, 1990; Lombardo & McCall, 1984; Namie, 2000; Namie & Namie, 2000a; Baron & Neumann, 1998; Robinson & Bennett, 1995; Ryan & Oestreich, 1991).

Furthermore, according to the research, abuse in the workplace is associated with a host of serious adverse effects on an individual's physical well-being, psychological or emotional well-being, work performance, and social relationships. Examples of effects on *physical* well-being include sleep disorders (e.g., nightmares, insufficient rest), headaches, backaches, fatigue or exhaustion, illness, hyperactivity, weight changes (e.g., significant increases or decreases), irritable bowel syndrome, heart arrhythmia, skin changes, ulcers, substance abuse (first-time use), and suicide. Some *psychological or emotional effects* of abusive workplace behavior are depression, anger, rage, helplessness, powerlessness, cynicism and distrust, self-doubt, guilt, shame, embarrassment, insecurity, disillusionment, poor concentration, lowered self-esteem, aggression or revenge, hypervigilance, panic attacks, and posttraumatic stress disorder (PTSD). Negative effects of abusive behavior on *work performance* include reductions in job effort, extra effort, commitment, and satisfaction and morale and include increases in absenteeism and turnover or attrition. *Social effects* noted in the literature are isolation and loss of friendships (Björkvist, 1994; Davenport et al., 1999; Hornstein, 1996;

adverse effects

Keashly et al., 1994; Leymann, 1990; Lombardo & McCall, 1984; Namie, 2000; Namie & Namie, 2000a; Northwestern National Life Insurance Company, 1993; Pearson, 2000; Ryan & Oestreich, 1991).

> At faculty meetings he believed that there was only one voice that should be heard, his. He thinks that he is a people person because he can make almost 70 people sit there and face him. His faculty meetings usually go on over an hour and no one else speaks. Now, occasionally, he will ask if there are any questions. We have one or two people who will ask questions and he is bru-tal with them. He will say, "I am not going to talk about that with you now," and "That is not what I wanted to hear," or "I don't like that." He would say, "I told you what we are going to do. Were you listening to me, were you listening to me?" He would say, "If you have anything to say during the fac-ulty meeting, don't!" One time, he pulled out the teacher notebook of rules and went through almost a hundred pages of "You don't do this . . . don't you ever. . . . I mean it . . .!" He was ranting and raving. "I don't want to hear a damn word out of any of you! You don't understand what I am trying to do." We "aren't professional." He said he had no idea what "louses" we were, and he would never blah, blah, blah. Somebody asked him a question and he went into full ballistic mode about how we were awful and how we had all betrayed him. He was walking back and forth in front of the group . . . you know, like Captain Queeg. He yelled and cursed. By now we were all just kind of blown back against our chairs and watching him rage on. No one was asking any questions and everyone was afraid to move. We felt that if we stood up or said anything that it would all be targeted at us. . . . After, we all ran out like rats off a sinking ship. (Victim of principal mistreatment)

Examination of the research on abusive bosses (versus coworker abuse, for example) has revealed a number of disturbing findings. First, abusive conduct by bosses is commonplace in a wide range of both for profit and nonprofit organiza-tional settings. Second, studies indicate that bosses (e.g., superiors, managers) are most frequently workplace abusers rather than an individual's coworkers; in vari-ous studies, bosses have been identified as engaging in abusive conduct toward subordinates between 54 and 90% of the time (Björkvist et al., 1994; Einarsen & Skogstad, 1996; Hornstein, 1996; Keashly et al., 1994; Namie, 2000; Namie & Namie, 2000a; Northwestern National Life Insurance Company, 1993; Pearson, 2000; Rayner, 1998). Several scholars have persuasively argued that they expect abusive conduct by superiors to increase given organizational changes such as the growth in diversity, a decline in unionization (Yamada, 2000), and increases in electronic monitoring (Hornstein, 1996).

Third, the research on abusive bosses indicates that victims of this type of abuse seldom have viable opportunities for recourse. Studies emphasize that because of organizational culture (e.g., a "macho culture") and off-putting management practices (e.g., a cavalier attitude about abuse, attempts to justify abusive conduct), victims' complaints about abusive bosses usually result in (a) no action (i.e., no response) from upper-level management or administration and departments of human resources, (b) efforts to protect an abusive boss, or (c) reprisals against the victim for registering complaints (Bassman, 1992; Davenport et al., 1999; Hornstein, 1996; Keashly, 1998; Keashly et al., 1994; Leymann, 1990; Namie, 2000; Namie & Namie, 2000a; Pearson, 2000; Rayner, 1998). Unfortunately, efforts by victims of abuse and their colleagues to "blow the whistle" on workplace mistreatment and wrongdoing in general have not produced better results.[3]

> I dropped a hint to the school accreditation reviewer that all is not well in Camelot. The next day at a faculty meeting, the principal said that something had occurred that was a cloud on our whole school. She said that the reviewer heard that everything they would see at the school was a sham. She reminded us that if we dared to speak up about anything that was negative about the school, it was grounds for dismissal. The principal said, "How can a Judas betray us like this!" She said she would contact the three teachers on the review committee and get them to tell her who it was. Her final words were, "I want all of you to work to find out who this traitor is!" The next day she called an emergency faculty meeting, expecting someone is going to cave in and confess. . . . At the beginning and at the end of every faculty meeting, she said she did not get mad, she got even. People learned real quick that if you did talk, there were repercussions. I am a single mom and I have got to put my kids through college. I don't want to lose my job. I thought, "That can be the groundwork for her to try and get rid of me." (Victim of principal mistreatment)

Finally, David Yamada (2000), a Professor of Law at Suffolk University Law School, after examining existing legal possibilities for victims of workplace abuse—Intentional Infliction of Emotional Distress (IIED, Title VII of the Civil Rights Act of 1994), Americans with Disabilities Act (ADA), National Labor Relations Act (NLRA), and the Occupational Safety and Health Act (OSHA)—concluded that, despite the serious adverse consequences such conduct has on victims, existing laws are clearly inadequate in providing legal protection from the kinds of abusive boss conduct noted above. Put bluntly, most of this abusive conduct is simply not illegal and thus there are no legal remedies available to individuals who are not, for instance, victims of racial discrimination or sexual harassment. To remedy this, Yamada has developed a new legal theory—referred to as intentional infliction of hostile work environment—that would provide protection, self-help, and compensation to victims of a superior's abusive conduct as well as punishment for the superior.

THE IMPORTANCE OF THIS BOOK

Practical Implications for Educational Practitioners

> I have learned silence from the talkative, toleration from the intolerant, and kindness from the unkind; yet strange, I am ungrateful to those teachers. (Kahlil Gibran, in Bartlett, 1968, p. 976)

The leader has to . . . analyze and monitor his or her own affect, to "know thyself." If the leader is volatile, labile, impulsive . . . [it] can lead untold organizational actors to uncalculated calamities. . . . It is especially important to be aware of the dark side of personality, which acts so as to weaken will and frustrate the commitment to values. (Hodgkinson, 1991, pp. 138-139)

We have noted that our purpose in writing about principal mistreatment is to contribute constructively to solutions at all levels. We believe our findings, as troubling as they are, have special significance for prospective and practicing administrators and teachers. To test this notion, we created a 2.5-hour presentation and discussion of our research findings about principal mistreatment for school administrators and teachers taking graduate coursework at a major research university. Following this presentation, participants were given 30 minutes to respond to a survey that included one open-ended question: *What importance, if any, does knowledge about principal mistreatment (abuse) of teachers have for your development as an educational leader?* Over 300 administrators and teachers responded to this survey between 1999 and 2001.[4] The following quotes were drawn from the survey:

> When people are mistreated at work, their focus of attention is diverted from completing their work to trying to understand and manage the mistreatment . . . in other words, to *surviving*. A fearful and stressed teacher will generally downshift to the lowest mode of functioning. Creativity and innovation suffer. Paths of communication change in the school as teachers either talk among themselves or shut down entirely. Mistreatment of teachers is especially damaging because such mistreatment is often clearly visible to students. Even when mistreatment is more subtle, the subliminal perception of it by students is certain to undermine teachers; in fact, in some cases a mistreated teacher may become angry and the anger may be directed back toward students. Students then resort to further aggressive behavior as they internalize the hostility that has been directed toward them. . . . Thus, not only do teachers suffer, but the bullying is passed down the line. The implication for my development as an educational leader is that . . . I must be very mindful of how I treat other people. What goes around comes around in many destructive ways. (Teacher)

> Teachers often perceive abusive or harmful behavior as the status quo; they become socialized to accepting abusive behavior from administrators without realizing they have a right to fair and respectful treatment. (Teacher)

Without exception, those who responded affirmed the merits of studying the mistreatment problem and suggested a number of immediately practical uses for our findings. Respondents typically used phrases such as "very important," "extremely useful," "incredibly significant," and "shocking but extremely significant" to characterize the importance of the topic for their professional development.

They reported that knowledge of the "negatives," that is, "what not to do as an educational leader," is as important as just studying the positive, effective things. Specifically, respondents reported that such knowledge provoked in them a long-term commitment to a "truly reflective" orientation to school leadership, based on an understanding of how *personal factors* (e.g., one's weaknesses, values, assumptions, attitudes, behavior) alone or in conjunction with *organizational conditions* (e.g., stress, accountability expectations, unreasonable expectations by superiors) can lead to the abuse of teachers:

> These materials make me take a serious look at my weaknesses, examine myself, see if I say or do these things . . . things I am not aware of. I am better able to watch myself and won't be taken over by power and become a bullying principal.

> I have some deep thoughts about abuse. I do feel that I have some characteristics that some would take as abusive, such as sarcasm and intimidating looks. I know that I am by no means abusive, but have bad days. I definitely worry about how others perceive me. The presentation today has allowed me to see myself in a different light. I think back to some of my days in the classroom and I know that there are things that I need to work on. . . . It is important to study principals' mistreatment of teachers. We need to know the effects of our actions. In class, we have talked about communication and trust. These two factors can be destroyed by even a hint of abuse.

> This information will help me be aware of my natural tendency to seize power and control my surroundings. In my classroom, at one time, I was a control monster. This happens to a lot of teachers.

> This topic has made me do some real soul searching. I was an assistant to an abusive principal. I will always remember what this did to teachers, their families, and students. We must continually think about our values and never allow power to corrupt us.

Some respondents indicated that the "subtle cruelties" perpetuated by principals discussed during the presentation were intriguing; most, however, were deeply moved by the gamut of "crippling effects" principal abuse has on teachers and educational processes:

> I have seen many teachers' lives ruined by an abusive principal, but I never before realized the magnitude of the negative experiences that abused teachers can suffer at the hands of their principals.

> Until you are a victim of that kind of abuse, you can't understand the chain of fears that can result. They can stay with you forever.

> My parents always taught me the importance of treating everyone with respect. They had experienced the devastation mistreatment can bring to others. Having lived through an abusive school regime, I saw the pitfalls

yet I never understood the effects, sometimes permanent, on teachers and students, until I read this material. I now doubly see the importance of mutual respect in the educational workplace. Anything else would be detrimental to the educational cause: that of instructing students.

Our presentation had special significance for teachers and principals who had been victimized by principals (and others) at some point in their careers:

During the presentation, I began to feel the exact same feelings I felt during a three-year period of emotional abuse by a principal. I compiled a journal during our discussion to relieve my physical reactions. All of us must work to understand this problem and take responsibility for it.

It is very powerful and affirming to hear Dr. Blase confirm some of the emotions I have had when I have felt mistreated by a principal and assistant principal. My principal is not an abusive boss, but by oversight or lack of communication, I have felt offended by some of his actions. My first reaction was, "What have I done?" or, "What's wrong with me?" Then you feel disoriented; this comes from erratic feedback. I have been used to praise, recognition, compliments, and respect. When that was withdrawn, I had reactions similar to abused teachers. If my reactions came after such small actions by my principal, just think how devastating regular, consistent, ongoing abuse would be! Awareness of these effects should help prepare me to avoid acting in inappropriate ways as an administrator. I am committing to at least a yearly evaluation of myself as a leader that offers an opportunity for teachers to anonymously give me feedback so I can respond and work on changing my behavior in a timely and public way.

The most important thing for me as I develop as an educational leader is to guard against behaving in an abusive way. After seeing the video and participating in class discussion, I reflect back to two years ago when I feel I was a victim of mistreatment by a varsity coach under whom I worked. I remember how vulnerable I was and how naïve I was going into the newly acquired, sought after position. My boss consistently snubbed me, called me out in front of the other players, and made me feel inferior and foolish. I feel like I am a very strong person but the effects of his position and his mistreatment had me questioning myself on a daily basis. I felt I was "asking" for the treatment I received; I constantly asked myself what on earth was I doing to upset this man so much that he would treat me in this fashion.

Clearly, individuals derive meaning from direct experience with and reflection on the problematic aspects of life (Bandura, 1977, 1982; Blumer, 1969). Vygotsky's (1978) theories of verbal self-regulation and internalization and Tharp and Gallimore's (1988) application of these theories to teacher education demonstrate that systematic and rigorous reflection (i.e., cognitive and metacognitive as well as cycles of inter- and intrapsychological processes) on social and linguistic life experiences contributes significantly to an individual's professional development. Put differently, prospective and practicing administrators and teachers can be expected to develop important insights about effective school leadership and teaching through systematic reflection on both its positive and its negative elements.

Lombardo and McCall (1984) studied successful executives who had been victimized by abusive bosses earlier in their careers. These researchers found that executives derived some of their most profound lessons about effective leadership from reflection on abusive experiences. Blase and Blase (1998) reported similar findings for teachers preparing for careers in educational leadership, as did Ginsberg and Davies (2001) for administrators generally. Clearly, these data strongly confirm the significance of knowledge of and reflection on the negative for professional growth as a leader (Butler, 1996). Without such reflection, administrators routinely fail to recognize and confront personal values, attitudes, and behaviors that contradict their own espoused theories of effective leadership, and this failure can produce substantial adverse outcomes for individuals and organizations (Argyris, 1982, 1990, 1994; Bass, 1981). This latter point is especially significant in light of countless studies that demonstrate that some school principals typically employ leadership approaches that adversely affect teachers as well as classroom instruction (e.g., Blase, 1986, 1990; Blase & Blase, 1998; Diehl, 1993; Farber, 1991; Malen & Ogawa, 1988; McNeil, 1988), and in many cases, they may not be aware of the consequences of their actions (Adams, 1988, Gunn & Holdaway, 1986; High & Achilles, 1986; Reitzug & Cross, 1994). Indeed, few people are without personality characteristics that, in positions of leadership and under various organizational conditions, could result in the mistreatment of others (Ashforth, 1994; Barreca, 1995; Kets de Vries, 1989). The role of reflection in vigilantly safeguarding one's leadership praxis from misuse of position and power cannot be overemphasized.

Respondents to our questionnaire also reported that the topic of mistreatment should be directly addressed in administrator and teacher preparation programs; individuals should be equipped to deal with a variety of possible "work realities," both as administrators and as teachers:

> Being forewarned is forearmed. Teachers who are aware of this study will better understand what is happening and what to do in an abusive situation.

> Leaders of the future should be educated to know the temptations of power and that abusive behaviors only elicit aversive responses.

It is interesting to note that educational scholars have argued that power, both its effective use and particularly its misuse and abuse, is addressed inadequately, if at all, in most university-based administrator and teacher preparatory programs (Blase, 1991b; Blase & Anderson, 1995; Nyberg, 1981).

Finally, respondents emphasized that the topic of principal mistreatment of teachers "must be brought out into the open." One called it "educational leadership's dirty little secret" that must be given serious public attention by academic and professional educators. Without public and professional recognition of the problem, respondents asserted that administrators and teachers would be "afraid to talk about this horrible problem candidly and honestly," and without such dialogue, improvement would not result.

Practical Implications for District Office Personnel and Boards of Education

This book can be a valuable resource for central office personnel and boards of education throughout the United States. Individuals in these positions are legally, professionally, and ethically responsible for the general welfare and safety of teachers and the conduct of school administrators. Specifically, this book has implications for the recruitment, hiring, professional development, and termination of school-level administrators; it also has clear and compelling implications for developing viable policies (e.g., antiharassment policies, antimobbing policies) and procedures (e.g., mediation, grievance) to protect and provide relief for victims of mistreatment. Without protective policies and procedures, teachers subjected to mistreatment by school principals have little recourse (Davenport et al., 1999; Keashly et al., 1994; Namie & Namie, 2000a; Yamada, 2000). The role of district offices and boards of education is important in light of research on workplace abuse indicating that upper-level management in organizations usually ignores or colludes with abusive bosses when victims make formal complaints. Moreover, they may inadvertently contribute to the problem through the attitudes they convey about teachers and the expectations they have for school-level administrators (Davenport et al., 1999; Keashly et al., 1994; Namie & Namie, 2000a). Implications of our findings about principal mistreatment for district office personnel and school boards are discussed fully in Chapter 7.

ABOUT THE STUDY

What types of principal conduct do teachers define as abusive? What effect does such conduct have on teachers, teaching, and learning? How does a principal's abusive conduct undermine teachers' performance in the classroom and in the school in general? These are some of the basic questions we used in our study to examine how teachers experience abusive conduct by school principals.

Over a 1.5-year period, we conducted several in-depth interviews with each of 50 teachers who had experienced long-term (6 months to 9 years) mistreatment by their principals. The sample consisted of male ($n = 5$) and female ($n = 45$) teachers from rural ($n = 14$), suburban ($n = 25$), and urban ($n = 11$) school locations. Elementary ($n = 26$), middle or junior high ($n = 10$), and high school ($n = 14$) teachers participated. The average age of teachers was 42; the average number of years in teaching was 16. The sample included tenured ($n = 44$) and nontenured ($n = 6$), and married ($n = 34$) and single ($n = 16$) teachers. Degrees earned by these teachers included B.A. or B.S. ($n = 7$), M.Ed or M.A. ($n = 31$), Ed.S ($n = 11$), and Ph.D. ($n = 1$). The mean number of years working with the abusive principal was four. Forty-nine teachers resided in the United States and one resided in Canada. Fifteen of the teachers we studied were with an abusive principal at the time of this study; most others had experienced abuse in recent years. In total, these teachers described 28 male and 22 female abusive principals.

Examination of the personal and official documents submitted to us and reports from those who had worked with and referred us to the veteran teachers we studied suggest that the teachers were highly respected, accomplished, creative, and dedicated individuals. In most cases, they had been consistently and formally recognized by their school and district not simply as effective teachers but also as superior teachers; in many cases, such recognition for their exceptional achievements as public educators extended to state levels.

Symbolic interaction theory was the methodological foundation of our study. This approach focuses on the perceptions and meanings that people construct in their social settings (Blumer, 1969; Mead, 1934), in other words, "What goes on inside the heads of humans" (Meltzer, Petras, & Reynolds, 1975, p. 55). Consistent with research of this nature, no a priori definitions of principal abuse were used to control data collection. Such an approach would have limited teachers' freedom to discuss their personal views and experiences of principal mistreatment (Bogdan & Biklen, 1982; Glaser, 1992, 1998; Strauss & Corbin, 1998; Taylor & Bogdan, 1998). Our study conformed to guidelines set forth for inductive, grounded theory research and therefore emphasizes meanings of participants and the generation of descriptive, conceptual, and theoretical results.

All the findings discussed herein, drawn directly from our data, focus on teachers' perspectives on principal abuse and, in particular, the conduct teachers define as abusive and its adverse effects on their psychological or emotional and physical or physiological well-being as well as their performance in the classroom and in the school. The relevant literature is included throughout this book in the context of specific findings of our study.

We present here categories of abusive conduct and effects for the group of teachers we investigated; individual profiles of principals and teachers are not presented. *Thus, it is important to note that each principal identified by individual teachers engaged in a range of abusive behaviors described in the following pages, and each teacher, supervised by such a principal, experienced most of the major categories of deleterious effects we describe.* It is also important to reiterate that our study, being exploratory in nature, did not indicate the pervasiveness of the mistreatment problem in the United States.

To investigate the broad question, "How do teachers experience significant long-term abuse by a school principal?" we used a snowball sampling technique to identify teachers who had been victimized by school principals (Bogdan & Biklen, 1982; Taylor & Bogdan, 1998). Between two and four in-depth structured and semistructured telephone interviews were conducted with each of our research participants. In total, 135 hours of interviews were completed. The personal and official documents we collected were used, in part, to confirm the credibility of teachers' interview data as well as their overall effectiveness as teachers. In addition, we used a variety of techniques to determine the trustworthiness and reliability of teachers' reports. Given the sensitive nature of this study, however, no identifiers (e.g., a teacher's gender, school level, and subject matter specialization) appear alongside verbatim quotes presented throughout the chapters. And, of course, pseudonyms are used. (See the Research Method and Procedures section for protocol details.)

AN OVERVIEW OF THE BOOK

What does principal mistreatment of teachers look like? In this chapter, we have presented a brief overview of the professional literature on the problem of workplace abuse in general, a summary of findings from a survey regarding the practical value of our study, a discussion of the importance of this book for district office personnel and boards of education, and a description of the study upon which this book is based. Chapters 2 through 6 discuss findings drawn from our study. Chapters 2, 3, and 4, respectively, describe increasing levels of mistreatment: *Level 1 (indirect aggression—moderate), Level 2 (direct aggression—escalating), and Level 3 (direct aggression—severe).* In reading these chapters, readers will see that mistreatment takes many forms including verbal and nonverbal, indirect and direct principal behaviors. Mistreatment also ranges from behaviors such as denying resources to teachers to sabotage and public criticism, and, in its most aggressive forms, from explosive and threatening acts to forcing teachers out of their jobs.[5] What effect does principal mistreatment have on teachers, teaching, and learning? In Chapters 5 and 6 we describe effects on teachers, ranging from humiliation and lowered self-esteem to pervasive fear, severe depression, physical problems, and effects on one's home life, as well as effects on classroom instruction and the school as a whole.[6]

What can be done to overcome this serious problem? Chapter 7 summarizes our findings and conclusions and presents suggestions for overcoming the mistreatment problem including individual, organizational, and legal remedies.

Finally, we provide a detailed discussion of the research methodology employed in our study in the Research Method and Procedures section at the end of the book.

NOTES

1 The Campaign Against Workplace Bullying. P.O. Box 1886, Benicia, CA 94510. 888-FIX-WORK.

2 Davenport et al. (1999, p. 191) describe myriad psychosocial and financial costs associated with workplace abuse. One notable example is described by Pfaffenbach (2000): In a 2000 decision that included a strong statement against workplace bullying, Chief U.S. Magistrate Judge Robert B. Collings upheld a jury's award of $130,000 (for interference with advantageous relations) and $400,000 (in punitive damages) against Direct Federal Credit Union and its president, who had retaliated against employee Celia Zimmerman for her gender-bias claim. Although her gender-bias claim had been rejected by a jury, Judge Collings noted that the president "acted with a vindictive motive and . . . undertook a deliberate, calculated, systematic campaign to humiliate and degrade [Ms. Zimmerman] both professionally and personally" (p. 1). Pfaffenbach also noted that Ms. Zimmerman had been awarded $200,000 for her uncontested claim of retaliation.

3 In the past several decades, people have blown the whistle on a range of wrongdoings including environmental protection violations, racial and gender discrimination, and government fraud (e.g., toxic waste buried at Love Canal, Space Shuttle safety problems, and blocked career advancement for African Americans at Texaco). Approximately 60% of whistleblowers are fired or forced to resign. Despite the risks inherent in whistle-blowing, experts report a steady rise in the number of suits filed with the U.S. Justice Department, as well as a jump in the proportion of females initiating such lawsuits (from 25 to 50%) (Kiger, 2001). This latter indicates a growing, gender-free consciousness and concern for the tragic consequences of wrongdoing despite the possibility of reprisals and other negative effects.

4 The 300 prospective and practicing administrators and teachers who completed the questionnaire were between 22 and 51 years of age; 41% were male and 59% were female. Virtually all disciplines in education were represented.

5 Levels of mistreatment are not correlated with the degree of harm to the victim; this varied from one teacher to another.

6 Pseudonyms are used throughout.

2 The Many Faces of Moderate Mistreatment

From Discounting Teachers to Offensive Personal Conduct

The true leader . . . is the one who knows how to balance reflection and action by using self-insight as a restraining force when the sirens of power are beckoning.

— Kets de Vries (1989, p. 221)

The great man is powerful, involuntarily and composedly powerful, but he is not avid for power; what he is avid for is the realization of what he has in mind: the incarnation of the spirit. So long as a man's power is bound to the goal, the work, the calling, it is, in itself, neither good nor evil, only a suitable or unsuitable instrument. But as soon as this bond with the goal is broken off or loosened and

*the man ceases to think of power as the capacity to do something but thinks of it
as a possession, then his power, being cut off and self-satisfied, is evil and corrupts
the history of the world.*

— Martin Buber (quoted by Kets de Vries, 1989, p. 221)

With the arrival of the new millennium, a handful of published news stories appeared chronicling cases of alleged teacher abuse by American school principals. The stories of an exceptional teacher from Idaho who went, in one year's time, from "Teacher of the Year" to "teacher out on his ear" (Geery, 2001, p.1) and of "Dirty Dan," a Seattle principal who was charged with everything from sexual harassment to a vindictive management style and an uncontrollable temper (Bush, 2000) are but two in a list of alleged horrors in American public schools. Whether or not accusations prove true in these two controversial cases (both educators claim cadres of supporters and detractors), and whether the principals involved prove to be "bully bosses," these cases have, at a minimum, brought national attention to a problem that must be confronted: abuse of teachers by school principals.

It has often been said that people might be led, but they won't be driven. Principals, by virtue of their position, possess enormous power that may be used in constructive or destructive ways. Unfortunately, some principals use their power in ways and to achieve ends that substantially harm others. In this and the next two chapters, we explore principals' abusive behaviors as well as the possible causes of such behavior.

WHAT IS POWER?

Generally speaking, social power is the capacity to influence others; it is exercised through social interaction. Power can be derived from one's position in an organization or personal attributes (e.g., interpersonal skills, creativity). The psychologist Rollo May (1972) described five types of social power:

- Exploitative power (power over others)
- Manipulative power (power over others)
- Competitive power (power against others)
- Nutrient power (power for others)
- Integrative power (power with others)

Specifically, May (1972) highlighted the distinction between power over, which is destructive, and power with, which is constructive. Power for and with (nutrient and integrative power) are other-oriented power in caring for another and exerting oneself for the sake of another. For example, a teacher who demonstrates caring for the welfare of students reflects a "power for" nutrient orientation. Similarly, a principal who shows support for a teacher in conflict with a parent is reflecting a "power with" orientation. The reader may recall that Gandhi and Martin Luther King, Jr. used these forms of power in dramatically positive ways.

On the other hand, May (1972) noted that power comes in many social forms and carries risk; it may be used in abusive and even corrupting ways. Jean de la Fontaine declared that "Anyone entrusted with power will abuse it if not animated with the love of truth and virtue, no matter whether he be a prince or one of the people" (*Webster's Book of Quotations*, 1992), and, as mentioned in Chapter 1, in 1887, Lord Acton wrote, "Power tends to corrupt and absolute power corrupts absolutely." Both Josef Stalin and Adolf Hitler represent strong examples of the latter.

In Chapter 1 we indicated that this book is based on interviews conducted with teachers primarily from across the United States who experienced long-term patterns of mistreatment by principals (Blase & Blase, 2001). In analyzing our data, we found that principals who mistreat teachers are power overoriented in the worst sense: They engage in numerous destructive behaviors toward teachers; they misuse formal authority as well as personal types of power. Principal mistreatment includes indirect and moderately aggressive behaviors, such as ignoring, insensitivity, stonewalling, nonsupport in confrontations with parents, withholding resources, withholding professional development, withholding and taking credit, and favoritism; direct and moderately aggressive behaviors, such as spying, sabotaging, destroying teacher aids, stealing, and publicly and privately criticizing; and direct and severely aggressive behaviors, such as lying, being explosive and nasty, threatening, writing reprimands, giving poor evaluations, mistreating one's students, forcing one out of a school or teaching job, sexual harassment, and racism.

In essence, we have organized the behaviors mentioned above according to level of aggression as Level 1 (indirect aggression—moderate), Level 2 (direct aggression—escalating), and Level 3 (direct aggression—severe) principal mistreatment (see Box 2.1); these categories of mistreatment are discussed in this and the next two chapters. Please note, this heuristic does not imply that Level 1 principal mistreatment behaviors resulted in less harm to teachers when compared to Level 2 or Level 3 behaviors; to the contrary, the degree of harm related to any single aggressive behavior varied from one victimized teacher to another, as one would expect. Our study focused on long-term mistreatment; therefore, teachers discussed the cumulative effects of a collection of abusive principal behaviors. (For comparison, we present Leymann's 1993 list of 45 mobbing behaviors in Box 2.2. Mobbing behaviors are essentially the same as mistreatment.) Before proceeding, it is important to emphasize that all teachers we studied experienced a range of both less and more severe forms of mistreatment over a substantial period of time. This chapter describes the somewhat less severe, although clearly destructive, forms of principal mistreatment. In Chapters 5 and 6, the effects of principal mistreatment—teacher disorientation; humiliation; feeling ostracized; lowered self-esteem; effects on one's relationships, classroom instruction, and school; fear; anger; depression; physical damage; and harm to one's personal and family life—are discussed in detail.

Box 2.1   Principal behaviors by mistreatment levels and effects of
mistreatment

Level 1 Principal Mistreatment Behaviors (indirect, moderate)

- Discounting Teachers' Thoughts, Needs, and Feelings
    Ignoring
    Personal Insensitivity
    Stonewalling
- Isolating and Abandoning Teachers
    Controlling Teacher-to-Teacher Interaction
    Failing to Support Teachers in Difficult Interactions with
        Students and Parents
- Withholding Resources and Denying Approval, Opportunities, and Credit
    Withholding Resources and Denying Approval
    Obstructing Opportunities for Professional Development
    Withholding or Taking Credit
    Docking Sick Leave
- Favoring "Select" Teachers
- Offensive Personal Conduct

Level 2 Principal Mistreatment Behaviors (direct, escalating)

- Spying
- Sabotaging
- Stealing
- Destroying Teacher Instructional Aids
- Making Unreasonable Demands
    Nitpicking
    Overloading
- Criticism: The Ubiquitous Form of Level 2 Mistreatment
    Private Criticism
        Direct Criticism
        Stigmatizing and Pejorative Labeling
        Intentionally Vague Criticism
        Use of a "Snitch's" Information to Criticize
        Gossiping
        Soliciting Others
    Public Criticism
        Front Office
        Faculty Meetings
        Classroom
        Intercom
        Lunchroom
        Hallway
        Other Places

Level 3 Principal Mistreatment Behaviors (direct, severe)

- Lying
- Explosive and Nasty Behavior
- Threats
- Unwarranted Reprimands
- Unfair Evaluations
- Mistreating Students
- Forcing Teachers Out of Their Jobs (Reassigning, Transferring Unilaterally, Terminating)
- Preventing Teachers From Leaving or Advancing
- Sexual Harassment
- Racism

THE EFFECTS OF PRINCIPAL MISTREATMENT OF TEACHERS

- Wounded Teachers: Early Emotional Responses
  Trapped
  Fearful and Angry or Outraged
  Preoccupied, Stressed, and Traumatized
  Corrupted and Guilty
  Diminished Sense of Professionalism
  Shock and Disorientation
  Humiliation
  Loneliness
  Injured Self-Confidence and Self-Esteem

- Damaged Schools
  Damaged Relationships
  Damaged Classrooms
  Impaired Decision Making

- Severely Damaged Teachers
  Fear and Anxiety
  Anger
  Depression
    Feeing Isolated
    Feeling Trapped
    Feeling Unmotivated
  Oceans of Tears
  Revivification: Experiencing It All Over Again
  Physical and Physiological Problems
  Intention to Leave One's Job
  Effects on a Teacher's Personal and Family Life

Box 2.2 45 Mobbing Behaviors

First Category: *Impact on Self-Expression and the Way Communication Happens*

- Your superior restricts the opportunity for you to express yourself.
- You are interrupted constantly.
- Coworkers restrict your opportunity to express yourself.
- You are yelled at and loudly scolded.
- Your work is constantly criticized.
- There is constant criticism about your private life.
- You are terrorized on the telephone.
- Oral threats are made.
- Written threats are sent.
- Contact is denied through looks or gestures.
- Contact is denied through innuendoes.

Second Category: *Attacks on One's Social Relations*

- People do not speak with you anymore.
- You cannot talk to anyone, i.e., access to others is denied.
- You are put into a workspace that is isolated from others.
- Colleagues are forbidden to talk with you.
- You are treated as if you are invisible.

Third Category: *Attacks on Your Reputation*

- People talk badly behind your back.
- Unfounded rumors about you are circulated.
- You are ridiculed.
- You are treated as if you are mentally ill.
- You are forced to undergo a psychiatric evaluation/examination.
- Your handicap is ridiculed.
- People imitate your gestures, walk, voice to ridicule you.
- Your political or religious beliefs are ridiculed.
- Your private life is ridiculed.
- Your nationality is ridiculed.
- You are forced to do a job that affects your self-esteem.
- Your efforts are judged in a wrong and demeaning way.
- Your decisions are always questioned.
- You are called demeaning names.
- You are faced with sexual innuendoes from others.

Fourth Category: *Attacks on the Quality of One's Professional and Life Situation*

- There are no special tasks for you.

- Supervisors take away assignments, so you cannot even invent new tasks to do.
- You are given meaningless jobs to carry out.
- You are given tasks that are below your qualifications.
- You are continuously given new tasks.
- You are given tasks that affect your self-esteem.
- You are given tasks that are way beyond your qualifications, in order to discredit you.
- Supervisors cause general damages that create financial costs to you.
- Supervisors cause damage to your home or workplace.

Fifth Category: *Direct Attacks on a Person's Health*

- You are forced to do a physically strenuous job.
- Threats of physical violence are made.
- Light violence is used to threaten you.
- You are physically abused.
- You are sexually harassed.

SOURCE: Leymann, H. (1993). *Mobbing* (N. Davenport, Trans.). Hamburg: Rowohlt Taschenbuch Verlag GmbH. Translated in Davenport, N., Distler-Schwartz, R., & Pursell-Elliott, G. (1999). *Mobbing: Emotional abuse in the American workplace* (pp. 36-37). Ames, IA: Civil Society. Reprinted by permission.

I'M THE BOSS!

To paint the picture broadly, we share general quotes from a variety of teachers in our study, quotes that reflect the essence of teachers' perspectives of their abusive, domination-oriented principal. Such principals appear to be preoccupied with power over others in an absolute sense; they are extremely coercive, directive, rigid, and closed-minded.

We called the principal "Hitler" because of his dictatorship style. He harassed and abused many teachers. One teacher he singled out; he wanted to get rid of her. He yelled at her in front of others, and the teacher gradually lost her self-confidence and her ability to plan and teach. She withdrew, and she had health problems. Even her dentist said that she was under a lot of stress. Her hair was falling out and she often broke out in hives. She stayed in her room and did as she was told. Since her ideas were rejected or ignored, she stayed away from committees. All year she seemed depressed. She began to have marital problems. Her morale was the lowest. . . . She is at another school now, and she is a leader. She has a new life, she is in good health, and she has so much to offer.

She just really rules the roost. She was like a rooster, and the school was her domain. You only spoke in hushed tones. You didn't cross her. She was raised in the military, and she was just like a drill sergeant: arms crossed, back straight, head up. She walked around with a lot of confidence. She let you know that she was the boss and she was going to do anything that she wanted to. It was that simple.

He didn't say, "I prefer to be called Dr. Johnson," he said, "I am to be called Dr. Johnson." The message was: Don't mess with me. I am the big guy around here. I am the principal; I am going to put you in your place. It is really too bad that we get these kinds of characters in the principal-ship … these intimidators, whose only supposed skill is motivating people through fear.

His manner of speaking to me is always very abrupt, blunt, cold, sharp, to the point, uncaring, dominating, and top-down. Everything is about power. He makes you feel like he is the boss and you are the subordinate. He will go to any lengths to put pressure on you to make sure you act in a subordinate way.

He was this way to everybody and about everything: If a kid was coming down the hall and not doing something right, he would give them the maximum punishment. He would go to games and pull students out just to show how important he was. In all types of occasions and in dealing with teachers, it was clear that he wanted everybody to know he was the person in charge of virtually everything.

I think that she just enjoyed the feeling of power. She enjoyed the feeling of knowing that she made somebody upset. She liked seeing somebody cry. She thrived on confrontation. She even gossiped about teachers to other teachers; she was hoping that it would get back so that people would be bickering. It was just part of her feeling of power, knowing that she could evoke that kind of emotion in us.

He was the principal now and he expected me to look up to him and treat him like the top person on the totem pole. When I told him that I might be at another school in the morning for a meeting he said, "If you are not here, don't call the secretary, call me. If you can't get me, call my assistant. If you can't get her, call the counselor." Then he stood up and leaned over his desk and smiled and said, "Because that is the pecking order around here."

She is very loud. At meetings, she stands erect with all of us seated. She speaks in a loud voice and she consistently wears power suits and heels. She is in it for power. Those of us who dare to question anything are in jeopardy. Little did I know.

She wanted total control over people, but when she got it she didn't respect them. She destroyed one guy, criticizing him all the time and saying that she was not going to hire him back. Many times I would see them after school together, sitting and talking. He was always doing little brown-nosing types of things. She had him under her control and he became her lap dog.

LEVEL 1 PRINCIPAL MISTREATMENT: INDIRECT AND MODERATE AGGRESSION

As long ago as 1936, Beale wrote,

> Often a principal can call a meeting of teachers to "discuss" some measure of vital concern to them, make his own views known, awe the opposition into silence, and actually get a unanimous vote of approval for something that the majority of the teachers oppose, all because it is unwise to cross the principal in a thing he wants. The general climate of schools and the undemocratic rules under which they are administered tend to make principals autocrats and teachers yes-men. Most teachers' conferences, committees, or councils are supervised if not run by the principal or at least are dominated by his known wishes because it would be reported to him who opposed him. Teachers' meetings in which teachers freely and frankly discuss problems and come to uncontrolled decisions are rare, and they occur only under unusually liberal principals. Democracy has not yet been applied to schools. Clashes with the principal over method, ideas, or conduct usually lead to discrimination if not penalties. A principal can make a teacher miserable by imposing unpleasant or heavier duties or by requiring of him strict adherence to rules or standards only laxly applied to others. The situation is made worse by the fact that autocracy or inefficiency or even immorality cannot be safely opposed in a principal in the many systems where his appointment has depended upon political or social influence. (p. 602)

As noted in Chapter 1, Keashly's (1998) thorough review of the literature on workplace abuse yielded seven dimensions of emotional abuse. Such abuse, she found, derived from hostile workplace conduct, was frequent, and resulted in severe and long-term effects on people. These effects are often similar to what people experience when subjected to racial and sexual harassment. Keashly concluded that emotional abuse

1. Includes verbal and nonverbal modes of expression

2. Constitutes a pattern, is repeated

3. Includes behavior that is unwelcome, unwanted, and unsolicited

4. Violates a standard of appropriate conduct toward others

5. Results in harm or injury

6. Is intended to harm or could have been controlled by the actor

7. Involves power differences

All the aforementioned dimensions of workplace abuse are reflected in our findings. For an overview of primary research findings of workplace abuse research completed prior to our study, including the behaviors of those who mistreated or abused others, the effects of those behaviors, and typical responses of mistreated people, please refer to Chapter 1 or to Table 2.1 (also see Cleveland & Kerst, 1993; Fitzgerald & Shullman, 1993; Keashly, 1998; Northwestern National Life Insurance Company, 1993).

In general, mistreated teachers experience strong feelings of powerlessness, among others, in an atmosphere of coercion and domination by their principals. Indirect, albeit destructive, forms of principal mistreatment described by teachers in our study included both nonverbal and verbal principal behaviors. Next we discuss five types of Level 1 principal mistreatment behaviors.

Level 1 Principal Mistreatment Behaviors

- Discounting teachers' thoughts, needs, and feelings
- Isolating and abandoning teachers
- Withholding resources and denying approval, opportunities, and credit to teachers
- Favoring select teachers
- Offensive personal conduct

Discounting Teachers' Thoughts, Needs, and Feelings

Mistreated teachers in our study frequently found themselves ignored or snubbed by their principals; principals were also insensitive to teachers' personal needs. More specifically, abusive principals stonewalled, and they avoided responding to teachers' direct questions.

Ignoring. When mistreatment occurred through face-to-face interaction, principals typically displayed offensive nonverbal behaviors, especially ignoring or snubbing a teacher. Such behavior was always a part of a more extensive pattern of abuse.

In my technical drafting class, I have to constantly be moving around the room. One day the principal said he saw a student put his head down, but I did not see it. It didn't happen. When I received my evaluation the principal had given me an NI [needs improvement] for that. I said, "Dr. Dunn, I did not see that." He got very upset and looked at me like, "You are going

Table 2.1 Findings of Workplace Abuse Research: Behaviors, Effects, and Responses

Behavior	Effects on Target	Target's Response
Nonverbal	*Physical Well-Being*	* Doing nothing
Aggressive eye contact (glaring at, casting "meaningful" glances)	Illness Sleep disturbance Fatigue	Ignore person Avoid person Seeking social support, talking with others for support and ideas
Ignoring; silent treatment	Headaches	
Intimidating physical gestures (finger pointing, slamming things down, throwing objects)	*Psychological/Emotional Well-Being*	
Inappropriate or excessive use of memos, e-mails	Lowered self-esteem Cynicism, distrust Anxiety, nervousness, job-related tension	Seeking an exit Quitting Transferring Absenteeism
Verbal (direct)	Depression	Looking for good in the
* Yelling, screaming	Anger, resentment	person and situation
Cursing at person	Helplessness or	Confronting
Having angry outbursts, tantrums	powerlessness Suicide	Asserting Threatening
Being nasty, rude, or hostile	*Job Related*	Defying
Accusing of wrongdoing, blaming for errors	Decreased job satisfaction	Having others intercede ** Filing a complaint
Putting down, insulting, belittling comments, name calling—often in front of others	Increased turnover Increased transfers Planning to or thinking of leaving	** Speaking to higher-ups . Having colleagues speak to abuser
Threatening job loss or change	Absenteeism	Other
Discounting or dismissing thoughts or feelings	Lowered productivity Disruption of communication with	Appeasing Enduring Denying
Making personal criticism of features irrelevant to job (appearance, family, friends)	superiors and coworkers	Detaching Relabeling Illusory control
Giving excessive or harsh criticism of work or abilities		
Verbal (indirect)		
Spreading untrue rumors or gossip		
Breaching confidentiality (sharing private info about person or other workers)		
Assigning meaningless or "dirty" tasks as punishment		
Making unreasonable demands for work		
Withholding or denying opportunities or resources		
Taking credit for work		
Other		
Physical contact without harm		
Sexual harassment		
Racial harassment		

SOURCE: Adapted from Keashly (1998), Cleveland and Kerst (1993), Fitzgerald and Shullman (1993), and Northwestern National Life Insurance Company (1993).
 * frequent
** infrequent

to question me?" After that, he wouldn't even acknowledge me walking down the halls. He would just turn and keep walking.

I went to introduce the principal to my husband. She looked at me, turned around, and just walked off. She was flat out rude. I couldn't believe that someone would stoop so low. If we passed in the hall, she would turn and walk the other way or she would give me a dirty look. She even snubbed me in the store. I remember saying, "Hi," and she turned and walked off. I feel like I am dealing with a middle schooler.

The cold war . . . I was essentially frozen out. He didn't acknowledge me in the halls, always looked the other way, never said hello. He didn't even evaluate me, but just filled out the form and put one phrase in there criticizing me for disagreeing with the direction of the building. He just turned brittle cold.

The only time she would speak to me [was] if it was an absolute necessity. It really gave me a cold feeling. Even if I walked into the office she would turn her back to me. She would speak to another teacher who was with me, but she never spoke to me. In meetings she would give me the evil eye. After I resigned as department chair, she gave me a smirk like "I got you."

Rather than smiling or saying "Good morning, Mrs. Babbitt, how are you? I've come to watch your class. Carry on," he was very cold and gruff, stiff, silent, no smile.

[We had] a disagreement . . . [and she] stated that she was the boss and I was the subordinate. Since that first incident, this principal has been cold to me, turns her back, ignores me.

He was like a little strutting rooster. He would walk down the hall and pass within six inches of my face and he would turn his head the other way, not say hello, not give eye contact.

He said hello to the other two [teachers], mentioning their names and making eye contact. I was not greeted by name, gesture, or eye contact. That is very impolite, and I still feel bitter.

Personal Insensitivity. Teachers described many abusive principals as extremely insensitive to personal matters, even illness.

From 10:00 a.m. until 2:00 p.m., there was constant screaming and yelling of children on the playground, within 10 feet of my trailer. I started getting migraines, so I spoke with the principal many times about it. The children could have played kick-ball on the other side. My doctor wrote a letter about it, but the principal refused to move those children to the other area where they could play.

I had a respiratory infection for years and my internist did all kinds of tests and never could pin anything down. I said to my doctor, "Do you think the wet carpet in my classroom could have anything to do with it?" He said, "Yes, it harbors mold and bacteria, and that is the only thing it could be." I cut a snip out of it and took it to my doctor. He wrote a letter to the principal about taking the carpet out. The principal completely ignored me. I wrote several letters to the superintendent. Finally the superintendent had it taken out. I haven't been sick since.

We would try to get to work even if we were on our death beds. If I called her to say, "My child is very sick, and I won't be able to come in today," she would just hang up on you. I never got a response other than that.

Several principals even failed to learn teachers' names:

There were about five of us who were around the same age and all blond. I worked for him for five years and still, at the end of the fifth year, he might call me Sue, he might call me Lydia. He just never got our names right. When you work for someone for five years, they should be able to call you by name!

Stonewalling. Teachers viewed stonewalling as a form of principal mistreatment:

He never responded to my memos. I asked him about getting a substitute for the Jewish holidays and he didn't respond. I asked him about going to the gifted convention and he didn't respond. I asked him about getting reimbursed for what I spent on items I use in my classroom and he didn't respond.

He never had time to talk to me, although he was in his office watching the baseball game. I remember asking the secretary, "Is Sam available?" and her always saying, "No, he can't see you right now."

Isolating and Abandoning Teachers

Abusive principals frequently isolated teachers by preventing their contact with others, especially colleagues, and by neglecting to support teachers in difficult encounters with students and parents.

Controlling Teacher-to-Teacher Interaction. A common complaint was that abusive principals attempted to control teachers' interactions with colleagues:

He doesn't want us talking about the school in the lounge or in the community; he says, "That is gossiping, and I want you to shut up." He said, "I told my wife to shut up. It took years before she stopped." He'll go on like that at faculty meetings.

He called me into his office and said, "Where were you on Friday night? Now think really hard. . . . Your coworker told me that you were at such and such a place and that you were talking to another teacher from our district. You know I won't tolerate that."

She is power crazy. She would split up teams of teachers just because they worked well together.

She threatened all of us from day one not to talk during our planning period with other teachers because that was just an unprofessional thing to do. She said, "It promotes gossip." She didn't even want us in the lounge during our planning period. She would say, "You don't need to say anything to your friends." You couldn't say anything negative about the school. It was just a control thing.

Failing to Support Teachers in Difficult Interactions With Students and Parents. Teachers indicated that abusive principals frequently failed to support them in confrontations with problematic students.

She always told us, "I am going to support the children, not you."

A child slapped a teacher in the face. This was extremely disrespectful and the teacher wanted some sort of disciplinary action. The principal wanted just a discussion and told the teacher to take the child back to class. As they were walking out, the child slapped the principal on the butt, for which the principal put the child in the "time out" room as punishment. The teacher felt that it was not fair.

Discipline got out of control in the school. It was horrible. I was bitten, kicked, and hit by a five-year-old child on a daily basis. After trying everything including calling parents, counselor involvement, etc., I went to my principal. She would keep the child for 15 minutes, letting her color, play, and do play dough, rewarding her instead of punishing her. Once, when I was bitten by her to the point that my hand was bleeding, my principal said, "I know that hurt."

In *all* cases of nonsupport with students, abusive principals were "shamelessly unfair"; they not only failed to properly investigate problems, but they also often blamed teachers for the problems.

She told me that she needed to discuss a student. I went to see her, but she kept hedging and trying to get me to say something that never happened. Then she told me a student's father reported that I had slammed the student against the wall and grabbed him and that his best friend confirmed the story. All that had happened was that I had kind of got between some students and put my hand up so that nobody got hit, just one of those things that happens a hundred times a day. The principal said, "It would be perfectly understandable if you lost it with the kids. I know how they can get to you, and I know that you have been under a lot of stress lately. It wouldn't surprise me if you did something like this. Why don't you admit that you did? It would be a whole lot easier for you. Just tell me you did it." In other words, it was not convenient for her to take time calling in witnesses. This is so hard to talk about [teacher is crying]. The next day the principal called me into her office and again said, "It would just be a whole lot easier if you just admitted it." When I met with the father, I explained. He believed me and it was no big deal. By then I was having anxiety attacks, trouble sleeping, nightmares, diarrhea, losing weight. That kind of thing happened to many teachers. They were accused of abusing the kids, and in each case she said the same thing, "Why don't you just admit it; it would be a whole lot easier for you."

I had kids out of mental institutions, out of jails. It was really a rough place. I had one kid who had murdered. But referrals were looked on very negatively in that school. You had to handle your own discipline. You could expect an attack from the principal if you didn't.

One child ended up going to the hospital and being committed. He threatened this fifth-grade teacher saying that he was going to kill her. The principal wouldn't do anything because he didn't want any negative attention brought to his school. God forbid that he help the child. The teacher said that if the student threatened her again, she was going to call the cops. He did. He tried to hit her. The principal didn't do anything about it. The teacher's life was hell after that.

If a child had a behavior problem identified through the support team, he would just say that the teacher had poor discipline. . . . He would pound on his desk and yell.

In other incidents of nonsupport, principals failed to investigate problems, unfairly blamed teachers, and also gave them written reprimands.

I had put one little girl's head in my hands to get her to look at me. I certainly did not jerk her the way the principal made it sound, like I was a child beater. He called me a liar and said that I was defying him. He got students to testify against me and put a letter of reprimand in my file. He then refused to tell me who testified.

Two boys were engaging in noisy horse play, pushing and shoving. Finally in a loud voice after not getting their attention several times I said, "When I say stop, you need to stop." I got a memo later from the principal. He said that I thoroughly embarrassed him in the front office in front of students, staff, and parents, by raising my voice. He followed it with a written reprimand. I said, "What would you suggest that I do? Please advise." He never responded.

Several teachers explained that abusive principals, again without investigating problems, verbally mistreated them in front of students.

You could not depend on him. I had finally gotten fed up with a student who was fighting in the hall. The principal just said, "Well, what do you want me to do about it?" Another time, I was fussing at two girls who were arguing in the hall and the principal came in and jumped on me. He corrected us [me and another teacher] in front of students. Once I said to him that I think that the students get the point about clearing the halls; I stood out there this morning. The principal just screamed at me, "Who gave you permission to stand out there?" I started crying. Tears just filled my eyes.

In addition, we found that abusive principals typically failed to support teachers in conflicts with parents.

A father who had recently been released from a mental hospital entered my classroom carrying a bag with what appeared to be a machete handle sticking out. He began to thump his son on the chest with such force that the child fell backwards, pinned against the wall. He was screaming so loudly other teachers came. One went to get the principal. The principal simply laughed, did not come to my room, and made no pretense later that he had misunderstood. He did not accompany me when I had to go to court. I felt unsafe, alone, and abandoned.

You couldn't depend on her to stand by you. She would contradict herself. At first, she would be very supportive of the teacher. But when she met with the parent she would turn around and wouldn't stand by what she had told the teacher.

You always hope that your principal would be supportive, but she was not in the least bit supportive. I was caught completely off guard when a parent went on and on about me and the principal was very silent.

Many abusive principals unfairly and routinely blamed teachers for any problem that occurred between them and parents:

I felt like I was not respected by her. She didn't care to listen to what teachers said. If you had a problem with a child and you tried to solve it on your own or with the parent, but the parent got upset and blamed you, not the child, she would take the parent's side against you.

Parents would show up without an appointment and the principal would call on the intercom and say they are on their way down. I told him repeatedly, in private, that I wanted parents to make an appointment. He would call me to his office for the weekly harassment meeting. He would tell me any and every parent complaint that happened that week. I believe hardly any of them ever took place. He said, "I don't want to tell you who it was, you might take it out on the kid." I said, "Give me a break. You call me in here and rake me over the coals, and you aren't going to give me a chance to defend myself or correct the problem?"

If a parent complained, the principal would not wait to see what the situation might be. He would just call you up to the office, or stop you at the door and usher you into his office. Then he would yell and use profanity.

Moreover, teachers reported that abusive principals reprimanded them for problems in the presence of parents:

> She would say that you were the person with the problem and not the child. . . that you were making the child have low self-esteem and act out in class. It was your fault. I wasn't even in the conference with the parent and the principal asked, "What exactly is it that you were doing to her child?" She accused me in front of the parents without even investigating. When the parents left, the mother said, "I know that you didn't do anything wrong."

> He did not back you in front of the parent at all. He would scold the teacher. He was probably counting on the parents to keep him at that school. I had a seventh-grade boy stealing popsicles. His parent said, "Well, was the door locked to the teachers' lounge? If it wasn't, you can't expect them not to be stolen." The principal told me to drop it.

Withholding Resources and Denying Approval, Opportunities, and Credit

Abusive principals mistreated teachers by withholding necessary resources and denying approval, docking a teacher's sick leave, obstructing teachers' opportunities for professional development, and withholding (or seizing) credit for work-related achievements.

Withholding Resources and Denying Approval. The commentaries of many teachers identified principals who unfairly withheld resources or denied approval essential to their work with students. The experiences of a music teacher and an art teacher, over a number of years, were particularly destructive:

> She moved me and my classes into the gym lobby with no place to store my students' instruments. The bathrooms had that old urine smell, the heat didn't work, and there was no air conditioning. She denied all my requests to play at the hospital or to go to the symphony, and all requests for funds for the music program. She wouldn't repair instruments. She denied my requests to create a fundraiser. She cut rehearsal time. She did this to let me know that she was the boss, she was in charge of the school and I jolly well had better learn that. It gets worse. I was placed in a closet, eight feet wide and thirty feet long. This storage closet was my orchestra classroom. The parents said, "Look, this situation is just awful." I was in the closet for five months.

> He completely withheld art supplies. I shared half of a single-wide trailer and for four years asked him for a clock, three trash cans, a small table, and shelving for a paper cutter. I asked that they take the old carpet out. He did anything he could to make my life miserable. There was no water and

finally the sink came in but with no faucets. He said, "Why don't you come down here on a Saturday and make the maintenance crew some cookies. Maybe they will put the sink in for you." He completely ignored me.

Several teachers described principals who withheld needed resources or denied approval for things like student projects, planning time, access to telephones, or field trips.

I had never even taken a picture with a 35-mm camera, but he forced me to take the yearbook sponsorship anyway. He made comments to me like, "You could be put in another school anywhere in this county teaching any level or doing things other than teaching," and, "I can find somebody else who will take your schedule." He would agree to provide resources I needed but when the time came and he hadn't followed through, he would call me a liar and say that I hadn't asked him to do anything. I would end up like a chicken with my head cut off running around, stressed out, trying to get the job done.

A major corporation sponsored a competition about designing a future idea. This is a great way to teach research writing. My assistant principal signed off for us to enter three kids in the competition. One of the groups won. We were featured in the newspaper. The principal went ballistic. She was angry that I had entered us in a competition that associated a school with a product. She said that it was against district policy, but refused to give me a copy of the policy. I knew that it wasn't true because another elementary school had gotten a front page spread for the same situation. She took something that could have been so positive for the school, the community, our program and created a series of roadblocks.

I was the youth corps coordinator for our district's student job program. The principal disallowed my making calls to the prospective employers to place my students. She said that I was tying up the lines and didn't want me to use my planning time. I said, "How do you expect me to get this job done?" She said, "You will just have to figure that out."

The kids had been working hard all year long. I really made them toe the line. They were excited about a huge field trip. It was going to be great. Three days before the trip the principal decided that we couldn't go. . . . I said, "You signed off on the approval sheets. It put me behind the eight ball." He said, "You will just have to give the mini grant back."

Docking Sick Leave. One teacher described a case of withholding that took the form of inappropriately docking her accumulated sick leave:

For three years, I wrote the entire staff development plan. One year he had pulled me out of class and put a parapro in my class so that I could write, but later he docked my sick leave for it. I was trying to bank my leave so that I wouldn't have to pay out of my disability insurance. He lied another time. He put me in a room, gave me a laptop and for three days I wrote. I am talking from 6 in the morning until midnight and then some. He docked me the sick leave and charged me for the sub that he put in the room who was, by the way, one of our parapros. I was valuable enough to write the damn thing, but he penalized me!

Obstructing Opportunities for Professional Development. Our data reveal that some abusive principals undermined teachers' efforts to initiate and involve themselves in professional development opportunities:

> I had this idea to initiate professional growth plans that focused on trying to discover ways in which teachers can help each other grow. It was meaningful professional growth. . . . I certainly was aware that people had been victimized by this principal, and I had observed people being embarrassed publicly. I had even cradled people who were crying and angry and disenfranchised. I had spent countless hours supporting others who had been hurt and damaged by this principal. . . . She said, "Forget it [professional development]." She hid behind saying that people were too burdened. She didn't want to come out clearly as abusive. I felt that this was abusive because she is the one who told me to try it. She criticized what I was doing to make sure it became an unacceptable and undesirable thing for teachers to do.

Withholding or Taking Credit. All the teachers we studied indicated that their principals refused to recognize or praise them for work-related achievements. Principals were often seen as conspicuously withholding such recognition and praise:

> You never got any praise from her. You were just expected to do it or else.

> At the faculty meeting the principal mentioned two male teachers who were doing a presentation at a state meeting and said they were phenomenal, but never mentioned me.

> I brought in $34,000 worth of grant money one year. Someone sitting next to me in a faculty meeting brought in $600. The principal had her stand up at the faculty meeting, had her talk about it, and praised her. This was done to make me feel bad.

> The principal took a full academic year to learn my name. The first time she entered my classroom she said, "Oh, so you do have students." By the end of my second year, her rudeness achieved new levels. She acknowledged a number of others who had contributed to relatively small parts of a project, but she never thanked or even acknowledged my extensive efforts on big projects. I also organized the technology inservice but was never thanked; in fact, she thanked someone else!

Taking credit for a teacher's accomplishments was also discussed:

> I asked him, "Why did you sign the grant that I wrote?" He said, "Well, central office would question it. As long as you are my employee, your work is my work and I get the recognition."

At my vocal music programs, she would get up and take credit for outstanding student performances. This also implied to parents and students that I was incompetent and not doing my job, so she had to take over.

His thing was always to take credit and be the center of attention. The discipline committee developed a schoolwide plan, and he didn't have anything to do with it, but on the front page of the policy he wrote [his own name as developer of the plan].

He always claimed credit for new ideas that I brought to him. He stated in front of others that I worked for him, not with him.

Favoring "Select" Teachers

All teachers we interviewed attributed the practice of favoritism to their principals. According to our findings, favoritism refers to inequitable treatment of faculty; select individuals are rewarded while others are punished or neglected or both. Directly and indirectly, principal favoritism reinforced domination of mistreated teachers. Some examples of rewards to favored teachers include being released from attendance at meetings, being assigned better students and classrooms, receiving positive evaluations, receiving support for advancement, and receiving public recognition. Clearly favoritism toward others exacerbated teachers' feelings of mistreatment by principals.

Sheppard and Lewicki (1987) explain that favoritism serves an important function in controlling workers, and it adds insult to injury in the case of a mistreated worker; the abused person now observes others being treated well—a double whammy that severely violates fairness norms. The effects of all this, described in detail later in this book, are far reaching and damaging with respect to a teacher's emotional, physical, social, and professional well-being.

Some people have never gone to one PTA meeting and they have never been written up for failure to go. I missed only one meeting, and she wrote me and others up for failing to complete duties and responsibilities.

It is important to her that people realize that if they don't play ball they will get hurt. For instance, they might have their favorite classes taken away, be put in different rooms all over the school in order to inconvenience them, have permission to go to a conference denied, and certainly would not be allowed to teach courses they wanted to teach.

Some faculty members were her pets, people who agreed with her, never questioned, and just toed the line. It didn't matter what they did, they were going to get super great ratings. Her pets felt like I deserved her mistreatment.

She withheld her signature [from my application for an administrative position in the district] on the basis that there were others that should be ahead of me. But I realized that she wasn't being systematic at all. The others were her pets. That same spring, I went for a job at another school, thinking, "I had better get out of here and go somewhere they will back me."

He gave [a favored teacher] a plaque at a faculty meeting. He said, "Here is a teacher who has been supportive of her principal. She has not gone outside of this school talking about me behind my back. She has been here to help. I am giving her the Principal's Support Award."

There was a strong element of unfairness. One teacher, who had a very strong friendship with the principal, ruled the school, and anybody who crossed that particular teacher would have the wrath of the principal on them. Ninety percent of the principal's abuse was a result of this pet teacher, who was so hated that other teachers would automatically shut down around her. She was up for Teacher of the Year the first two years and nobody would even consider her. As a result, people who were Teachers of the Year were shunned and ridiculed by the principal.

Even mistreated teachers who had been favored at one time by their abusive principals described similar patterns:

Before, I was one of his favorites. I could get away with anything. I could leave early, get there late, practically do anything I wanted. Other teachers would be reprimanded or punished for the same thing. He totally discriminated against teachers he didn't like. . . . He wrote up a teacher he didn't like for being one minute late to her class, but he would come in late himself!

I hate to say it but pretty much whatever I wanted I got. If I needed money for the cheerleaders, a class change, help with a student's behavior, it was taken care of.

In addition, being a favored teacher frequently required, according to our study, that such teachers "spy" for their principals. This issue is discussed fully in the next chapter.

We learned that she had a couple of people keep tabs on the faculty for her. They reported to her exactly what they heard among faculty.

Moreover, as mentioned earlier, favored teachers supported abusive principals in a number of ways that reinforced the principal's domination of targeted teachers and intensified their sense of mistreatment. To illustrate, they encouraged others to comport with the principal's agenda, demonstrated their appreciation for the principal publicly, criticized other faculty, represented the school with external evaluation agencies, and colluded with the principal on decision making.

He had a group of "yes people," particularly the coaches. As the union representative, I circulated a letter to all teachers laying out their rights, saying that they couldn't be required to serve on certain committees and so on. The coaches wrote back across the letter, "Just do it." It's that Nike slogan. Don't question, don't argue, don't complain, just charge forward. We don't need to think or have questions.

If a teacher comes in and has something to say or disagrees—even in a nice, tactful way—that is a threat to his authority, and he gets very defensive. It's the same even if I just want to offer a suggestion, it's the same thing. The outspoken people are the targeted people. The others are always chatting with him, bending over backwards to get along, and bringing in baked goods and coffee on his birthday. They seem to be fine.

The favored group of teachers are wise to the game, cynical, superficial, don't work very hard, report to her on other faculty, and are willing to carry out brutal orders and say hurtful things to people. They are willing to help the principal exercise her authority by extension.

It's racial. Anybody who ever dared to speak up was not chosen to be on the committee that would meet with the accreditation representatives. She put the wealthy whites on committees, but the blacks, the sucker-uppers who do what she says, she appointed as committee chairs.

Her little cliques would meet without the rest of us and decisions would be made.

Being favored by an abusive principal was not without its costs; indeed, the practice of favoritism was in many respects simply another type of principal control of selected teachers. Two teachers previously favored disclosed the following:

I became one of his pets, which I didn't like. He would call me at home and talk to me about the school, or I would end up staying a full day to talk with him but only get paid half time. I would go to all these meetings and take on different committees because I felt like I had to give the extra time. More and more was expected of me. He gave me more of the academically advanced children and children whose parents would be involved in school, and that continued as long as I pleased him. As long as you were the "yes man" he did you favors. But, you felt guilty and you would see the way he treated the other teachers that didn't conform. When I went to him and told him that I didn't want to be a pet anymore, that's when he started abusing me.

I felt continual pressure to volunteer for certain things. I was constantly getting notes in my box to go to this meeting or do something. I certainly was expected to do more than the average staff member. If I told her I couldn't do it, then I was not looked upon favorably.

In essence, the practice of favoritism by abusive principals had several general adverse consequences for teachers, individually and collectively. First, favoritism, because it violated fairness norms central to school culture (Becker, 1980; Blase, 1988b; Dreeben, 1968), greatly exacerbated mistreated teachers' sense of injustice and feelings of anger, fear, and depression. Second, favoritism fractured the political culture of the school; it resulted in cliques, "in groups," and "out groups"; increased distrust; and decreased communication among teachers. Clearly, faculty support for mistreated teachers was problematic under such circumstances.

Offensive Personal Conduct

Two mistreated teachers complained that their abusive principals displayed offensive personal habits and unprofessional conduct; such habits and conduct negatively affected school morale and school climate. One stated,

> He'd always corner me and give me mean, really mean looks. I was very intimidated. He was my principal, my boss, my superior. He would shrug a lot, blow, and like just breathe heavily. He would stand real close to me.

Another principal's personal habits were especially repulsive:

> He had disgusting personal habits. He would walk around the school building or around you, at faculty meetings, or anywhere, and he had uninhibited flatulence. He was always burping and blowing his nose between his thumb and his forefinger in front of everybody; he never used a handkerchief. Other bodily sounds were emitted as well. He was a gross individual, and this reflected on our school as a whole.

Some teachers reported that their abusive principals were also generally unprofessional in their conduct:

> He spent a lot of time doing personal things during the day. He liked to polish rocks. He had some kind of machine in his office where he polished rocks. It was his hobby. He also had old cars that he would work on; he would pull them up to the front and spend time during the day working on his cars.

> He took away the student health clinic so he could have a second office. One day, I was walking down the hall and my kids starting sneezing. We were, like, "What is that smell and where is it coming from? It smells like vanilla." People started laughing, and we found out he had been lighting scented candles in there. The smell is in the school and the candles are glowing.

Other teachers noted that several abusive principals had affairs with their colleagues:

> There was one teacher in particular who spent so much time with him, like hours in his office. She would just leave her classroom unmanned.

> All three of his marriages were to kindergarten teachers. He had affairs with them in the building. The last one was married at the time they had an affair, openly, in the neighborhood. They walked around after school holding hands, that kind of stuff. Of course, it got around to the district and she had to move to another school. He was fired the next year.

There has always been a rumor of affairs that he has had. Those women tend to be secretaries or parents who are volunteers. They seem to stay after school every night with him.

THE VICTIM'S PERSPECTIVE: WHY IS THIS HAPPENING TO ME?

In their seminal studies of the efficiency and effects of democratic versus autocratic leadership styles, White and Lippitt (1960) revealed that autocratic leadership (absent the abusive behaviors discussed throughout this book) results in submissiveness, hostility, discontent, and dependency in followers. Without exception, we found that teachers attributed mistreatment to an inordinate need, on the principals' part, to control and dominate teachers ("She is a control freak." "It's all about power over people."). We also found that teachers who are victimized by authoritarian (abusive) conduct characterized by manipulation, self-aggrandizement, self-centeredness, angry outbursts, and other abusive actions often attribute the problem to principals' "insecurity" (Levinson, 1968). Whyte (1994) writes,

> We have all met in the workplace malevolent characters who bear a grudge against life. Or those who carry a streak of grudge. Try to confront them with their minor cruelties and you are likely to be threatened yourself. They have all the rationales and all the evidence. Their wound is too tender, the grief too raw, and their own sense of righteousness too strong. They have condemned part of their existence to the cellar and they will not forgive it for having hurt them so cruelly. Not only do they have that initial cruelty to face but their own cruelty laid on top of it. They must now forgive not only life but also themselves for having compounded the wrong with a greater wrong. (pp. 196-197)

Other causal theories offered were, "He enjoys putting people down," "She wants to squash any disagreement," "She's vindictive," and "He is a sexist pig." (See Riehl & Lee, 1996, p. 873) for more on how "[s]ocial patterns of power and domination are often closely associated with gender." See also *Note* at the end of this chapter.) Possible causes of principal mistreatment are fully examined in subsequent chapters.

In Chapter 3, we examine some of the more aggressive forms of mistreatment observed in our data: Level 2 principal mistreatment behaviors, which are direct and escalating.

NOTE

In July 2001, ABC News produced a special, *Powerfully Nice,* noting that although women occupy about 12% of executive jobs in the United States, to achieve these positions, they were often tough and forceful. Many are now finding that they have been *too* tough on people; some of these women are being sent to a corporate coaching program called "Bully Broads" to learn ways to temper and improve their approach to leadership.

3 Escalating Mistreatment of Teachers

From Spying to Criticism

In the societies of the highly industrialized western world, the workplace is the only remaining battlefield where people can "kill" each other without running the risk of being taken to court.

— Heinz Leymann, Swedish father of the international antibullying movement (cited in Namie & Namie, 2001, p. 91)

Equivalent drive-by shootings occur every day in the corporate office. One deadly manipulative conversation or maneuver can finish a life' s ideals in a moment. Young spirits can shrivel and die on contact when ambushed by the orphaned and disowned shadows of many corporate cultures.

— Whyte (1994, p. 157)

This chapter describes some of the direct and escalating aggressive forms of mistreatment observed in our data: Level 2 principal mistreatment behaviors. These include spying, sabotaging, stealing, destroying teacher instructional aids, and making unreasonable work demands—as well as one of the more serious and most prevalent mistreatment behaviors, unfair and harsh criticism of teachers' work and abilities. We begin with a general discussion of authoritarian and control-oriented types of leaders and why people consent to such indefensible attempts to control them.

THE AUTHORITARIAN OR COERCIVE LEADER

When Lee (1997) asked thousands of people, "When do you feel comfortable making others do what you want?" they responded, "when enforcing safety measures, meeting deadlines, averting potential or present threat to life or property, preventing moral or ethical violations, and dealing with those who have limited or impaired abilities." Obviously, school principals face situations in which such reasons for controlling others may apply. Yet, when no adverse conditions exist, some principals predictably resort to coercive (i.e., punishing) forms of control such as bullying, force, and intimidation to achieve their ends. Why? Emotional factors that trigger the use of unwarranted forms of coercion in some people include impatience, tiredness, anger, lack of skill, lack of hope, insecurity, threats to ego, an inordinate need to control, and a myriad of other thoughts and feelings. In addition, social factors—social modeling, mob psychology, a need to create the illusion of control, short-term payoffs, and peer approval—may trigger the use of coercion (Lee, 1997).

According to Lee (1997), one can employ a soft or a hard approach to control and coercion. The soft approach is characterized by misleading, beguiling, deceiving, seducing, deterring, diverting, saddening, discouraging, inhibiting, or tricking others. Suppressing, forcing, controlling, intimidating, bullying, threatening, scaring, belittling, prohibiting, disparaging, emasculating, and disenfranchising are examples of the hard approach.

We have already presented many instances of both approaches to control from our study. Plainly, the abusive principals described thus far fail to exhibit positive forms of power associated with honorable people (e.g., persuasion, patience, gentleness, acceptance, kindness, knowledge, discipline, consistency, and integrity) (Lee, 1997). To the contrary, the coercive behaviors—as exhibited by principals in our study—create adversarial and hostile relationships associated with compliance, resistance, revenge, sabotage, distrust, or revolt. It should be emphasized that when principals treat teachers coercively, they often produce the very behaviors they may have been attempting to avoid (Hornstein, 1996).

Of course, not all forms of control are harmful. To illustrate, authentic praise by a principal for a teacher's effective use of an instructional strategy may produce teacher acquiescence based on consent. In fact, Blase and Kirby (2000) found that a principal's use of positive forms of control can have significant positive effects on teachers. However, the excessive use of these types of control by a principal results in less control by teachers; its use limits teachers' voice, professional discretion, and efficacy, among other things. Malen and Ogawa (1988) found that principals' inappropriate use of control is alive and well even in purportedly shared-decision-making schools. Similarly, Blase and Blase (2001) discovered this in the shared-governance schools they excluded from their study of empowering principals. Unfortunately, authoritarian and coercive leaders in general have a tendency to misuse power and harm others because they consistently seek compliance and domination. They simply are not demanding leaders or leaders with high expectations, which can be a positive approach to leadership (Hornstein, 1996); rather, they are abusive leaders. This is an important distinction. Studies have demonstrated that, given the significance of the principalship to teachers, the repeated use of just one negative coercive strategy by a principal (e.g., criticism) can depreciate a teacher, personally and professionally, and produce adverse affective, cognitive, and behavioral outcomes for teachers, which, in turn, negatively affect student learning (Blase, 1988a; Blase & Blase, 1998; Malen & Ogawa, 1988).

POWER IS SEDUCTIVE

Any inequity in power may be disruptive to interpersonal relationships; such inequities can undermine a leader's ability to maintain close, friendly relationships with others who are less powerful (e.g., Kipnis, 1972; Sampson, 1965; Sorokin & Lunden, 1959). Why? Researchers have shown that having "power over" others increases the likelihood that the powerholder will manipulate those with less power (Kreisberg, 1992). Having power also appears to lead to the development of a cognitive and perceptual system (or habitual way of thinking) that leaders use to justify the use of power to manipulate subordinates (Adams & Balfour, 1998; Kipnis, 1972). In addition, the subordinates' behavior itself (e.g., the mere appearance of a powerholder often causes changes in subordinates' posture, demeanor, and activity) may reinforce a powerholder's "exalted" perception of self (Kipnis, 1972; Ott & Russell, 2000). Teachers, for example, often change their behavior when a principal is present; their subordinate status provokes an attentive watchfulness and tuning of their responses to the moods and requirements of the principal (Blase, J., 1997, Blase, J. J., 1988b). By implication, principals would tend to be more unguarded and may exhibit a certain "habitual haughtiness" and superiority that is associated with the bearing of power and authority (Ott & Russell, 2000). In fact, in his study of 200 professionals, Kelley (1992) found that, according to followers, 40% of bosses had questionable leadership abilities; only one in seven leaders presented a potential role model to be emulated; less than 50% instilled trust; and nearly 40% had ego problems—that is, bosses were often threatened by subordinates, they needed to assert their superiority, and they never shared the limelight with others. Our data demonstrate that such descriptors are especially applicable to abusive principals.

WHY PEOPLE CONSENT WITHOUT QUESTIONING

Kelley (1992) also found that 30% of those surveyed often or always accept what bosses, teachers, doctors, and other authority figures tell them without question. Kelley wrote,

> Much of our social structure reinforces the leader's final authority and the follower' s duty to obey. Religion teaches not to question God's laws or

purpose, obedience is explicitly codified in military law, and when a coach tells you to run laps or a supervisor tells you to write a report, your immediate presumption is that you will do it. To obey is expected and rewarded, and to disobey requires explanation and the risk of punishment. The leader then benefits from the presumption of expertise, legitimacy, and trust, while followers have to overcome considerable social conventions to challenge the leader's position. (1992, pp. 169-170)

Similarly, Kreisberg (1992) argues that "the pervasiveness of domination throughout the world suggests that it is commonly maintained through more subtle processes than the exercise of brute force. Domination is perpetuated through the ability of those who dominate to gain the consent of the oppressed without the awareness of the oppressed that they are participating in their own suppression" (p. 14).

In addition, de la Boétie (1975) notes that self-deception can deprive people of freedom; that is, those who passively consent to others' power and control eventually find themselves victims of their own obedience. This passive consent is "the tyrant's best friend, whereas education about the nature of consent, freedom, and power is his greatest enemy" (p. 54). De la Boétie saw organized withdrawal of people's consent as the only remedy for state tyranny, and he suggested that this is best used when those who are tyrannized have thoughtlessly deceived themselves into obeying and thus made the tyranny possible. Knights and Willmott (1985) also note that individuals' unintended responses and passive consent to their situations often reinforce the conditions of domination and disenfranchisement. Finally, in his extensive review of related evidence, Martin (1986a, 1986b) found that individuals often accept injustice without responding, even when being unfairly treated personally.

Clearly, the consent of the oppressed is central to understanding the psychological bases of the exercise of power, including a powerholder's imposition of control over others. Nyberg's (1993) work is instructive along these lines. He described different forms of consent based on the quality of information one has when deciding to consent to another's use of power:

- Acquiescence under threat of sanction
- Compliance based on partial or slanted information
- Indifference due to habit and apathy
- Conformity to custom
- Commitment through informed judgment

The first four types of consent are not based on informed judgment. Nyberg argues that, in a democracy, consent based on informed judgment should be a political and social ideal.

In sum, control and domination are based on power inequities in a given situation and this allows an individual (or group) to control the behavior and possibly even the thoughts and values of others to fulfill their desires (Kreisberg, 1992). Dominated people are known to suffer "in the box"; they withdraw, suffer diminished self-concept, experience fear, tend to be cautious, and experience depression as well as other adverse psychological, social, and political outcomes. Indeed, although people in organizational settings need leaders, they do not want or need to be dominated or exploited (Gibb, 1968). When control is necessary, it is the positive form of control based on consent that tends to be effective; Louisa may be Thomas's boss, but Thomas's conduct should be based on his informed consent, not on Louisa's domination of Thomas.

In the following two sections, we present our findings about Level 2 principal mistreatment behaviors, i.e., direct and escalating aggression. Principals' authoritarian and coercive orientation as well as teachers' acquiescence (based on fear) are vividly apparent.

LEVEL 2 PRINCIPAL MISTREATMENT: DIRECT AND ESCALATING AGGRESSION

The results of our study indicated six forms of escalating mistreatment of teachers by principals; these behaviors comprise direct and escalating aggression against teachers.

Level 2 Principal Mistreatment Behaviors

- Spying
- Sabotaging
- Stealing
- Destroying teacher instructional aids
- Making unreasonable work demands
- Criticism

Spying

Most of the teachers who participated in our study accused their principals of personally spying on them. For example, some abusive principals ominously situated themselves in hallways near teachers' classroom doors:

> I would be lecturing and he would come and stand in the doorway behind me, where I couldn't see him. My kids would see this and tell me later, but I just tried to downplay it. . . . It's embarrassing. The one day that really got me was when he did it and the kids later asked, "Why does Mr. Blake give you a hard time?" . . . I felt like the warden is walking by looking in my prison cell!

> She used to hang around outside my room eavesdropping on me. The students also would tell me that she would stand outside the lounge door to listen during teacher conversations.

Some principals surreptitiously used the intercom to listen to classroom activity:

> One blatant way she abused power was by listening in on the intercom. We were unable to discern when it was on. We were told that our classroom teaching became the entertainment for her and select friends in the office.

> The intercom comes on any old time and you know that she is listening to you. That is terrible! One time I did stand up and say, "I am not going to put up with this." . . . That escalated her listening in on my room.

In addition, several teachers reported that their principals monitored their telephone conversations:

> He would listen in on a personal phone call. He would come up close to hear and then question you about it later. Like, if you made a medical appointment, you would have to describe your symptoms to him.

Most of the teachers we interviewed indicated that abusive principals also solicited the services of other, favored teachers to spy on them:

> The favored group of teachers are wise to the game, cynical, superficial, don't work very hard, report to her on other faculty, and are willing to carry out brutal orders and say hurtful things to people. They are willing to help the principal exercise her authority by extension.

> She had some pets who were her stoolies and you knew right fast who they were. Any little thing that would happen on a hall would go through the pipeline straight up to her. She would praise and support the stoolies. You didn't say anything about them.

In a couple of cases, teachers were not sure if, in fact, certain teachers were informants for the principal:

> We had a joke that the lounge was bugged, because he seemed to know everything that everybody said. I don't know if there really were some teachers going to him and repeating things, but we didn't dare say anything about him in the lounge.

According to our data, some abusive principals used parents to spy on teachers:

> It's constant harassment from this man and the parents who are basically snooping for him. He started bringing this woman down to "help" me, supposedly. So, I said, "I do not want any help, there are already 37 people in my half of the trailer." He said she was going to be in there anyway.

> She had a group of crony parents who were up at the school every day. They were her little kitchen cabinet. They were always looking around the

school and going back and telling her about teachers. Then the teachers were getting called in on this and on that. If any of her crony parents' kids gave you a problem, you knew you better not say anything about it or you were going to get it.

Sabotaging

Teachers disclosed that principals manipulated other faculty to sabotage efforts designed to benefit students or colleagues:

I was asked in a district meeting to give my feedback in reference to developing exploratory classes. Now, if you ask my opinion, you need to be prepared to hear what I'm going to say. I'm not going to kiss up. They asked me and I told them what I thought. The principal didn't like what I said. When I was awarded a grant for a project, she did everything she could to sabotage the project. Word got back to me that the principal said no one was supposed to help me, and she made sure that no one did. In essence, the grant I got was wasted.

I informally went around to a few people and asked if they would be interested in this project to support teacher development. They were. When she got wind of this, she went around to her inner group and said, "This is a lame brain idea, a very flaky and stupid thing, and anybody who gets involved is a real loser and will be seen as working against the administration."

Stealing

Several abusive principals were accused by teachers of stealing from them and others:

You never left your biscuits or your pastries out! If you happened to have a drink or coffee on your desk, he would take the food into his office and come back and take your drink to wash it down with. If we ever confronted him about stealing our lunches and snacks, he would just deny he knew anything about it. But, you had just seen him take it! The secretary in the office one day brought pizza and he just walked by, with her at her desk, and grabbed up the whole plate. Then came back and grabbed her soda up and washed the whole thing down. There was never a word like, "Oh, I am sorry. Was that your lunch?" It was pretty commonplace. He would raid the refrigerator in the teacher's lounge, too.

The principal said, "I hope you didn't mind but I sold my pickup truck yesterday afternoon, and the only way that I could sell it was if I threw your air conditioner in with it." It was a new, very expensive air conditioner! I was shocked, but I was afraid to say anything. My husband had a fit.

I had my suspicions in November when I lost my diary. I kept it in the room. I would write things down that the principal did as they happened. I turned the room upside down to find it but never did. I am convinced to this day that he took it.

One teacher reported that her principal stole school funds, money that otherwise could have been used for instructional and extracurricular activities:

I figured that she was skimming between $1000 to $2000 a month. She had a little scam going with snacks. She would never let the PTA see how much money was collected. She would sell little cups of ice cream and stuff, believe it or not. The secretary was picked up by the police, and she was charged with theft and convicted. The principal was never even reprimanded.

Destroying Teacher Instructional Aids

Some abusive principals literally destroyed classroom instructional aids or ordered teachers to remove them from their rooms. The experiences of two veterans, both highly recognized teachers, are especially poignant.

I had a beautiful loft in my room with pillows and a huge bookshelf that you could convert into a stage. It was great. The principal ordered it destroyed. But I went over his head—a bad thing, according to him. I asked the county warehouse people if they had to take the loft. They said no. So, I wanted my husband and some men to dismantle it so I could store it in my basement. When I came back one day after lunch, the warehouse people had axed the reading loft! The principal also ordered me to move a shelf from under the blackboard that was so convenient for the children. Everything that I have ever learned about math and teaching supports using concrete objects. He said the solid oak desk in my room was really a piece of junk and we were going to get rid of it. . . . I had a guinea pig and he made me get rid of it. He said that it was unhealthy and dangerous; if a child was bitten, we could be sued. [Reading from her journal:] He stripped away everything that made my room unique, that makes teachers special, sets one teacher apart from another. A package that says to children here I am, examine me, question me, shake, rattle, and roll me and I will open up for you and reveal everything. What happens when a teacher is stripped of her style, when, year after year, her brightly colored package is picked at? Off come the ribbons, the bows, the brightly colored paper. What is left is a shell, an empty box. I was a teacher who had a special style of teaching. But everything that made me special has been done away with. Circle meetings were stopped. The Friday workshops were ceased. I have lost so much of myself. The more bookwork, page work, and blackboard work that I do, the less alive the students seem; I can see a change. The light went out of their eyes. I was told I needed to control them rather than making learning a joint venture. I became a teaching box—filling up heads with information so that they could pass the test. I want to work in an atmosphere of ease and acceptance, not constant anxiety. I want to work where teachers, all teachers, are appreciated, not just a chosen few. I was Teacher-of-the-Year, sponsored the educational fair, won first place in other competitions, and was nominated for teacher of excellence. But all that was me is gone now. I want out.

My classroom is a potpourri of lots of different resources, books, equipment, and all kinds of things. I am a teacher of gifted children. But the principal said to me, "You are considered the best teacher in the school, and I have heard only wonderful things about you. I know that you are a perfect teacher, but I repeat again, no child can learn in that filthy mess! Get rid of all of it!" Nobody could believe that he was doing this. I wasn't allowed out of my classroom for weeks. He made me throw away thousands of dollars worth of resources. I kept thinking, I have to see somebody to see if I can retire. I will just clean up as if I am retiring.

Making Unreasonable Work Demands

In conjunction with a larger pattern of mistreatment, teachers were also subjected to mistreatment with regard to work standards (i.e., nitpicking) and unreasonable work demands (i.e., overloading):

Nitpicking

Principals nitpicked about time or micromanaged teachers' time.

At 8:00 every morning, he was in the parking lot with a sign-in sheet. As people pulled in, he would write down their time. If they got there at 8:02 or 8:03, at the end of the day, he would announce over the intercom, "Ms. So-and-So needs to stay until 4:10, Ms. So-and-So needs to stay until 4:07." I had a fish tank in my room and one of the fish died. I wanted to replace the fish during lunch, and it took me 25 minutes. I had to stay 25 minutes later that afternoon because I left during the day to go get the fish.

He was very big on this time thing. He actually put in a time clock for us to punch in on. At a faculty meeting, we made the comment that we felt this was very blue collar, not professional treatment. You couldn't be late, not one minute late for any reason. He said that we are blue collar types if we can't be on time.

A teacher arrived at school with a lot of stuff in her car, so she unloaded it. A student stopped her on the way in, and then she went back to get the other load. But it was after 8:00 when she came back into the building. Even though she had already been in the building, the principal marked her as tardy.

Every morning she stood by the clock. At 7:45 on the dot, she would pick up the clipboard with the sign-in sheet and highlight every name that hadn't signed in. Teachers were very upset. Some got there only a couple of minutes late and others had been there since 7:00 working but hadn't signed in yet.

At that point, he started clocking me to make sure that my class ended exactly on time and that I had five minutes between classes. He was outside my door many, many, many times to make sure that I ended at exactly at 10:11. It wasn't even an even number, 10:11.

Every morning he would come out into the halls, and his favorite thing to say to teachers, which he said very sternly, was, "Get to your stations!" Those were his favorite words.

Overloading

Teachers reported that principals occasionally overloaded them with work that they considered trivial in nature:

The last week of school is so very difficult, it can be stressful. While students are still in your classroom, teachers are expected to do cumulative folders, record skills, grades, attendance, and so on. The principal came around and told the teachers to check each other's folders and sign affidavits. I was crushed that she felt after teaching eight years I needed four other teachers to check my work. Our attendance codes were very clear and easily understood by any auditor who would check our roll books. But no, she told us that different codes needed to be filled in for 25 students times 180 days. That was around 5000 codes. Teachers had hateful looks on their faces. Everyone was mad.

A few teachers experienced work overload as a major form of ongoing mistreatment:

That year, the principal made me take study hall and work on teen parenting as well as full-time teaching. It was illegal, but I was stuck. He was audited and cited for that by the state.

During one of the incidents that I had with the principal, after I told him that I wanted to transfer, he said that he had ways to make people regret the choices they made. He made me teach all the lab classes and also take the yearbook sponsorship.

I was handling textbooks and teaching an extra sixth period. I was also given permanent bus duty. So, I asked, "With all my other extra duties, what is the reasoning?" She said, "Because I said so." I thought that [so much work] was humanly impossible and resigned as department head.

A teacher's workload, described as "too difficult and excessive," was a dominant form of one principal's mistreatment that spanned several years:

I certainly was expected to do more than the average staff member. I was pressured to volunteer. I had notes in my box to go to meetings. I was on committees. I did workshops for seven years. I was grade-level chair for five years (which was supposed to be rotated). It was a lot of extra work. I was not getting paid extra. . . . Once I said, "Working with some of the faculty is really pretty tough." She said, "Oh, I know, but you always do such a good job. I know that so-and-so will never get this done and you will." My seventh year was by far the worst—when I wouldn't do something she was not very pleased. When I had a problem with two teachers she just said, "You are wasting my time and I am sure that you will be able to handle this." It was that kind of thing: Just go handle it. Now I am in a worse position than before. I feel like I am getting it from all ends.

Criticism: The Ubiquitous Form of Level 2 Principal Mistreatment

Keashly (1998) found that emotional abuse in the workplace often includes excessive or harsh criticism, for example the following:

- Putdowns, insults, belittling comments, name calling (often in front of others)
- Criticism of one's work or abilities
- Personal criticism of features irrelevant to one's job
- Spreading untrue rumors or gossip

In the remaining pages of this chapter, we discuss the many forms of principal criticism described by teachers including several types of private criticism (i.e., direct criticism, stigmatizing and pejorative labeling, intentionally vague criticism, use of a snitch's information, gossiping, soliciting others, and public criticism). All the teachers we studied indicated that their principals unfairly and routinely criticized them.

Private Criticism

Private criticism took six forms:

Direct Criticism. Teachers explained that they were privately and routinely criticized for a range of issues, such as classroom teaching, plan books, classrooms, use of keys, conduct of department meetings, dress, getting pregnant, ink color, and behavior at faculty meetings. Principals' criticism was usually conveyed with strong negative affect, both verbal (e.g., yelling) and nonverbal (e.g., pounding the desk). Such criticism was also considered "unfair" and "unjustified." For example, principals criticized teachers' instruction and planning:

Because some students complained, the principal called me in and said, "I think you are expecting too much from these students." I said, "These kids are used to playing and watching movies all day. They were far below grade level and I pulled them up to grade level." But even when they misbehaved on the bus, I was bawled out.

He would bring teachers into his office and intimidate them. You could hear him pound on his desk and yell at them for all kinds of things. He took my plan books every week and graded them in red ink. He'd write ugly comments. He would leave little notes in teachers boxes about things that weren't true, like "Your class was noisy." He would sit in your classroom and later leave a note that would say, "I was disappointed in your English lesson today." He would just make things up!

According to teachers, principals privately criticized them for what the principals defined as "messy" classrooms:

The principal would say, "Your room is too cluttered and you need to clean it up!" I have boxes and things stacked around on top shelves, but it is not at all unattractive and it is certainly not messy. I just have work centers. The teacher two doors down was a whole lot worse than me, but he wouldn't fuss about that. I had many parents requesting that their children be put in my room, but no matter what research or ammunition I had to back up what I was doing, once he set his mind to something, that was it. He said, "You are becoming known as the play teacher."

In the morning of the first day of teaching, after a week full of beginning teacher meetings, the new principal came into my room and asked, "What would the superintendent say about this classroom?" I said, "That this is a very creative class and that a lot of learning goes on in here." He said, "No, he would say this is a mess!" With incredible force, he ripped a stray piece of paper off the bookcase and said, "This is what I am talking about! This room is a wreck! No child can learn in this room! I want this room cleaned up, everything thrown away." I said, "Mr. Wilson, this is a discovery room, an art room. All of these supplies are things that we need to create projects." He pulled out some film and said, "I have taken pictures of every single nook and cranny of your room, every drawer and every closet. Your room is a mess!" I almost got hysterical because I had never been harassed like this before. I have been here 28 years and I have never had a problem. I have been Teacher of the Year and I was the Honor Teacher of the County. It is not like I don't know what I'm doing.

One teacher was rudely criticized because she asked to borrow some keys.

Standard operating procedure was that he would blindside you. When you are sick or if your mother just died, he pulls you into his office for unbelievable scenes. When I needed his keys to classrooms to fix machines, he started screaming at me that I didn't want those keys, that I didn't understand anything, that I wasn't a professional. I was so upset . . . I couldn't stop crying. Then he went on a tirade about how the faculty doesn't understand, he has done everything for them, and they have betrayed him.

Another principal criticized a teacher for how her department conducted its faculty meetings, among other things:

He said to me, "You better learn how to run a department meeting," but he was never explicit about any problem. Once he got in my face and accused me of allowing kids to smoke. . . . At a meeting with him and my union representative, he said, "Your perception of me was totally false; I haven't treated you badly, never." So I pulled out my journal and started reading quotes from him. . . . He wouldn't apologize.

Teachers' dress was frequently a topic of unfounded principal criticism:

My colleague was ridiculed and berated by the principal because she didn't get permission to wear jeans. The principal pulled her in the office and ripped her apart, told her that she was immature and she still belonged at college, she didn't have any business being in a school, and she needed to grow up. A very dear friend who happened to be Teacher of the Year was told by this same principal that she has a reputation for being lazy. The principal just basically got enjoyment out of getting people to cry. It's a power thing for her. She called another teacher all kinds of unprofessional names.

A teacher discussed how her colleagues were criticized for being pregnant:

A teacher said she was thinking about starting her family but she wanted to wait and see if the principal would retire, because the principal had previously confronted people about being pregnant. That's against the law! The principal would say, "What poor timing. How dare you think you can have a baby at the beginning of September!" One of the teachers miscarried; she was devastated. She said she thought it was from the stress at school.

One teacher described what her principal did when she had used a particular color ink on a form.

One morning I found a note in my box that said I had signed my report cards with the wrong color ink, blue instead of black. The principal pulled me out of class into the hallway and said, "You were told this was the way it was to be done, and you have not followed those directions!" I apologized twice but he kept berating me. The next day, I got a reprimand in my box. I was totally humiliated as a professional.

Teachers were privately criticized for their behavior at school faculty meetings:

He called me into his office with the assistant principal and chewed me out. He told me that my attitude was unacceptable, that I sit in faculty meetings and stare out into space. I said, "You have pushed me into a corner and I live in fear every day of what you might do to me, like you have done to others. I don't like this feeling and the way you treat me, and I am angry."

One new principal unfairly criticized a teacher for securing a coaching position by going to the superintendent "behind his back":

He said very loudly, "I see you have gone behind my back." I thought, "Who is he talking to?" I didn't have a clue as to what the problem was. I asked what he was referring to, and he said, "We don't need to get into that." Then he started on another tirade. He kept repeating, "You have gone behind my back, and if I am going to run the ship, I have to have a tight ship and everyone has to be loyal." I had never been chewed out before. I had always been told by administrators that we are really glad you are here. This was foreign to me. The chair that he had for me to sit in was very low. This guy has set up this little room for these kinds of interrogations. He was yelling and red in the face. I finally got that he was upset about my appointment (prior to his arrival) as wrestling coach. . . . Then he started off on another tirade about the chain of command.

Needless to say, principals' criticisms of teachers included countless other issues (e.g., failure to complete tasks, unprofessional conduct toward students, matters of delegation, a teachers' acceptance of a new position in the district, and general incompetence). And most important, criticism was, teachers reported, based on false or manufactured information and was thus considered grossly unfair. In most cases, principals were accused of failing to conduct proper investigations (or any investigation) of the issue at hand before attacking the teacher; in other words, accusations without investigation were commonplace.

I work out of the district office during preplanning. Well, my coordinator got an e-mail from this principal about my performance, that I had not gone over to meet him and that after talking with faculty members at his school, he found out that I had done nothing for the special ed program all last year. He questioned whether or not I would be able to act professionally or hold my own around top professionals from the county like our superintendent. Both my coordinator and I were shocked! I went over to the school to ask the teachers if they had any complaints against me. They all went "What? Get out of here!" because they really do like me.

When two other teachers failed to do their part of our group work, I was the one disciplined. I started getting called into the office more and more for a lot of minor things. . . . At any given moment, I might be called to the office and chastised for something. It was almost every week.

The principal who had hired me seemed to be calling me in once a week with some concern. He fussed at me for having delegated something to a band booster parent. When I said I was sure he delegated things to his staff, too, it really set him off! He yelled at me. He seemed to interpret this to mean that he could not do his job without help. He was a very physically imposing man and he turned red and his temples and jaw muscles pulsed angrily.

My principal played favorites. He gave a rival candidate a copy of the interview questions for the assistant principal position. When I got the position, he stated that the only reason I got the job was because of who I knew. Later during the year, he would not even look at me.

Stigmatizing and Pejorative Labeling. Unjustified principal criticism of teachers was frequently nonspecific; it consisted primarily of pejorative labeling, such as accusing individuals of being negative:

As the union representative, I wrote a letter to the principal saying there was no educational substance behind his approach and that my students weren't learning anything. He wrote back, "You are just being negative and unwilling to change. Your attitude is the problem and you are undermining the staff and morale." He circulated the letter to the whole staff. I filed a grievance that forced him to back down. After that, it's been a cold war.

She said, "You have changed . . . become a negative person, not positive, don't care about kids, and are not a valuable asset to the school." She felt somebody was making me be this negative person, else why would I vote against the pay-for-performance program?

I had requested repair for our old and obsolete makeshift computers. The principal called me and accused me of being a complainer, a negative influence on the kids and other faculty members. He said that I was self-serving and did not look out for the school or its reputation.

Intentionally Vague Criticism. In other cases, teachers reported that principals' criticism was intentionally vague:

I asked him what else was I doing wrong. He said, "I have concerns." I said, "Okay, what are those concerns?" He said, "No, I just have concerns." He was sitting at his desk. He had me sit down and just kind of stared at me. I said, "Is there a problem?" He said, "No, there is not a problem," and just maintained his silence. . . . I felt he was trying to intimidate me.

Using a Snitch's Information to Criticize. Moreover, our data indicate that principals intentionally made unfounded criticisms they claimed a third party (e.g., teacher, student) had initiated or reinforced. Nonattendance at an assembly, having a negative attitude, yelling at students, and use of student worksheets are but a few examples of this kind of criticism.

The principal came over the intercom, very loud and angry. She told me to come to her office immediately. She blasted me out for not being at the assembly. But my assistant was with the kids and their behavior was fine. I had taken 30 minutes to get an upset child and a very upset mother on their way (I was upset, too). She told me in a very hard tone that maybe I needed to think about another job. She said that I was negative and that other teachers had said the same thing.

I was called into her office about the fourth or fifth week of the first year. She said another teacher had told her that I had referred to a child as "stupid." Her tone was very harsh. I sat there trembling. (I can feel my insides trembling now.) I hoped that my face was not reflective of my feelings. I thought I was going to burst into tears. I said to her as calmly as I could, "I did not say that. I did not do that. I would never do that. That is not a word that I allow the children to use. I certainly would not say that." She would not tell me who had heard this. . . . "You are the most negative person on my staff," she said. That was the last straw for me. I walked out. No sooner did I get out of the office [than] I was in tears. Some of the teachers came to me and knew immediately something awful had happened, but I didn't feel like I could say anything because supposedly somebody had said untrue things to the principal and I didn't know who.

She called me into the office and said, "A number of parents have brought to my attention that you were screaming at the children and we can't have that." I couldn't believe that a principal was saying that! She was just lying. I said, "Get those people who told you this, and I want to meet with the superintendent right now!" She said, "I don't quite remember who they are."

He lied. He said five parents had complained about me. The whole thing was made up except for one parent who had actually complained. The principal decided to make this a lot bigger than it was. He said, "You seem a bit defensive about this." He put his elbows on the desk and leaned over and said, "Let me tell you something. If your test scores are not where they should be this year, you will appear before the superintendent." I said, "Fine. I am not afraid to meet with him and tell him what I have done during the year." When I walked out of the office I heard him say to the assistant principal, "Good job," as in "we intimidated her, really scared her."

During a faculty meeting, an overwhelmed kindergarten teacher was listening but also trying to catch up on some paperwork. She got called into the office and told how rude she was. He called her all kinds of unprofessional names and told her that parents were talking about her behind her back. None of this was true.

Gossiping. Sometimes principal criticism was indirect and took the form of gossiping to other teachers and even to parents:

We caught the principal all the time telling one teacher what another teacher had said, and it was always something derogatory. He was trying to pit teachers against each other, and I think he enjoyed knowing that he made someone upset or seeing someone cry. He used to call me to his office and make me listen to him talk about other teachers. I felt very uncomfortable.

The principal went to the black teacher and told her that the white teacher had complained about her. Then the black teacher jumped all over the white teacher. The principal never addressed the fact that one teacher was not doing her duty. She just liked to see teachers fighting. That's how she is.

Soliciting Others. One teacher disclosed that a principal tried to solicit her help in disparaging a vice principal who had gained popularity during the principal's absence from the school:

The vice principal wrote me a bad letter of reference. When I confronted him, he admitted that it was based on hearsay. I said, "You have cost me a job, cost me a promotion, and cost me a chance to get ahead in another setting!" Then the principal, who was threatened and dethroned by the assistant principal's popularity as acting principal during her illness, asked me to grieve the assistant principal for having done this. Now she is going to exercise some muscle, and one of the things she would like to do is nail the vice principal.

In one case, the help of another principal was solicited:

He's gotten his friends to harass me. He got another principal to write me a letter about my teaching saying, "Let me tell you what you can do to be a better teacher. You are too theoretical, you don't need to apply research in the classroom." I don't even know this woman!

Public Criticism

Our data indicate that teachers were also publicly criticized and humiliated by principals and that such criticism was based on fallacious or distorted information and was accompanied by strong negative affect and offensive nonverbal behavior. Principals criticized teachers in the presence of others in the school's front office area, at faculty meetings, in classrooms, over the intercom, in lunchrooms and hallways, and in other places, as the following examples illustrate:

Front Office. Teachers described abusive incidents by principals that occurred in the front office area of their schools:

I sent an abused child with blisters on his back to the principal, but he sent the child back and told me, "This needs to be ignored because it is not good for school-community relations." So, I ended up going to our juvenile court judge who called the principal and had the principal report it to Family and Children Services. I was in the office and happened to be down on my knees filling out something and he said, "Ms. Jackson, that's where you belong, on your knees." He said it really mean, like I should be subservient. Then he walked into his office and slammed his door.

I was the speech therapist and I serviced the children for that school. There was a child whose family was putting pressure on this principal to get their child serviced. The paperwork hadn't come through the unit yet and I was waiting. The office was crowded with secretaries and teachers going in and out. The hallway was crowded with teachers and parents going in and out. The principal stopped me in the doorway and asked me if I had started seeing this child. When I told the principal I was waiting for paperwork before servicing a special child, his face turned all beet red and he started shouting. He wanted to know if I knew who he was. He was furious and screaming and hollering: "Do you know who I am? I am in charge here!" People were staring. I was shocked. I just couldn't believe that a person who was in a position of authority was behaving in such an unprofessional manner. I was physically shaking hard for 15 or 20 minutes. I was so angry that he had abused his authority by treating a teacher that way.

I had been waiting for the principal in the office area, doing a good deed, trying to help the secretary. When the principal arrived, I jokingly said, "I am glad you finally got back." She flew into a tirade saying, "I don't care how long you have been waiting. What do you think I have been doing, standing around the corner picking my nose?!" It was awful. I was so embarrassed. Everybody had the same dumbfounded look on their faces. I froze. I was in shock. She had these kinds of incidents with other teachers . . . bawling them out in front of their students and coworkers. It was embarrassing. I was disappointed and hurt. It was a public reprimand.

This new teacher, Jane, was basically trying to protect the principal when she reported that the principal's pet teacher was making derogatory comments about her [the principal] around the school. The principal then twisted it around and made it look like Jane was a troublemaker and that no school wanted her anyway. She made all the teachers in a grade level march in the office and sign a form in front of Jane saying that she lied. Teachers were afraid and felt terrible but thought their jobs could be threatened, so they went along. Jane ended up hospitalized for a nervous breakdown.

I was trying to explain an error about directions on a form to the registrar. The principal started jumping on my case like I had no business questioning that! She was real harsh. She yelled, and I kept saying, "Wait a minute," but she just kept on and on. She was screaming. She looked at me with fire in her eyes!

Faculty Meetings. Many teachers' mistreatment experiences included frequent public ridicule of themselves and colleagues at faculty meetings.

> At one of the first faculty meetings he told us he was locking the supply closet. We took it as an affront to our professional status. We weren't used to being treated this way. Some teachers went to talk to him, but he blew it up into an argument. He had gotten red in the face in that meeting, just a hateful look on his face. He slammed his fist down on the table and we all just kind of jumped back. We have never been faced with something like that before. . . . We got a letter in our boxes that said if other incidents like this turned up, he would put a letter in our files downtown. He said that he didn't need to justify his actions to us. He said, "Things are going to be the way I say they are going to be! You are not going to tell me how to run my school. Things are not going to be done the way they were in the past. I am here to straighten you teachers out!"

> No matter what you did, you were criticized. I would come in early and work late, and he said, "If you have to come in early and stay late, you are not organized! You don't know what you are doing!" He said this at a faculty meeting. At another faculty meeting, he said the same thing about teachers who come in on the weekend and work. These teachers are so conscientious they want to work during off time. They want to get things ready for the kids, to be prepared, and he criticized them for it.

> Another bad part was embarrassing teachers in front of other teachers. He was notorious for keeping teachers at meetings until 5:00 or 6:00. At one meeting, I got up to leave to meet my father to pick out my mother's tombstone. I was halfway across the room and he screamed at me, "Do you have a problem?!" I said, "I told you earlier I was going to meet my father to pick out my mother's tombstone." . . . I said, "My working hours are 7:30 to 3:30 and it is 3:30 now and I am leaving," and I left.

> If a teacher asked a question, he would say things like, "Ms. So-and-So, did you understand what I said? Could you explain it to the other teacher because obviously she wasn't listening."

One teacher reported that her principal's criticism during a faculty meeting took the form of mocking her:

> While I was speaking during a faculty meeting and offering to help get a gift for our visiting review people, the principal was whispering and mouthing my words to the group. She was mocking me in front of the staff. She was also saying, "I've already taken care of that, blah, blah, blah. . . . We have got it all together." She didn't stop me to say it, she mouthed it to the faculty who were then laughing. The sucker-uppers laugh on cue. She'll do that kind of thing with anyone who would dare speak up.

Classroom. It was not uncommon for abusive principals to criticize teachers in their classrooms, in which students and others were present:

> All of a sudden my door was opened and pushed very hard, enough that it slammed into my desk. I was shocked. This immediately got the attention of my student teacher and the children who were in the classroom. He said to me in a very loud voice, "Is there a reason why you have taken it upon yourself to move my belongings out of the media center?" I explained I had inquired about borrowing the media bookshelf and was told I could. But he said in a hateful, loud tone that he wanted those things in the library exactly where he had placed them. I thought, "This behavior is not appropriate." Meanwhile there are 20 eight-year-olds that are looking at him with their mouths open because he has a loud voice. The student teacher is sitting there scared to death. I am trying to defend myself.

> During one fire drill one of my students left a rock inside a door so that we could come back in that door later (it was close to my classroom), but we ended up going around to the front of the building. Somehow, the principal found that rock and came around asking who did it. This one little guy was going to raise his hand and admit that he did it. But I didn't want him to suffer any kind of abuse, so I said, "I did it." She started to yell and holler on and on, to take me down in front of the students. Her voice was on fire. The students were in shock. I was embarrassed. I guess I probably turned pink or a couple shades of red. I didn't say anything back. She didn't give me a chance. When she got through talking, she turned and stormed out. Everybody was quiet.

> The principal told all teachers that had decorated classroom doors for the holiday to have a hole a certain size so that he could look in [through the glass] if the door was closed. But I always teach with my door open. He came by with a little knife and in front of my students, cut the paper on my door. Then he started yelling at me, saying that I had not followed his rules. He yelled loudly and pointed at me. Three or four of my kindergarten students who were on the rug doing story time were crying as he was pointing and yelling.

> He came to my room mad, yelling at me in front of students. He demanded that I tell him who in my department made certain statements about the t-shirts. After he left, my students made comments like, "Man, what's wrong with him?" I cried. Later, when I was on committees, I felt I could not be honest because I was afraid that someone would tell the principal my opinion about something, that he would disagree, and that he would come down to my room and blow up at me. He had humiliated me in front of my students. From that point on I became a "yes, sir" girl.

Intercom. Teachers were criticized by the principal over the intercom while students were present in the classroom.

When something had not been filled out she would call me on the intercom and argue with me with children in the room. I found this very unprofessional. She came into my room to observe one day, and a little girl was loud. So later she got on the intercom to argue with me in front of the kids about our different views of the way children should behave in the classroom. She said, "I don't want to hear another sound in that room," that sort of thing. It was really unprofessional.

She would come on the intercom and chastise the faculty with the students in the classes. My students would say, "Wow, she sure is mad at you!" She never investigated anything before spouting off. She had a very short fuse and a very quick temper and wanted to be in total control. If she could not have total control, she got very upset.

If the principal wanted the phone, she would get on the PA to teachers and say, "Teachers, get off the phone! I need to use it. This is not a social hour!" It made you want to say, "Heil Hitler!"

I had a suggestion I shared with other teachers and wrote a memo to the principal. She sent the memo back. Furthermore, she called me over the intercom two weeks later and publicly criticized my idea in front of other teachers and students. She was loud and very impolite. It created a scene! I never wrote another memo to her again.

Lunchroom. Several teachers discussed principal criticism of them that occurred in the school cafeteria:

She would yell at teachers quite often on the PA as well as in person, and in the lunchroom lobby in front of all the students. . . . She pointed her finger about three inches from one teacher's nose and was just blasting him right there in front of the entire lobby. She said he was not being professional, he should not joke around with students, and he should keep his voice down because he was irritating. A hundred students were present. I was standing there, too. I can remember thinking if that were me I would just die.

This is so typical of him. He walked in and we were all eating lunch. He asked, "What are we having?" We named the two entrees, and I said, "Listen, try the fish." Very rudely he said, "You don't have to tell me what to eat! I'll try whatever I want!" It was said to humiliate me and it did! I immediately started crying and left the lunchroom.

One day I had some rectal bleeding, and my doctor told me to report to the emergency room. My assistant principal wanted to know what my symptoms were. A week or so later the principal came into the lunchroom and, in front of other teachers, said, "You know it wouldn't surprise me if a lot of the teachers in this school had hemorrhoids. We have so many anal types."

Hallway. Teachers were berated in the school's hallways with others present:

There were students waiting in the hall to see the nurse, teachers running off copies, and parents there, too, when the principal started venting about my students' behavior! She just flew off the handle! Everyone was shocked. Finally she stepped into her office, and I shut the door behind us. She vented for two minutes, and then I just walked out.

Students were fighting in the hall, so another teacher and I ran out to stop it. All of a sudden, the principal came by and said that we were being way too loud. He corrected us twice in front of the students. I tried to explain, but the principal stood there and just screamed at me, saying "Who gave you permission to do that?" . . . Tears just filled my eyes. He gave me the cold shoulder after that.

One day a teacher came to me and said, "I am upset. I have never had anything like this happen to me before. Dr. Swift caught me in the hall and came right at me. He started yelling in my face. He took his finger and poked it in my chest." He told her that she could make no decisions about what class she would teach. He said, "I make the decisions around here, and you jump when I say jump!"

Other Places. Teachers described instances of public criticism that occurred in the parking lot, at a principals' meeting, in the principal's office, at special events, and in memos to the faculty:

My principal and I had an agreement that I could leave five minutes early at the end of the day because I teach a pullout program in the morning. The first time I walked out of the building five minutes early, the principal started running after me and yelling at me, "Where are you going! It's not time yet! Get back in the building!" Even if I had been wrong, I don't think screaming would have been the way to handle it. I was very shaken.

I was furious that he had taken my letter and distributed copies of it at the principals' meeting; not because it was a bad letter, it was an excellent letter, it made me look like a shining star. . . . But I don't want my name vented around in front of principals and supervisors in any way.

I had an incompetent parapro who couldn't correct the children's work and did not know how to do math. The principal called us both in to her office and in front of the parapro told me I was expecting too much from her and I needed to give her more time. She totally degraded me in front of the parapro.

At the end of the year, we had a potluck luncheon, and we were sharing stories, but the stories that she and the assistant principal shared were really cruel stories—embarrassing incidents—about teachers. For the second year in a row, she referred to a teacher who was stood up at the altar. Who wants to be reminded in front of a 100 people that you had a wedding shower but were stood up at the altar and you're not married!

Every day a three to four page memo was sent out to faculty members, mostly about teachers and what they had done wrong. "Mrs. Wilson, you will not park in the back of the building. I expect you to park in your assigned parking place."

In this chapter, we have seen that authoritarian and coercive principals engage in myriad forms of Level 2 mistreatment, including spying, sabotaging, stealing, destroying teacher instructional aids, and making unreasonable work demands, as well as frequently criticizing teachers, both privately and publicly. Unfortunately, these forms of emotional abuse result in intense fear, which compels teachers to acquiesce to such treatment. In Chapter 4, we will examine Level 3 principal mistreatment behaviors, the most severely aggressive of all forms of abuse derived from our study.

4 Severe Mistreatment of Teachers

From Lying to Destruction

A significant amount of abusive boss behavior is the result of enduring, malignant forces that exist inside the bosses themselves. [It is] gratuitous abuse. When sheer malevolence is responsible for the active disrespect of subordinates, it has nothing to do with uncontrollable explosion ignited by job-related stress. Instead, this abuse represents bosses' self-serving efforts to enhance their own feelings of power, competence, and value at subordinates' expense. It is born of bosses' characters. . . . [It] is abuse for the sake of abuse. Malignantly motivated bosses experience temporary relief, and sometimes even ghastly pleasure, because they have diminished another human being's sense of power, competence, or self-worth.

— Hornstein (1996, pp. 48-49)

A cursory look at behavior in organizations suggests that Machiavelli is still active among us, doling out advice. His ghostly hand would seem to have scripted a memo that distorts or omits information; his spirit would seem to have encouraged meetings to be held to decide what had already been decided, or rewards to be promised but never given out.

— Greiner & Schein (1988, p. 58)

We have seen that principals who abuse teachers do so in a variety of verbal and nonverbal ways and that such abuse includes Level 1 (indirect, moderate) and Level 2 (direct, escalating) principal mistreatment behaviors.

Unfortunately, the reality of principal mistreatment includes even more devastating forms of abuse, glimpses of which have been foreshadowed in Level 2 behaviors. Indeed, in many respects there is only a thin line between these two levels of mistreatment. In this chapter, we discuss the most aggressive and severe, perhaps evil, types of abuse that appeared in our study data. These Level 3 principal mistreatment behaviors include lying, being explosive and nasty, threatening, giving unwarranted reprimands, giving unfair evaluations, mistreating a teacher's students, forcing teachers out of their jobs (reassigning, blocking transfers, making unilateral transfers, and terminating teachers), preventing teachers from leaving or advancing, and engaging in sexual harassment and racism.

A review of the literature on abusive bosses reveals that such individuals engage in similar verbal and nonverbal behaviors (e.g., accusing one of wrongdoing or blaming a person for errors; yelling, screaming, cursing, being nasty, rude, or hostile; displaying angry outbursts or tantrums; and threatening job loss or change) (Cleveland & Kerst, 1993; Fitzgerald & Shullman, 1993; Keashly, 1998; Northwestern National Life Insurance Company, 1993). Teachers in our study described similar behaviors; they also reported that such conduct seriously threatened and damaged them both personally and professionally.

Thus far, we generally have examined the characteristics of authoritarian or coersion-oriented leaders, the different ways in which subordinates consent to the unwarranted use of power, and the negative feelings that such power provokes. Our study confirms that principals who mistreat teachers exhibit comparable characteristics. Before presenting our findings on the most severely aggressive level of principal mistreatment, three questions are briefly explored: Why do people abuse their power? What causes people to use power aggressively or in "evil" ways? What are the consequences for people who demonstrate courage in the face of negative use of power by superiors?

WHY DO PEOPLE ABUSE POWER? EXTERNAL INFLUENCES

> Not all expressions of power . . . relate to the process of getting work done. Also present in organizations are power strategies designed solely to promote selfish objectives. Highly personalized objectives such as promotion, money, status, and job survival can dominate individual behavior more than work-related objectives. (Greiner & Schein, 1988, p. 59)

Since the time of Plato, wise men have argued that power must be tamed lest it degenerate into despotism (Winter, 1973). Chaleff (1995) suggests that it is essential to challenge the use of abusive power early on; such challenges become increasingly difficult when power becomes entrenched. Chaleff also contends that it is very difficult for people to confront abusive administrators because this puts them at even greater risk. Consequently, abusive leaders frequently continue on their course of destruction against individuals and this is ultimately destructive to the organization as a whole.

Power in and of itself, of course, is morally neutral; it can be developed and used for good or for evil purposes (Sampson, 1965). Arthur (1992), for instance, described the "power hungry" type of executive who is able to ascend to the top position in an organization without challenge. Such a person may arrive at the top through influential people, money, political connections, or the failure of the screening process. Moreover, after arriving at the top, one's motivations may change; having power is a difficult responsibility. Those who are prudent use power sparingly; however, others are tempted to test and misuse power, to expand power, and to experience the excitement of power. An example of the latter is Richard Nixon; the power of his office overwhelmed him and induced him to exercise it in areas that led to his downfall. Nixon's case demonstrates that the evil acts of leaders frequently corrupt followers and cause them to perform evil acts themselves (Chaleff, 1995). Corruption is corrupting.

Kipnis's (1972) research on the "metamorphic" effects of power has shown that individuals can be significantly transformed as a result of gaining power. Kipnis found that after acquiring power, individuals typically

- Increased their attempts to influence those who were less powerful
- Devalued those who were less powerful
- Attributed the cause of a less powerful person's efforts to themselves, rather than to the less powerful person's motivation to do well
- Viewed less powerful people as objects of manipulation
- Preferred maintaining psychological distance from less powerful people

Put differently, Kipnis (1972) demonstrated that power affects a powerholder's self-perceptions; the powerholder tends to develop an exalted and vain view of self-worth that inhibits compassion for others. He also noted that many who hold power value it above all else and pursue the acquisition of more power; power often becomes an end in itself, results in abuse, and thus cannot be justified on ethical or moral grounds.

Why do some people abuse their power? Kipnis (1972) listed the following *external* factors that may cause administrators to misuse power and engage in behavior that Kipnis labeled *corruption*. By implication, we suggest that abusive principals may react to the following external influences by misusing their power:

- Standards
- Expectations of superiors
- Rules
- Policies
- Curriculum requirements
- A diversity of goals that fracture the principal's work
- Assessment and test scores
- A bureaucratic hierarchy
- Lay control of schools
- Community pressures
- Parents

From studies of different types of corrupt rulers, including monarchs and democratically elected officials, Sorokin and Lunden (1959) concluded that regardless of how a person acts in private affairs, as a state official that person is likely to behave in Machiavellian and cynical ways in matters of policy and politics. Stated differently, the private and public behavior of even elected leaders often depicts a striking contrast, much like Jekyll and Hyde. That is, leaders use one set of principles that determines actions at work and another that determines actions at home. The authors identified factors, including criminalizing influences, that corrupt state officials and that result in what they call "predatory" leadership:

- Paralyzing elements, such as the incessant bombardment of contradictory interests of various groups and people; thus, one's moral integrity and mental sanity may become fragmented, confused, and contradictory.
- The effect of having power, that is, becoming intoxicated with power. This is based on the belief that one is chosen or anointed and thus is above the "common herd," possessing the absolute moral and legal perception of right.

It is interesting that Sorokin and Lunden (1959) found that in democracies elected officials not only became victims of such corrupting factors, but their criminality rate was higher than that of despotic rulers.

WHAT INTERNAL FACTORS CAUSE PEOPLE TO USE POWER AGGRESSIVELY OR IN EVIL WAYS?

In addition to external influences, internal factors such as professional incompetence and a range of personality disorders (e.g., narcissistic personality, authoritarian personality, closed-mindedness, anger disorder) may cause leaders to abuse power (Allcorn, 1994; Davenport et al., 1999; Fromm, 1947; Hornstein, 1996; Kets de Vries, 1989; Namie, 2000; Peck, 1983; Rokeach, 1956). The prospect of personal gain or the temptation to "line his or her pockets" is another factor; in such cases, power becomes a means to an end (Kipnis, 1972). Other internal factors include lack of interpersonal skills and lack of ethical principles (Namie, 2000).

Kets de Vries (1989) posited that the best way to understand leadership is to study the inner world of the leader, the psychological forces that make up his or her personality. In his overview of the spectrum of leadership types, Kets de Vries explained that certain mixtures of styles can make for a very successful leader, but other styles can be dysfunctional and even abusive. For example, a style of paranoia and detachment is associated with ineffective leadership; this was also reflected in our data. By contrast, Kets de Vries stated that a self-oriented, narcissistic personality may produce a leadership style that is considered by some as the sine qua non of leadership, a conclusion also supported by Yukl (2001); however, such personality characteristics are frequently associated only with aggression and evil conduct.

Hans Toch (1984), in *Violent Men*, has identified a host of human motives that may cause leaders to use aggression and even violence against subordinates:

- Reputation defending: One who has a reputation to uphold, realistically or not, may use violence or aggression.
- Norm enforcing: Those who believe that it is their mission to enforce universal rules and conduct may use aggression.
- Self-image compensating: One strives to maintain an image of himself or herself through aggressive or violent means.
- Self-defending: Those who, perhaps because they were abused in childhood, believe that others are likely to be dangerous.
- Pressure removing: Fears, pressures, and frustration of social life or economic situations may build up to a point of explosion.
- Bullying: Some people gain pleasure from intimidating or terrorizing others.
- Exploitation: This is like bullying, with the additional gratification of forcing others to comply to do one's bidding.
- Self-indulging: Sadistic individuals deliver noxious stimuli to others, which may in itself be gratifying.
- Catharsis: Catharsis that follows aggressive or violent acts will cause such acts to be repeated.

Level 3 principal mistreatment behaviors toward teachers are severely aggressive and may be provoked by several of the preceding motives.

A Note About Evil

The definition of *evil* found in the *Oxford Dictionary of English* describes the antithesis of good, in all important respects. Katz (1993) states, evil is

> Behavior that deprives innocent people of their humanity, from small scale assaults on a person's dignity to outright murder. [This definition] focuses on how people behave toward one another—where the behavior of one person or an aggregate of persons is destructive to others. (p. 5)

Accordingly, one can conceive of a continuum of evil ranging from white lies (see Bok, 1989, for a compelling argument that even a white lie potentially has serious consequences), for example, to more extreme forms of evil such as the defamation of Native American populations, the Holocaust, and the corrupt dynamics of organizational culture documented in the space shuttle Challenger's destruction (Adams & Balfour, 1998).

In his book, *People of the Lie,* M. Scott Peck (1983) argued that evil masters of deceit have a need to dominate others. Moreover, they conceal "ordinary evil" from themselves as well as from others. "The evil are people of the lie, deceiving others as they also build layer upon layer of self-deception" (1983, p. 66). Peck has suggested that psychiatry recognizes a new type of evil personality disorder, which is characterized by

- Consistent, destructive, scapegoating behavior that may be quite subtle
- Excessive, albeit usually covert, intolerance to criticism and other forms of narcissistic injury

- Pronounced concern with one's public image and self-image of respectability, which not only contributes to the stability of one's lifestyle but also to pretentiousness and denial of hateful feelings or vengeful motives.
- Intellectual deviousness with an increased likelihood of a mild schizophrenic-like disturbance of thinking during times of stress. (1983, p. 29)

Peck's definition of evil is not limited to acts such as murder; he states that "evil is also that which kills spirit" (p. 42). The essential attributes of life, according to Peck—sentience, mobility, awareness, growth, autonomy, and will—can be seriously damaged or killed without destroying another's body, for instance, as is done in child abuse. Like the abusive principals described in our study, some people simply have a strong desire to control others, to foster dependency, to discourage others' thinking for themselves, and to limit unpredictability and originality; the evil character type avoids inconveniences by transforming others into automatons and robbing them of their humanity (see, for example, Fromm, 1964).

Peck (1983) also discusses group evil; that is, when a group's behavior is strikingly immoral, such as people's actions during the My Lai massacre. As a group, the participants passed the moral buck, the cover-up was immoral and a huge lie, and those who witnessed the atrocities failed to report them for fear of ostracism and worse. In this case as in others (e.g., the tobacco industry's cover-up of the carcinogenic and addictive properties of tobacco), lying (and other forms of deception) was both a symptom and a cause of evil (Peck, 1983).

In *Unmasking Administrative Evil*, Adams and Balfour (1998) set forth the premise that evil is inherent in the human condition. They argue the following points.

1. Administrative evil is a result of the modern age and its technical, rational approach to problems. This form of evil has many masks, and thus ordinary people are inclined to do evil, even when they do not intend to.

2. Overt invitations to commit evil are rarely issued; rather, they come in the form of expertise or proper language or are even packaged as a good project. This represents a moral inversion, where evil or destruction is redefined as good and worthy.

3. In modern organizations, people engage in patterns and activities that result in evil because of what occurs under their level of awareness; thus, they are not aware that they are committing evil until after the fact, and often not even then. Social and public policies also result in evil at times because of instrumental or technical goals that contradict ethical considerations.

4. Because of the many masks that administrative evil wears, one can adhere to public service ethics and at the same time participate in great evil, not realizing this until it is too late.

In our study, principals' use of deception against others was a core theme and was strongly linked to very damaging effects on teachers. Victimized teachers believed that most of the principals they described intended to harm and even destroy them and that many such principals were quite aware of the damage they caused. For instance, most principals failed to investigate issues before attacking the teacher. And, when teachers confronted abusive principals about their conduct and its destructive effects on them, such principals typically denied all allegations, blamed the teacher, and engaged in further reprisals against them (see Bok, 1989, and Lewis & Saarni, 1993, for discussions on the self-protective function of deception and lying.

WHAT HAPPENS TO THOSE WHO RESIST OR DEMONSTRATE PERSONAL COURAGE IN THE FACE OF ABUSE OF POWER?

A review of the relevant research literature indicates that bosses in organizations frequently lie, cheat, and deceive in order to protect themselves and the organization from dissenters, even when the dissenters' actions are consistent with law, organizational policy, or professional ethics. Blacklisting of whistleblowers, for example, is but one well-documented form of retaliation against those who complain about unethical or corrupt practices (Glazer & Glazer, 1989). Clearly, the teachers we studied expected abusive principals to go nuts; that is, lose control and retaliate by becoming more intensely abusive if they complained about mistreatment. Our data indicate that principals viewed teachers who complained as very threatening, and they used extremely vicious methods to suppress, punish, and intimidate them. As might be expected, teachers rarely spoke out against mistreatment because of fear of retribution. Only a couple of the teachers we interviewed successfully fought back when mistreated, and in each case they had unusual resources; for instance, one was personally acquainted with the superintendent. Scott's (1990) classic work on domination reminds us that subordinate groups rarely confront powerholders, at least not directly and not publicly. To protect themselves, dominated groups routinely exhibit a public performance of consent and deference, a display of "tactical prudence" (p. 15) that belies their true thoughts and feelings about the powerholder.

LEVEL 3 PRINCIPAL MISTREATMENT: DIRECT AND SEVERE AGGRESSION

In the following section, we demonstrate that Level 3 abuse of power by principals abounds in our database and that teachers' attempts to curb such abuse (as with Levels 1 and 2) were typically met with further abuse.

Level 3 Principal Mistreatment Behaviors

- Lying
- Explosive and nasty behavior
- Threats
- Unwarranted reprimands
- Unfair evaluations
- Mistreating students
- Forcing teachers out of their jobs
- Preventing teachers from leaving or advancing
- Sexual harassment
- Racism

Lying

Most of the teachers we studied identified principal deception and, in particular, blatant lying as a common form of principal mistreatment. Lying was associated with other forms of abusive behavior, such as nonsupport of teachers in conflict with parents and students, unfounded criticism (already discussed), unfair formal evaluations, and forcing teachers out (to be discussed) ("You can expect principals who do bad things to lie to protect themselves."). Further, this behavior was also associated with countless educational issues: principals lied about children's placements, faculty voting outcomes, teacher termination, library responsibility, authorization, and stealing funds, among other things.

> During a faculty meeting, I made a comment about placements, and the principal looked at me and became very, very defensive. Her neck turned bright red and she said, "I have never changed a child's placement over the summer because of a parent's request!" The room got really quiet, and I was really embarrassed. She had taken it as a personal attack. She overreacted. Everybody was just stunned. I apologized and said, "I didn't mean to insult you, I was talking in general." I tried to explain my remark and tried to pacify her. After the meeting a couple of teachers said that they couldn't believe her reaction. Everybody knew perfectly well that she changed the placement of children, that it was a real problem.

> She did the class lists, not me, but told parents I did it. She didn't want to take the flack from parents so she put it off on me. Parents complained. She blamed me and said to parents that if I really cared about their child I would have taken the time to make sure that they were placed appropriately. Some of the parents felt comfortable enough to come back to me. They knew that I didn't do this. She lied.

> We took a vote on participating in the pay-for-performance program, and most people voted no. However, the principal said it had passed. She was lying. In fact, she pulled everybody in her office one by one and asked us

why we had voted against it. She made you feel really bad for voting against it.

I was unwed and pregnant, and the principal was trying to establish grounds for firing me legally. So, he sent me this letter that had nothing indicating that their reason for termination was because I was pregnant and unwed. It indicated that there was something wrong with my teaching ability. He wanted me to sign it. My students were even being taken out of my classroom, one by one, and encouraged to say that I cursed them, which I didn't. They got a couple of students to say that I cursed all the time and that I used the Lord's name in vain and I used the word that rhymes with duck. I never did. It's not even part of my vocabulary. One time I did tell a child to sit down in his damn seat. One student told them, "I never heard Ms. Atkins curse and I am not going to lie!" Others said the same.

The form saying I conducted 55 hours of inservice had his signature and was put in my mailbox with a sticky note that said, "Please sign and return." I took it to him and said, "I cannot sign this because you know I did not do this inservice. I didn't even begin to do this." He is such a liar! All the teachers signed even though they never attended.

The new principal said, "The library was taken away from you for mis-management!" That was when I broke. I almost got hysterical because I had never been harassed like this before. This guy didn't know me from Adam. I said, "Mr. Prince, I don't know where you are getting your infor-mation; the library was neither given to me nor taken away." He also said he talked to my former principal, so I went to him and he said, "That man has never come to me. Does he even know what magic you do in that room?" He [the new principal] was out to get me, and nothing I could do was right. It didn't matter what I said or what I did. He made up things and acted on his own stories. . . . The lies just tore me apart. I kept think-ing, I can't do this. I can't stand in front of a classroom knowing that my administrator lies about me. He was getting to me big time. I wouldn't have gone to attorneys. I would have just totally slipped into oblivion.

When I got to the new school, I started getting these calls from my former principal asking, "Where is the check for $3,000 for the yearbook prof-its?" I had to go back over to that school and show him where I had entered it into the books. He still claimed he could not find the check and that I had never given it to him. He kept calling me at my job and harass-ing me to the point that the principal at my new school finally told him, "This is no longer this teacher's problem. You are going to have to deal with this yourself." He was trying to set me up for stealing that money, and he had probably done it. I shouldn't say that. I don't have any proof. But there were lots and lots of situations with other faculty members who resigned from extracurricular activities because money was missing, and they thought he was taking it. You can't imagine what it feels like to have somebody accuse you of stealing!

I asked my principal if he would please write a thank-you note to the company that provided the faculty luncheon dessert, and I put a reminder with the address in his box as he requested. Not only did he not write the thank-you note, but when the parent who owned the company saw him, he denied that he ever knew they had provided the food! With each lie, I and the other teachers became more distant, more isolated, and more depressed.

She would set her teachers up. For example, she told me to delete summer school test files from the school's computer. Her superiors found out this was done and were very angry. Instead of accepting the blame, she wrote me up. Without the support of my fellow teachers, who also heard her directions to me, I would not have a job right now. They took a risk and spoke up for me. They had been in similar situations with this principal.

Explosive and Nasty Behavior

When principal mistreatment occurred through face-to-face interaction, principals frequently escalated and became explosive and engaged in particularly nasty behaviors:

From the beginning, he singled me out for criticism. He criticized me publicly and loudly. . . . He would mock me in front of other teachers. . . . [H]e called me into his office and berated me for over an hour on the proper way to show respect to a principal. He called me a troublemaker. . . . He ridiculed me in a faculty meeting. . . . He said he would always take the word of a parent or student against me anytime.

He gets very stiff in the neck. He points his finger in your face, and he often swears heavily. When you get locked into his office and he slams the door, you know he is going for you. I have heard from several coaches that when it is man-to-man, he has threatened to strike them and it has ended in, "You son-of-a-bitch, if you ever. . . !" This makes me so upset. I just want to kill him. He seems to hit when you are most vulnerable.

He would address us at meetings by yelling, pounding his fist, and carrying on at length until his face was scarlet and the veins stood out on his neck. No meeting with this man was complete without our usual verbal beating. I believe this man thought that it actually helped us. Quote, "the beatings will continue until morale improves."

The principal came to the first faculty meeting of the year and told the faculty that they all looked fat. He yelled at the faculty about how sorry they were. If you made a mistake he would yell and curse. He called one of my department workers "lazy" and "a fat ass." He also told dirty jokes at meetings.

If the principal did not like what you were doing, he would call you into his office and yell at you, let you know he had the ultimate authority. He would say he made the decisions and if you didn't like it, you could leave.

He was scary . . . out of control . . . screaming . . . about to explode.

She was loud . . . had a crabby voice . . . negative. If she did smile, it was kind of a nasty smile.

Threats

Not surprisingly, teachers defined all abusive actions by principals as implicitly or explicitly threatening. That is, teachers experienced such conduct as putting them at risk, in danger, and in a state of fear. Teachers had similar feelings, however to a lesser extent, when they were not the target of abuse but had observed or learned about abusive conduct from others ("If he does this to others, he would do it to me").

When my teammate was seven minutes late, the principal came in with kindergarten students in the room, scolded my teammate, telling her that the next time she was late, for whatever reason, she would write her up and a copy would be placed in her personnel file. Two other adults were in the room at the time. I was fearful of being late. I would dream about oversleeping. I rushed around in the morning like a crazy person, afraid I would be late.

In addition, teachers reported that abusive principals, with few exceptions, directly threatened groups of teachers as well as individual teachers. Our data indicate that threats were usually overt, but at times they were implied. Specifically, principals would threaten groups of teachers to stop them from spreading rumors about the principal, making negative statements about the school to a review committee, losing games, their unprofessional dress, and so forth.

That was a terrible year. At faculty meetings he [the principal] would say people were spreading rumors about him that weren't true, stabbing him in the back. He said, "You might think that there is safety in numbers but I will get you, one by one. . . ." That's pretty threatening! I was very scared.

I was verbally abused by my principal repeatedly. I was coaching football, and after each of three losses, the coaches were called into his office and he yelled and screamed at us and called us names like "losers." He threatened us, saying if we didn't turn things around and win more, we could look elsewhere for employment next year. He was always very intimidating with every action he took. People were scared to death of him. This man went on to become superintendent of one of the five largest metro school systems in the state.

She came to a staff meeting one time with a pack of transfers and said, "Anybody that doesn't like it here, you can just get one of these. I have got plenty of them." Everybody shut up. . . . She would talk about people's clothes, the way they dressed. She said, "I am here to tell you folks, if I don't think you look professional, you will be going home and you will be docked for this time." . . . She said, "The thing that I want to get straight is I am here for the children. I am not here for you," meaning the teachers, and "I am going to support the children." She is going to blame you, cut you loose, or not support you. She also said, "It is going to upset your evaluation."

He would threaten us with transfers. . . . I felt absolute fear because the biggest punishment in the world—in the county—is to be transferred. There are many undesirable locations and it hurts your reputation.

At faculty meetings, her behavior discouraged any questions or opinions. She would say, "Do you want to work here or not?"

He said if we ever questioned his authority, he would write a letter and send it downtown to our files.

Individual teachers were threatened for a wide range of reasons, for instance, to coerce a teacher to change a student's grade, for conduct toward a student, for expressing opinions that disagreed with the principal's, for confronting a principal for his conduct, for making a request to central office for needed resources, for use of personal days, and for having to miss PTA meetings. Control and domination were, in the teachers' perspective, the real reasons for principals' threatening conduct:

I had a senior [student] who in the last nine weeks of school decided he wasn't going to do a notebook. He flat [out] didn't turn one in. He was an athlete and he went whining to the assistant principal who was our football coach. He [the coach] called me in and said you have to pass him. I said, "He didn't do the work. I gave him extensions. I told him I would take his notebook late. I gave him every possibility. It's not my fault and I am not changing my grade." The next day the principal threatened me. He said if I wanted a job, I would change this kid's grade. He was furious. I caved in under the pressure, and I regret it to this day.

There was a parent who disagreed with a teacher who had taken a child out of the classroom to speak to him about not completing his homework assignments. With the parent there, the principal ordered the teacher to go back in front of the class and apologize to the child. He said that the parent would sit in and hear the apology. He also threatened to write her up and said to remember that she was not tenured, that he would be watching her every move and if she stepped out of line, she would pay for that. He said all this in front of the parent. She came to my room sobbing uncontrollably, like she could not get her breath, she was so upset. She felt threatened. She said she felt scared and intimidated and humiliated.

She asked me to tell the board person my opinion of exploratory classes. I did. Later that day, she point blank said, "I think you need to consider taking a sabbatical if that is your opinion." I was stunned, and I said, "I have no intention of taking a sabbatical. I am sorry if you don't agree with me." I never said anything rude. I just said what I thought. She demanded that I apologize for my opinion to the person from the board office.

I needed to miss a couple of PTA meetings because of therapy. The principal said, "No, it's not going to happen." I said, "Why not?" He said, "Because I am the boss. I say you are going to come to the meetings and you are going to come!" My therapist wrote a letter saying it was a medical necessity. He said, "I don't care," and if I didn't go he said he would "start the procedure to terminate your employment." It didn't matter that it is against the law to withhold medical treatment.

He said if I were to leave [resign] now, he would give me a good reference, but if I stay, there would be things that he could say about me. He said, "You are beginning a process that may have irreversible effects. Nothing you do will be overlooked."

In addition, principals wrote unwarranted reprimands, gave unfair evaluations, mistreated teachers' students, attempted to force teachers out of work, prevented teachers from leaving or advancing, and engaged in sexual harassment and racism.

Unwarranted Reprimands

Abusive principals constantly threatened teachers with written reprimands. Teachers described the use of reprimands as "grossly unfair," "irrational," and based on false accusations. Principals wrote teachers up for almost anything, for example, for being in a storage closet during class, a stolen video camera, use of the intercom, turning in a budget three hours late, and conduct toward students.

I was constantly intimidated and harassed. He sent me letters of reprimand, delivered during class and filled with false accusations. My students witnessed my reaction. I was not able to teach effectively. Once he cornered me in a closet and discussed inappropriate [sexual] topics, to which I would not respond. I then received a letter of reprimand for being in the storage closet.

The principal told the teacher that he would write her up for not knowing that somebody let a kid in the back door and he took a camera. The principal said that he'd either write her up or she could pay for a new camera. She was written up for being incompetent. She was a teacher that we had all nominated for teacher of the year.

She had a new rule at the school: "Do not communicate through the intercom system." Months after orientation, the secretary was calling me. But, I didn't catch it in time. So I buzzed back within seconds and said, "Were you trying to reach me?" Later the principal said that I was being written up for insubordination and defying her rule! I have never been written up in 26 years of teaching.

I had gone to the superintendent behind his [the principal's] back about a scheduling problem. At that point, all hell broke lose. He later said that I was not fulfilling my responsibility when a form was three hours late. I asked for a transfer. Within one week, I got another letter of reprimand about correcting a child. By the way, he made it sound like I was a child beater. He called me a liar and said that I was defying him.

Giving Unfair Evaluations

In all cases, teachers worked in school districts that required principals to complete "objective" teacher evaluations. These consisted of classroom observations, usually several per year, as well as conferences with the teacher. Such evaluations were described as important to the school district as well as to the teacher; in fact, most of the teachers in our study defined one negative evaluation as "seriously damaging" or "career ending" in their respective districts.

Our data show that teachers who were victimized by principals worked in a constant state of fear about evaluation. ("She would come in at any time and decide that she didn't like things. She did it to me, and I saw her do it to others." "We are always in a state of fear, and I am the breadwinner in my family.") Teachers' fears of unfair evaluations were exacerbated by their belief that no viable recourse existed to overturn such evaluations. ("As far as evaluations go, there is really nothing you can do. It doesn't matter what you say; it is there on paper, and you just sign it." "I was afraid of writing comments on the evaluation [because] he would think I would say he was lying, which of course, he was. . . . He would become even more vindictive.") It is important to mention that with the exception of beginning teachers who had not worked with other principals, all but one experienced teacher reported that they had, before mistreatment began, consistently received superior evaluations from former principals and even from their abusive principals.

In all cases, teachers stated that principals included flagrantly false information on their evaluations.

She lowered the boom and gave me the worst rating that I ever had in all my years of teaching. This had been coming on because I disagreed with her once. She had done this in the past to others. You name it, she criticized it. It was shocking. I had never had anything like that done to me, and in such a vindictive manner. . . . In the conference I said, "What you've written, it's not true." I was shaking like a leaf. . . . I went home that night and put together my version of the lesson, and some union people supported me. It was a very bad experience for me, awful. I am shaking as I am telling you this now. I stood up for myself because I wanted the truth to be known. I didn't care if I lost my job because I felt like everything was gone anyway.

The principal said he saw a student put his head down in class, but I did not see it. It didn't happen. Before he left my room, he said that I was not paying attention and that he would be back. He looked very hostile. On my teacher evaluation he checked two areas that needed improvement, and he wrote comments about things that never occurred. But I felt that there was nothing that I could do about it. I felt that if I wrote a comment at the end of the form, it would just make him angry because he would think that I was saying he was lying, which, of course, he was.

For many teachers, abusive principals not only made false representations on their evaluations, but they also violated district evaluation policies and procedures.

Our principal never came into my classroom, but he told me one day that although he didn't know what was going on down in my classroom, he didn't like it. He gave me a 50% unsatisfactory evaluation. This came out of nowhere. I had a super reputation and was consulting with other teachers because my program was so successful. Suddenly, with the change in principals, I was incompetent and unprofessional—awful things. It hurt. It was devastating. He has never come to observe me, but he went directly for my throat.

That man never stepped foot into my classroom for five years. My evaluations were fine, but then he began to become more critical and he gave me an awful evaluation. My [association] representative wrote to him saying, "When you are writing evaluations, you might want to have stopped in the teacher's classroom." He said that he had evaluated me informally when he passed my room in the hall and that he had spoken with a student about what the students thought of me. He made it clear that there was nothing that I could do to make him change his mind.

Teachers also reported that principals failed to give legitimate reasons, or any reasons whatsoever, when requiring them to submit to extended or special evaluations.

A group of us went to the board to complain about the principal. He [the principal] found out the names of every one of us and put all of us, every one of us, on extended evaluation, a form of probation or remediation. We never heard a word from the board about our complaints. We were all terminated that spring.

If he doesn't like you, he will have one of his administrators evaluate you almost every other day and all of your evaluations will be bad. He will literally hound you out of your job and make your life unpleasant. He had a central office supervisor come in and do a special evaluation of me. Afterwards, I asked if I could talk to the person. He said, "No, the central supervisor wrote you up." I thought, "Why is he saying it like that? He is trying to scare me." I never heard another word about this. I guess I did well.

He said that there was something wrong in my classroom, and he was going to have two people from the university observe my teaching. He told me that we would all get back together and talk, come up with some strategies. I was fine with that because I knew that I was a good teacher. I got the feeling he was looking for problems. He had gotten rid of teachers before. . . . I never got any feedback about their observations.

Several teachers indicated that abusive principals intensified their use of unfair evaluations when the teachers were consumed by personal life tragedies.

When my father was dying, I shared the fact that we had just told the hospital to let him die. The next day I was sitting at my desk, the children were quiet and on task, and here he comes to do an evaluation. I felt like a whipped dog; I didn't have any energy to get up and dance. He wrote a bad evaluation, and within two days he came back for a second one. When I signed it, I put down (for whatever good it does for teachers) that I wanted it to be on record that no observations were made until it was known that my father was dying or had died. The third evaluation came right after Dad died in April. I probably was a basket case at that particular time, but for the rest of the year I was a great teacher, and that is what should matter. He was so unfair.

A couple of teachers viewed principals' evaluations of them as absurd.

His big comment in the postconference was that I needed to work on having a more mature voice. I was 28 years old. He wanted a deeper, lower, more commanding voice. I said that my voice doesn't create a problem; the students are attentive. He just kept saying that with age my voice would deepen. He cited me on this on my evaluation.

A few teachers complained that principals had assigned them to teach courses for which they were not qualified and "promised" them that they would not be evaluated as a result.

I was told that I had to teach a class for which I was not certified, and I was told that I would never be evaluated on this class. But I was evaluated every time in this very class. My evaluations were poor. I signed the form under duress, due to pressure applied by the principal.

Mistreating Students

Our data indicate that principal mistreatment of students had harmful effects on both students and teachers. Generally, students were mistreated for what a principal defined as "misbehavior." Many were special education or behaviorally disabled students; others were regular students.

The principal and the advisor of special education programs brought a child to my room fighting, struggling, kicking, and screaming. They held him down in the middle of the room by his arms and put their legs over his legs to restrain him. Both of them were white, and he was a little African American child. When his mother came, the child called her a bitch. I had been relatively quiet, but then I thought that I would give it a try, so I said [to the child], "I am really happy that you are in my class and I think that it will be a nice experience for you." He told me to suck his dick. The two male administrators snickered; they thought it was funny. I shut up. This principal was going to gain total control over this child, show him who was boss. Eventually, the child got angry and called the principal, who was white, a "cracker." Immediately, the principal called the child a "nig-ger." My stomach just turned over. They struggled and the principal wound up hitting him in the mouth . . . his hand slipped. His lip split open and he was all bloody. I was sick to my stomach. I thought, "This is child abuse." I stood there frozen. I feel that I compromised myself morally for not stopping it. The principal was ignorant, mean spirited, and small. He is in a category of abusers who are just insensitive and stupid; they don't get it, and they don't understand that yelling at people is harmful to them.

I worked with a difficult population, so I apprised him [the principal] of the way I conduct my program. The first thing that he did was yell at a girl in my class. He read the riot act to this little girl and brought her to tears. She had been sexually abused by members of her family. I felt that he was way, way too rough, but I felt helpless. He humiliated her.

I had a new student who would have real temper tantrums for as long as three hours, but we would work through it. She would destroy the whole classroom. But she improved, so her tantrums were now like 45 minutes. The principal saw one and said, "We are going to suspend her. Children do not behave that way in my school, and she will go home!" . . . The child clutched me, crying and screaming. It took me and the mother 30 minutes to get her out of the school and into the car.

She told me to paddle the kids. I refused; that has no place in this century. She had a bigger paddle than any teacher. The kids would have to go to her and get paddled. It was dreadful, and I hope her days are numbered. She has injured a lot of children. I wouldn't allow it with a child of mine. The kids were scared to death. What I observed was just awful.

I had sent an ill child to him and he wrote back two times, saying, "This child doesn't seem to be sick enough to go home. She will stay until it is time to be dismissed." The little girl was truly sick and had an emergency appendectomy that afternoon. Her parents went to the school board about it. . . . His favorite thing to tell the children was, "I am going to be your best friend or your worst enemy." . . . Another time, he refused to deal with a child I thought was being abused. He told me, "This child needs to be ignored," so I ended up going to our juvenile court judge. He was a physically abused child.

He was biased. He didn't like the idea that Hispanic students had a right to be in school. He would raise his voice and show his obvious disapproval, curse them, and use profanity in dealing with them. I despised him for it. I tried to avoid him because I didn't like to hear his comments. It got to the point where some teachers were adopting his attitudes; they didn't like these children in their rooms because it meant extra work. They spouted off about these children and what a pain they were because they are non-English speaking. It infuriated me. It took me back to my personal experience with bigotry. I spouted off against their philosophy, enough that they shut up in front of me. I tried to be more of an advocate for the minority children. I knew that somebody had to.

At times, abusive principals undermined special education teachers and their students by engaging in actions that violated special education laws.

The principal was always asking me to bypass special education procedures. Before every meeting, there had to be a school-based administrative meeting, without the parent, to decide what to do. Then, if a parent wanted something different—like a less restrictive environment—we had to stop the meeting until we could go back and talk to the principal again. The message was, "We [the administrators] don't trust you, and we are going to watchdog you and make sure that you don't put special kids into regular classrooms," which was supposed to be our goal!

My six special education students disappeared from my classroom, one by one, into other programs, without my input. I told the principal that I was doing a self-contained program, but he merely said, "These are not special ed students." I said, "How do you know? The law says that you have to rule out learning problems and behavior problems." (I am tenured, so it would be difficult to fire me, plus I am good at what I do. I dot my *i*s and cross my *t*s.) He just didn't want my program on his campus. He did everything he could think of to get me fired, to find something wrong with my performance, to get rid of me, to make me quit. He eventually succeeded: I requested a transfer because he didn't afford these kids due process, and he refused to offer them special education services. Now, the person with the remaining students is not certified. These students should have been referred to my program.

Forcing Teachers Out of Their Jobs (Reassigning, Unilaterally Transferring, Terminating)

Most of the teachers we interviewed stated that they were subjected to a variety of abusive actions by their principals, such as unfair reassignment, forced transfers, and termination. In unilaterally reassigning teachers, principals changed their teaching locations, their professional responsibilities, or both.

One year we had 45 transfer requests. The ones who tried and couldn't get transferred, he put in trailers.

The principal said to this teacher, and I quote, "You have got yourself knocked up [pregnant] and you are out." She gave her a traveling remedial position between four classrooms. It was awful to watch somebody torture her, it wasn't physical, but it sure was mental. This teacher had been the principal's favorite. But the principal would turn on people unexpectedly, and they would just fall apart. The principal would smile, be nice, and all of a sudden, attack. She is sadistic. My friend tried to transfer almost every year for eight years, but the principal wouldn't let her out. She had supreme control.

He singled me out that year. He decided that I should no longer coach the basketball team even though we had won the championship both years and had never had parents complain. I had never known him to take something away from a person like that.

A teacher came by my room and said, "I think you are moving, because it is posted in the office." This was before the children had even left the building, when the parents would be coming through. Sure enough, there it was. She had moved me to the fourth grade, but I was not told. I was devastated. When I left school that day, I knew that I had to do something else. I definitely was not coming back to that building.

There was a teacher who was a screamer. She yelled all day because the students wouldn't stay on task. At a faculty meeting, the principal announced that that teacher would not be returning on Monday because she was being dismissed, that I would be taking her place, and that my current students would be split up among three other teachers. I had no idea that this was going to occur, and I was given no opportunity to say goodbye to my students. I had to move over the weekend.

Teachers also described several principals who, unilaterally and without consultation, transferred them to other schools.

At 8:00 a.m. on the first day of postplanning she said, "You are being transferred to Wilson School, and they expect you there by 10:00 a.m." I was totally stunned (I can't believe that I am getting upset now). I loved those kids. It was an inner-city school—I bought kids clothes, made home visits, helped kids study, was really involved. I felt like I was losing my family. Oh God, it did hurt! There is a process one goes through at the end of the year, in order to let go and relax for the summer. I didn't get a chance to go through it. There was no going out for drinks the very last day. I was uprooted all of a sudden. I started the next year at the new school embarrassed, afraid, and apprehensive about trusting people.

I was a full-time teacher with 12 years of experience. I was a state Teacher of the Year . . . very accomplished. The principal called me into his office and said that I would "no longer be working in that capacity." He decided that I would be used as a substitute for science teachers while they worked on projects. . . . Then, I was relieved of my duties for the failure of someone else, a person who had not done her job. I had been set up. The principal said, "It is my school, I can make that decision." I was told to clean out my desk. He also refused to meet with me. I reported to the other school the next day. That was the principal's way of washing his hands of me.

Abusive principals, again without just cause and without consultation, unilaterally attempted to terminate teachers.

He got rid of many excellent teachers who were recognized by their peers as hard workers, creative, dedicated teachers who would always go beyond the curriculum. He put them on professional development plans and even told one of them he wanted to move her out. She said to me, "This is my school and my community, and I want to stay here. He can't run me off." . . . But, his abuse got to be a serious health problem for her, and she finally left.

When the principal found out that I was pregnant, she asked me if I was married. I wasn't. She gave me three choices . . . marry the father, get an abortion, or resign. She actually wanted to fire me right away. She wanted me to agree to a termination. They had taken away my insurance, and they decided that I was on the wrong pay scale. I didn't have the extra $40 dollars to get a required fingerprint card done. It was a choice of the card (when I knew that I wouldn't be hired back) or putting food on my table and paying doctor bills. They terminated me for not doing the fingerprint card. They got away with this horrible thing based on the card.

In one case, ten teachers reported their abusive principal to the assistant superintendent, but never received a response. One teacher explained,

In March, the principal said, "I am not renewing your contract." I had perfect evaluations. But she said, "I am not required to give you an explanation about why. I am not renewing you." The next year, they installed her at central office, of all things, as personnel director. . . . She was responsible for my not being able to get a job in the public schools for the next two years. It is like somebody has stamped your application with a big, black X.

Preventing Teachers From Leaving or Advancing

Also frequently reported were principals' attempts to obstruct transfers of teachers, both within a teacher's district and to other districts. Typically, abusive principals wrote unjustified negative letters of reference to other school administrators in response to queries about teachers.

I thought, "I had better get out of here and go somewhere they would back me." I realized that my principal was not going to support me. You get lied to, you can't seem to get promoted. But, the fear of this woman is so strong in the district. She said that I can't get along with people. My friends in high places ran a check and found that no one would hire me—they were afraid to go against her reference.

On my reference form, she put me in the lowest 10% of people in intelligence. I said, "If you think that I am that stupid, I will get somebody else to write the letter." She said, "Oh, I made a mistake." When I asked for a letter, she didn't want to do it. I said, "If you say only that I have 'potential,' then if I mess up, it will be okay. If I do well, it would look good on your record." She said, "Okay," but then she couldn't spell *potential*. I needed that referral. I was desperate. It was a terrible situation. I felt like I was in prison, I had to get out.

At a union meeting, the president said that we didn't have to "do this parent-involvement thing. They can't force you." A young teacher spoke up and said, "But if we exercise our rights, we will be taken out of our subject area and we will never get a good job reference. You've got to be kidding!" Somebody told the principal what he said. When that teacher went for seven job interviews, he got seven defamatory references from the principal. On the eighth interview, he went to his old school and they chose not to even call her [his current principal]. He got the job and he got out. He was just sickened by the whole experience.

He said that he would not recommend me for a teaching position. I said, "You've got to be kidding!" He said, "What I will say is that you are an excellent teacher and you are wonderful with children, but you are a trouble-maker." He said, "I don't care if you think this is right or not." I didn't get the transfer. He wanted me to leave, but he didn't want me to leave for the school of my choice.

If you put in for a transfer and you didn't get it, you were on her list. One girl tried to transfer but didn't get it. Her next year, everything, to the most minute detail, was scrutinized. Any little thing was made into a big deal. She ended up resigning. She quit teaching. . . . When I applied for a graduate program, I went to the assistant principal for a recommendation. I did not put the principal as a reference.

In several cases, principals assured teachers that they would give them positive references; however, their assurances proved false:

The board office said that there was a problem with my references and that I better check them. I did. I was shocked. In her letter she said, "People have trouble getting along with her." That was the statement. She lied! The union said that it was a "wrongful reference."

Five years in a row, I tried to transfer, but the principal had been bad-mouthing me to other principals. I asked about it and he said, "I told that principal that you had made some mistakes as a young teacher."

Abusive principals also used negative letters of reference, even when prohibited from writing such letters, to undermine teachers' attempts to obtain new teaching positions in other school districts, in some cases, for years.

My principal defied a union agreement that prohibited him from giving job references about me; he gave reports for over two years. I had to take jobs outside education that were demeaning; they were far below my skill level because of him.

He had been prohibited by an agreement from the union from giving job references for me. But, he managed to blackball me anyway. I tried for four solid years to get another teaching job. I would have what I considered a good interview, and then I would never hear anything back.

Sexual Harassment

Several female teachers accused their male principals of ongoing sexual harassment; in one case, the harassment occurred over a period of nine years. Teachers viewed the principal's sexual harassment as obvious assertions of power and control.

It started my very first day on the job, when I was showing the children pottery. He came in and asked me to walk over to him, right in the middle of class. Then he said, "I just wanted to see you walk." He was smiling. Once I kneeled down to pick up the phone, and he said, "Don't bend down like that, my hormones are raging." I didn't make the call. . . . I walked out. He was constantly telling me how pretty and sexy he thought I was. . . . One day he told me that if I didn't go to this parade with him that I would be sorry. I did go. It was very crowded, and he had his hands all over me, on my shoulders and back and so forth. In the parking lot, he took his shirt off and pumped his chest up and flexed his muscles. He said, "I don't want this to turn you on. . . ." He made comments constantly. Then, at lunch he said, "I will never hire another fat teacher." He said he wanted them all good looking and built like I was, and that he would never hire a woman in particular with a big ass—he didn't care what her credentials were. I said, "Surely, you can't mean that," but he said that he did and I knew that he did. He is a male chauvinist pig. When I was divorced, he wanted to know about my new boyfriend and what kind of sex life we had. I knew that he would make life hell for me if I complained. There was nothing I could do. It went on for nine years, and I didn't tell anybody, ever, about any of this.

I had problems with him calling me to his office. He would close the door and say, "Does this make you nervous to be in here with me by yourself?" Then he would tell me inappropriate jokes. He was very flirtatious and very controlling, and he knew that he was making me nervous; the jokes were sexual. Once, he said, "I want you to come over here and stand behind the desk with me." He tickled the backs of my legs and said, "I have been wanting to do that all day." I got out of his office. The secretary was aware that he was harassing me and would look at me like, "I am so sorry." Once, he came by my classroom and poked me right under my arm, not a very good place to be poking a female. He just kind of laughed.

He made flirtatious comments like, "You really look nice today," and, "I really like what you are wearing." It was the way that he said it and the way that he looked at me. He made me feel uncomfortable. He said things like that when nobody else was around. . . . At a charity ball, he was there with his wife; he had been drinking way too much [and] when he saw my date and me, he made a comment that my evening gown was kind of low cut and he would very much like to touch me in areas that it was low cut. I was so shocked that I walked off. It was an awful position to be in. I was embarrassed.

Several other teachers described isolated episodes of sexual harassment that, in conjunction with other forms of mistreatment, had profound effects on them over the long run.

I asked him about leaving so I could go get a mammogram. He is over six feet, 250 pounds. He said, "Well, I am a doctor. Come into my office and I'll do the exam." He sneered and did that deep-throat-kind-of-laugh-chuckle-kind-of-thing. He thought that it was funny. I said, "I don't think so. Can I leave early?" Once, he told one of the ladies that so-and-so had had a breast reduction and that the school counselor had been outside the doctor's office looking for the breast to put it on herself. It was so inappropriate.

He always put his arms around this young female teacher and kissed her on the mouth. This was in a small community. The young teacher was victimized; she knew that she couldn't relate the incident because it would be a word-against-word confrontation. She had to withstand the abuse and futility of not being able to get help. It was very detrimental to her career, and she isolated herself from everyone.

Other teachers described incidents of sexual harassment that occurred at faculty meetings and other places.

He has an IQ of about 3. He and his wife had gone into Victoria's Secret and he started talking about these bikini panties at a faculty meeting. He said, "What do you call those? Crotchless underwear?" That is exactly what he said! It had no point—no relation to anything.

He has made sexual innuendoes and comments during staff meetings. He calls my coworker Sharon Stone and tells her how he likes her perfume. He touches her inappropriately.

Racism

Teachers defined six principals, three African Americans and three Caucasian, as racists; as with sexual harassment, they reported that racism resulted in poor school morale and poor school climate.

> A black teacher went to the principal because one of the little kids called him a nappy-haired gorilla. The principal said, "Oh, he was just teasing you." The principal made a comment to another teacher that that black teacher was the "best black he ever had working for him."

> He was definitely a racist. He didn't want to hire black people. He said that he had been made to hire a black teacher before and he had to hire two this year but he didn't want to. He never put black teachers in charge of prestigious committees. We never had a black Teacher of the Year. The black teachers were very strong, but didn't stay very long; the stress was too much for them.

> He said, "I don't particularly like you as a person, but I have been impressed with the fact that, even though you are white, you really seem to love these black kids."

> A teacher across the hall from me is alcoholic. She is sometimes drunk at school. Once, she threw up outside my classroom. [Her problem] was obvious, yet he [the principal] constantly put her as chair of various committees. She was black.

In this chapter, we have seen that Level 3 principal mistreatment includes aggressive, even evil, behaviors such as lying, being explosive and nasty, threatening, reprimanding, forcing teachers out of their jobs, sexual harassment, and racism. In the next two chapters, the truly life-altering, devastating, and far-reaching effects of these behaviors are discussed.

5 The Effects of Principal Mistreatment of Teachers

Lasting Wounds and Damaged Schools

Anger is the quintessential individual-signature emotion. I am what makes me mad . . . Revenge is the basic response to being hurt, humiliated, berated, having your esteem hurt. . . . It is a response to injustice, an attempt to restore equilibrium in relationships.

— Barreca (1995, pp. 196, 238, 241)

Regrettably, American teachers, individuals who perform one of the most honorable and important jobs in the country, all too often suffer society's lack of respect, criticism, and blame, as well as the government's blame for the short-comings and problems of our schools and society; such treatment causes teachers to experience a kind of existential insecurity, instability, and lowered self-esteem (Phillips, 1993). What happens when these omnipresent factors—a teacher's professional experience and society's indictment of teachers—are compounded not only by other factors such as low pay and poor school facilities, but also by mistreatment at the hands of an abusive principal? In previous chapters we have demonstrated that principals mistreat teachers in a variety of ways, such as forcing teachers to change grades, ignoring the needs of students with disabilities, publicly criticizing, violating policy, unfairly evaluating teachers, denying professional development opportunities, and engaging in deceptive and dishonest conduct. Abusive principals, by virtue of their mistreatment, intimidate teachers into submission and silence; this, in turn, requires that teachers make significant professional and ethical compromises.

In this chapter, we explore some of the seriously damaging effects of long-term patterns of mistreatment on the teachers involved in our study, mistreatment that lasted from six months to as many as nine years. Here, some of teachers' initial emotional responses to abusive principals as well as some far-reaching effects on schools are discussed. In Chapter 6, other effects of principal mistreatment, including the severe long-term emotional, physical, and personal harm that it inevitably produces, are examined in greater detail. Other research on workplace mistreatment (i.e., research described in Chapter 1) conducted in a large number of public and private work settings, both nationally and internationally, has generated findings consistent with those that follow.

THE ADVERSE EFFECTS OF PRINCIPAL MISTREATMENT

Our findings indicate that prior to mistreatment by their principals, few of the teachers we interviewed had any direct experience with workplace mistreatment—how it harms one's self, one's work, and one's personal life; nor did they know how mistreatment of even one or a few teachers could undermine an entire school, spreading fear and anxiety among their colleagues. Indeed, we found that principal mistreatment of even a few teachers often resulted in significant collateral damage to a school; widespread fear, resentment, distrust, and poor morale were common by-products of such mistreatment. We will briefly summarize aspects of teachers' common and pervasive states of mind—some of their most persistent emotional experiences—during mistreatment.

Wounded Teachers

As teachers in our study described their feelings that resulted from principals' use of a variety of aggressive behaviors (Levels 1-3) over the long term, it became apparent that they were deeply "wounded." Broadly speaking, teachers described a range of common, everyday feelings: feeling trapped, fearful and angry, preoccupied, stressed, and traumatized; feeling corrupted and guilty; and feeling a diminished sense of professionalism.

Trapped. Teachers initially felt "trapped" by their mistreatment ("in an iron cage," "damned if I complained and damned if I didn't," and "I was a prisoner").

Many teachers were important breadwinners in their families, and their need for an income, health insurance, or a letter of reference prevented them from leaving their jobs. Additionally, unresponsive central office personnel, weak union representation, and principals' manipulation of transfer policies exacerbated feelings of being trapped. In most cases, teachers believed they had "no choice but to submit" to the person who made them victims of "unjust" and "damaging" treatment. (Feeling trapped is also discussed in Chapter 6, as a dimension of depression.)

Fearful, Angry, or Outraged. Teachers also experienced chronic fear, anger, and outrage; furthermore, they were afraid to confront principals because of the likelihood of retaliation in the form of further mistreatment. Many "just lived in terror," they "shut up," "closed down," and withdrew emotionally and physically from involvement in work. Teachers' realization that they frequently did not have the courage to confront their abusive principals or maintain standards in their classrooms deepened their feelings of fear and anger. Mistreatment also produced harmful collateral effects: Other teachers usually "fell in line," pandered, and even became the principal's "pet" or "crony" to avoid mistreatment. Without exception, teachers were "outraged" toward principals for their mistreatment, for the favoritism the principals showed others, and for the damage caused to them, to their work with children and adolescents, and to their families.

Preoccupied, Stressed, and Traumatized. Although considerable empirical evidence shows that a principal's leadership approach can dramatically undermine teacher performance and school effectiveness (e.g., Barnette, 1990; Blase, 1986; Dworkin et al., 1990), the abusive principals we have described displayed no sensitivity regarding the damage they caused to teachers, nor to the related effects on their work in classrooms with students. At the same time, teachers were preoccupied with thoughts about their principal and their own survival. In many cases, the stress was seriously debilitating; in fact, about 10% of the participants in our study were diagnosed with symptoms of PTSD, a condition many people suffer when subjected to mistreatment at work over a long period of time (Scott & Strandling, 1994).

Corrupted and Guilty. Teachers felt "corrupted" and "guilty," for example, by being "forced" to change a student's grade, to violate district policy, and to remain silent about such matters. Our data also indicate that the principal's negative modeling influenced other teachers' behavior negatively, causing further collateral damage. Teachers spoke about how a principal's single act of abuse could set in motion a host of dysfunctional behaviors on the part of others and thus corrupt teachers and students in a given school. To illustrate, in one case, some teachers imitated the racism of their abusive principals. In other cases, teachers disclosed that students were forced to comply with the unethical demands of abusive principals; principals used students politically, coaching them to make false statements against victimized teachers. As one would expect, feelings of being corrupted and guilty further depleted teachers' self-esteem.

Diminished Sense of Professionalism. Throughout their ordeals, abused teachers were significantly less motivated and less creative in their instructional work; both teaching and student learning suffered dramatically. Teachers revealed that principals forced them to compromise professional ethics and, in particular, substantially compromise classroom instruction and their work in the school. Specifically, teachers explained that they "contrived" their teaching; in general, they "did the minimum" because of fear of further principal mistreatment and overwhelming stress. McNeil (1986) referred to this as "defensive teaching"; that is, simplification and fragmentation of instruction, removal of creativity and lesson complexity, and replacement of important instructional elements with control of student behavior (e.g., "keeping them quiet"). Teachers "worried constantly" about the damage done to themselves and their teaching.

All in all, our data indicate that mistreated teachers could not find within themselves, or obtain from other teachers or outside sources, adequate resources or the kind of support required to successfully counteract the emotional devastation they suffered. Most survived solely because they "learned to play the game," withdrew, or remained silent. In no case did school district office officials offer psychological support for victimized teachers or intervene to stop the reported mistreatment; indeed, in almost all cases such personnel were seen as directly "colluding" with abusive principals, "having the same mentality," or "putting their heads in the sand."

Initial Emotional Responses

In the following section, more detailed descriptions of teachers' initial emotional responses to principal abuse—feelings of shock and disorientation, humiliation, loneliness, and injured confidence and self-esteem—are examined in detail.

Shock and Disorientation. Teachers experienced a strong sense of disorientation and confusion as a result of mistreatment. In part, such feelings were directly related to not understanding the issue or problem that motivated principals' abusive actions toward them. Teachers used words such as "bewildered," "confused," "shocked," "disoriented," "helpless," "stunned," and "mystified" to describe feelings associated with early attacks by their principals.

It always bothered me that I never knew how to react or correct the problem; that was because I didn't know what the problem was.

I kept chalking it up to her being in a bad mood. I didn't make the connection between the fact that I had disagreed with her and the things that she was doing to me. I was real frustrated. Then I woke up and realized it wasn't just a bad day.

Unfortunately, teachers' sense of disorientation was not short-lived; nor was it merely an initial response to the sudden, out-of-the-blue nature of principals' actions against them. To the contrary, for most, such feelings persisted throughout their mistreatment experiences, in part because they were unable to understand why they were targeted and in part because they were unable to identify any course of action to resolve their situations.

> I couldn't understand what I had done to provoke this. I felt a loss of power, loss of center, loss of balance. I felt reduced, like when you have a parent who has turned on you. Our school was like a dysfunctional family and I was the abused child. I lost my confidence. I was becoming dysfunctional in my personal life. I had bad dreams. A call from the office would make my heart absolutely race. It is very painful, devastating. I felt sad, betrayed, angry, indignant, outraged, disoriented.

> At my first school, I was a workaholic. I would always go the extra mile. You could build on a vision. . . . I felt none of that mattered to this principal. I lost my motivation. After the first few incidents with her, I was in a state of shock; I never had a principal treat me that way.

> The new principal made me afraid to do anything. I became confused. If I referred a kid [special education referral], it might be that "you can't control your class." If I didn't, I was "neglectful." Damned if I do and damned if I don't.

> I felt like I was on a merry-go-round and I couldn't get off. I couldn't get his praise. I couldn't understand being put down. I mean, "nice job," a handshake, whatever. It never came and it still doesn't.

> I thought it was my imagination, that I was being paranoid, but my para-pro said, "Boy he treats you differently from the others." She had been in my room for about two weeks.

> I didn't know who to talk to, who to trust, who to confide in. Should I go to another school, another county? Look for some job besides teaching? Quit? I didn't know what to do; it was a terrible feeling. She had taken my comment very personally. I was stunned by her behavior. I felt betrayed. She had turned on me. We had had a very good relationship.

> I was always shocked and mystified. Her behavior was not professional demeanor. She was doing exactly what the no-nos were for me as a teacher.

Humiliation. Our study also demonstrates that principals' mistreatment provoked, early on, strong feelings of humiliation and embarrassment in teachers, especially when such treatment occurred in public places.

> Another bad part was embarrassing teachers. . . . My mother had died and he never said that he was sorry or even acknowledged her death. At one meeting, I got up to leave to meet my father to pick out my mother's

tombstone. . . . He screamed at me, "Do you have a problem?" I said, "I told you earlier I was going to meet my father to pick out my mother's tombstone and that is exactly what I am going to do. My working hours are 7:30 to 3:30 and it is 3:30 now and I am leaving."

I had been waiting for the principal in the office area, doing a good deed, trying to help the secretary. When the principal arrived, I jokingly said, "I am glad you finally got back." She flew into a tirade, saying, "I don't care how long you have been waiting. What do you think I have been doing, standing around the corner picking my nose?!" It was awful. I was so embarrassed. Everybody had the same dumbfounded look on their faces. I froze. I was in shock. She had these kinds of incidents with other teachers . . . bawling them out in front of their students and coworkers. It was embarrassing. I was disappointed and hurt. It was a public reprimand.

He raises his voice and basically puts people down. It's humiliating. At faculty meetings he will say, "That is a dumb idea," and that he doesn't want to hear that. He would say, "If you were listening to me you wouldn't ask that."

He made me feel silly and stupid. Other teachers were present when I got there and I just took it. I remember thinking, "I noticed that you, the principal, were abusing that child."

Professional staff and parents were there. She told me that I wasn't doing my job because she had to deal with discipline. Her tone of voice and her nonverbal language made it inappropriate.

She told everybody in the faculty about this embarrassing incident that this teacher had been trying to live down for three months and felt mortified about.

I was embarrassed when she got through talking to me and when she turned and stormed out. She was reprimanding me in front of students and other teachers.

Strong feelings of humiliation also resulted from other forms of principal mistreatment:

I put a lot of effort into trying to build this program, and then he turned and said that it was not working. I was devastated, humiliated. I had given all of my energy and training to that project.

It was extremely embarrassing. I felt like everybody knew that I was kicked out, transferred to a new school.

Loneliness. During the early periods of mistreatment, many of the teachers we interviewed received some support from other faculty; however, about half of the targeted teachers reported that individuals, and sometimes groups of teachers, began to ostracize them, typically because these teachers also feared principal reprisals for association or because they were "taking the principal's side" in the ongoing ordeal. Teachers experienced feelings of profound loneliness throughout their mistreatment experiences.

> We had always been a very close knit group, but now teachers treat me like I have the plague. They avoid me. We have very little interaction. I stay in my classroom and don't socialize, and I don't go to the lounge. One day, a colleague and I made an arrangement to trade hall duties, but then she canceled it and said, "No, I don't want to be indebted to you." She wants to be very neutral, because she is very uncomfortable and afraid of the principal. I am a very dangerous person to associate with.

> I went to my friends, my confidants, and said, "This is miserable, this is terrible." They looked at me as though I had obviously done something wrong and deserved what was happening to me. Their loyalty was to the principal. They were afraid about being mistreated too. They knew to play it safe, and they knew they had better stay away from me. They also didn't want to talk to me because they didn't want to know about it . . . it might make them feel badly. Well, if that is what they are going to do, I don't need that kind of friendship. I feel fearful disclosing things to them anyway.

> I got married that year. Anytime somebody got married or there was a birth of a child, there was some sort of recognition and people would attend the wedding. I had a lot of friends there, but few of them attended my wedding. They were afraid. One of my friends who did attend and stuck with me was treated like crap by the principal. Other teachers just kept their distance. I was the problem child.

> As union representative, I initiated a petition that most teachers quickly signed. The bulk of the staff voted to overturn the principal's plan but when they realized that push was coming to shove, most faculty would not relate to me. I did not have a support group. About a quarter of the faculty were actively hostile or at least on nonspeaking terms with me. We didn't speak for a couple of years.

> I was embarrassed. Some of the older teachers were saying that I was having an affair with the principal because he was always telling me to come into his office and close the door. I would walk into the teachers' lounge and the teachers would stop talking really quickly. I felt that they were talking about me, saying that I was fooling around with this terrible principal, but I couldn't say anything. I didn't know whom I could trust.

To avoid further principal abuse, at times even targeted teachers ostracized other targeted teachers:

> I am always afraid that I am not going to do something right and the principal is going to call me on it. The woman whom I am paired with in teaching is one of his bad eggs; she is always being yelled at and being

sent to the office. So I am afraid that if I am grouped with her, what she does will reflect on me. Then I think, "That is terrible to think; she is a good teacher." But, I am already in the dog house, and I don't want to be grouped with someone else in the dog house.

Teachers wouldn't be openly supportive, especially if they knew someone was about to be axed. You didn't want to be one of that person's big supporters because then you would be next. I didn't try to get very close to others. Everything was work related. There was never a "How is your family?" or, "Gee, I am sorry that you are going through a divorce," nothing on a personal level at all.

Injured Self-Confidence and Self-Esteem. Most teachers reported that, from the beginning, principal mistreatment seriously harmed their self-esteem. Specifically, both veteran and beginning teachers developed substantial self-doubt and loss of confidence in their ability and competence as teachers. Many teachers actually internalized, in varying degrees, principals' negative views of them, usually for years:

I had been given a program to work on because of my professional reputation and my skills in technology. Then, I was pulled out without notice and told things weren't working. I felt I was not successful, that I had no talent and I wasn't worth trying to fix. Then I was transferred to another school to teach in an area I was not qualified to teach and in a school I did not want to be at. It was quite a blow to my self-esteem. . . . [I] felt like I was a person of no value. I decided there wasn't any use for me to get a leadership degree, and that I would be horrible as an assistant principal. I began to doubt that I could do the job anywhere.

I was put down and getting the shaft. I felt I constantly had to justify myself. I felt worthless, useless, like I couldn't meet expectations. That was a lot of my problem. I lost respect for myself because I didn't stand up to him. I was afraid and I knew it. I wondered why he picked me out . . . Did he see me as a weak person and feel like he could manipulate me? He affected my self-worth.

My self-esteem suffered. You wonder whether you are a good teacher. Maybe it is true, maybe it is not. You start looking around, asking yourself, "Is it happening to everybody?" You feel you are losing your mind. As a little girl, I could never understand why my people let themselves be hauled off to the gas chamber; why didn't they stand up and say, "Hell no, we won't go there"? I let this man rule me as a dictator all the time, and I never spoke up for myself.

I had a lot of self-doubt after that first incident. I was worried that something I had planned for was going to come up every day. I questioned everything that I was doing. I was just sort of beating myself up every day.

My self-esteem was at rock bottom. I couldn't stop thinking about her [the principal] . . . which was also frustrating.

There was no value to what I said. He just thought that I was running off at the mouth. I began to doubt what I was doing. This was the first time I had questioned my teaching ability in over 20 years. I felt very devalued.

For relatively inexperienced teachers, abusive encounters with a principal were equally destructive of their self-esteem:

In my school, no one felt that they were competent. When criticism is all that you receive, it is hard to think of anything different, especially with no experience behind you. You start wondering.

I eat and sleep and think school and teaching. When he threatened my job, he threatened my whole definition of me. I was made to feel that I was irresponsible. I was questioning why I couldn't get this project going.

It destroyed my self-confidence. For a long time I did not think that I was a good teacher. I felt like I was a crummy teacher, like I didn't know what I was doing. I doubted my abilities.

Damaged Schools

Over time, principals' mistreatment resulted in far-reaching, destructive effects on schools, particularly with regard to relationships between and among teachers, their instructional work in classrooms, and collective decision-making processes.

Damaged Relationships. Historically speaking, most of the experienced teachers we interviewed reported that throughout their professional careers and in their work with former principals, they had been "totally" involved in their schools, and, in fact, frequently provided the leadership necessary to initiate innovative arrangements among faculty focusing on student development. Our data demonstrate that abusive principals severely undermined the development of innovative and collaborative structures among faculty as well as teachers' overall level of involvement in their schools. Consequently, in addition to ostracism by colleagues, *mistreated teachers typically withdrew from all discretional involvements*, such as committee work, schoolwide events, special projects, and staff development. When involvement was considered mandatory, such as faculty meeting attendance, teachers minimized their participation and, in general, maintained silence. Briefly, teachers indicated that such extreme responses on their part were designed to protect themselves from further attacks by abusive principals. These teachers became islands; support from others was limited and was often given only secretly because, as one teacher stated, "friends were afraid that they could become a target of mistreatment, guilt by association."

There were a lot of little cliques. There was no sharing among the faculty, no sharing of ideas or methods, no getting together and looking at students or doing assessments, none of that. Committees were few and far between and generally composed of her little pets. That is how all decisions were made. No one else wanted to be on the committees under these circumstances. We supported each other. I spent a lot of time on the phone with a really good friend . . . having a good long gripe session. She and I would make popcorn and just talk. Sometimes I would cry.

She had some pets, her stoolies, and you knew right fast who the stoolies were. She would praise them. You were very careful whom you talked with. People would gripe all the time. It was a mass exit at check-out time, a real indication that people are not happy. Teachers would push each other to get out of the view of the video camera in the hallway so they could chat about what they had heard about her that day.

I did not speak to the principal. . . . The last few years I don't think that the faculty laughed at all. I think that it is real important to have fun. I really miss that. Teachers would say, "You haven't done anything fun this year, played a joke on somebody . . . like cleaning up their desk or hiding their plan-book or messing up their chalkboard or changing all the alphabet and vowel cards around." I was afraid that I might get into trouble. At the faculty meetings, I didn't say anything. If you ever questioned anything or suggested anything, she would say things like, "Do you want to work here?" or, "If you have a comment that is not for the overall school, save it and meet with me." But we were afraid to meet with her. Your input wasn't desired.

At a faculty meeting, he said that if we went to the central office and gave information about him that he would find out who did it. He said, "You might think that there is safety in numbers but I will get you, one by one." . . . I didn't want to be involved in anything. Most of the teachers were like little islands. Everybody went into their classrooms and did their own thing, then left and went home. The faculty was divided. You never knew whom you could talk to and whom you didn't dare say anything in front of. There was very little talking. He had a few favorites, but he didn't have many teachers who respected him, but somehow he was getting information. We knew that the first-grade teacher would tell him anything. We didn't even get together for Christmas parties or anything like that.

Right away she started against the teacher to the point where she got other teachers to shun her. I agreed to do something, and some teachers said a lot of things about me. Some stopped saying good morning and started being real short. They would roll their eyes and do some body language. At holiday parties, attendance was extremely low. If she wasn't involved, attendance was up, like when we did the race for life for the cancer association. Trust suffered quite a bit. Even I was finding fault. I was short with certain people whom normally I could have fluffed off. Where normally most people would give and take, everything became like a life or death situation. Everything was negative. It was just the climate of the whole situation. Administrators set the tone of the school. When you get a totally negative feeling at the top, by the time that you get down to the teachers, kids, and parents, it is pretty bad. I felt very, very sad a lot of times because of what was happening to our school.

The extent to which many teachers withdrew from former social and professional commitments is noteworthy:

I withdrew from all professional organizations, except two. I just withdrew. I closed myself down. Before all this started, I was the State Teacher of the Year. I truly enjoyed teaching. I loved it. I thought that I would teach forever. I would come home happy every day. . . . I have always believed that we need to put a lot into our profession, that we need to work extra with other teachers and students. Before, I sponsored the science club, academic debates, the scholars bowl team, and students against driving drunk. I was senior class sponsor; I sponsored four committees at the school and county level. . . . I just withdrew from all of that. I was not going to put time and effort into a system that treated me that way.

I stopped doing most everything. I used to be on leadership teams, task forces, grade chair, the climate committee. . . . I did celebrations, action research, conference presentations, school improvement. Now, the only thing that I do, because I still just dearly love it, is technology coordinator. I dropped everything else. I am less open now, and my door is closed quite often. I am guarded and I am careful about what I say, always.

There were some teachers who felt like I deserved what she did to me, and there were some teachers who stood behind me. Her pets thought that I deserved it. I didn't get very much support from the other people because this woman was bullying them, too. . . . I did not stay a minute beyond my quitting time. There was a lot of whispering . . . that kind of thing. I did nothing I wasn't required to do.

It is horrible. Nobody is really speaking anymore; nobody is friendly. There is a big division in the school. It has become the black folks and the white folks against each other.

A couple of teachers indicated that although they withdrew substantially from schoolwide affairs, they were able to maintain some involvement:

I try to be as cautious as I can, and I don't do anything to fuel her fires. What I do is help on the margins. The reward for doing extra around here is punishment.

Only one teacher indicated that her faculty engaged in defiant actions when they were required to attend meetings:

During faculty meetings, he would read from his little typed list like we couldn't read by ourselves. People couldn't stand him. We would be talking, laughing, and cutting up—we made a fool out of him. We all hated his guts.

Although teachers directly targeted by principals significantly withdrew from schoolwide involvement, as described, our data also point out that principal mistreatment, particularly when it was widespread in the school, occasionally resulted in greater social cohesion among faculty. However, this was usually limited to a defensive banding together for social support and protection.

He came in to try and divide and conquer the faculty. It made us stronger. The faculty became very close and very tight. At meetings, the faculty sat there and looked at him and never asked any questions. I was not willing to go the extra mile; everyone felt that way. We would have attitude adjustment hours. As a senior prank, one of the students locked the gates to the school and the principal couldn't get in. Then, someone said that the faculty meeting had been postponed and we all cheered. On one occasion, the kids had taken pictures of his face and put it on top of a naked, very excited, well-endowed man and posted it all over the neighborhood. But really our morale was very low. Some of the teachers would just let it out and say that he was an asshole.

When teachers got together, they would share their complaints, get angry, and share frustrations. She treated everybody badly. It became a gripe session—everybody felt the same way about her leadership. It was constant dialogue between teachers about things that she had done, said, or didn't do. We would turn to each other for leadership because we didn't have a principal who helped us.

If anything, I think that the teachers were closer because it was such a stressful environment. People really pulled together. We did a lot of things socially. We would go to somebody's house after work and vent typical teacher-lounge stuff. He was constantly on someone, constantly picking at someone. People would say, "We know he is crazy; it is not you." . . . It was just a joke. That was the only way to deal with it.

It brought me closer to quite a few teachers. The secretary always looked so very communicative like, "I know what you are going through, and we all have to put up with a whole lot of shit." That is exactly how people are looking at each other. A teacher read me a story one of her students wrote about the principal. Students are feeling it too—it is unreal!

Unfortunately, repeated attacks and reprisals against teachers appeared, at times, to be a function of favored teachers, teachers who served as informants or spies for principals. Thus, abused teachers were typically alienated from others, their relationships damaged, and they had to rely on the social and professional support of only a handful of trusted colleagues. There were only a few exceptions:

I was not the only one she raked over the coals. I found out it was a kind of initiation. Once you have been talked to, in that fashion, you are part of the club. It made us very cohesive. We all had been abused, so we could empathize. When we needed stuff or support, we would go to each other. We had all been wrongfully accused, or chewed out, or were made the scape-goat. Even the people who had her ear knew that they were in a precarious situation. They would talk to both sides. We had their trust; there was nobody who was totally her person. We feared nobody on the staff as being the pipeline to her. We weren't afraid of each other in any way. If we wanted to feed ideas to her, we would feed them through these people—they were the bridges. We just kept the kids in mind, kept swimming, just kept going.

Damaged Classrooms. For most teachers, principal mistreatment had serious deleterious consequences for all major aspects of classroom life including the quality of instruction and social relationships with students. In general, teachers described feelings of "stress," "paranoia," "insecurity," "fear," "dread," "self-doubt," and lowered motivation with regard to classroom teaching:

My emphases and my thoughts went away from the curriculum as I won-dered where the principal was. I was paranoid. Was he coming to my class, what was going on? . . . I have avoided new ideas that I would have implemented in class because they would have involved the principal's support. I felt vulnerable. I knew the principal would not back me. My relationship with students became stressed.

I felt very insecure in class. I would second guess myself continually.

At first there was no effect. But, about mid-year, I became so angry, upset, paranoid, and preoccupied most of the time. I couldn't concentrate on teaching. My attendance was beginning to suffer. It was unfair to the students. One by one we were transferred by the principal to a counterpart program at the other end of the county.

I was afraid to ask for help, but I was still green and needed help, especially when dealing with special needs students.

More precisely, teachers disclosed that abusive principals forced them to employ traditional methods of teaching that they viewed as "rigid," "authoritar-ian," "dated," and "ineffective." Such methods emphasized lecture, rote and recita-tion, drill, and worksheets, and were associated with significant reductions in teachers' motivation, responsiveness to diversity, risk-taking, creativity and inno-vation, planning, preparation, and variation in the use of instructional strategies and materials. Furthermore, teachers described the increased use of authoritarian, control-oriented, impersonal methods of classroom discipline, an expectation of most abusive principals. Important adverse effects were also discussed for teachers' social relationships with students; reductions in teacher caring, patience, tolerance, and humor were apparent:

I was less motivated to try new things or even ask for advice on how to implement a new instructional unit and methods in my classroom. I was constantly angry with the students, but I couldn't show it. I had to internalize my anger to prevent trouble from students or parents because I knew that the principal would not support me. My authority in the classroom had been undermined; so I was very uncomfortable about how to deal with the students and the class. I did not try as hard or put forth the effort toward my classroom duties. Every teacher was guarded in the classroom and in discussions and conferences with parents. Eventually, coming to school and to class was a dreaded event. When I received letters of reprimand during class, my students witnessed my reaction. I was not able to teach effectively at all. At first, I tried to ignore the negative environment, but eventually I became withdrawn. I taught straight from the book. I put in as little time as possible. I didn't get very close to the students. My motivation for teaching became zero. I was constantly on edge. My nerves were shot and I would sometimes treat students in a negative manner because of the principal's abuse.

In my teaching, I was hesitant to try anything new. I didn't do anything different that would draw attention to me, especially anything that might not work the first time. . . . I have passed kids who failed just to avoid conflict with the principal. . . . In a strange way, I almost started treating children like he was treating me. I never berated them, but, when I would give directions, if a kid would ask about it, I would say, "You know what I just said!" I had no patience. I felt like I had to control the environment because, if I didn't, he would get me. I had kids with bracelets on their ankles, kids out of mental institutions and jails. They needed special service referrals. But I knew I couldn't do anything to set the students up for a referral, because the principal looked at that very negatively. Everything had to look good.

He wanted to see your tests, your worksheets. He wanted you to give much too much homework. For a child who doesn't have support at home, that breeds failure. He didn't understand children who came from environmentally deprived backgrounds. I had watched him paddle the children and scream and yell at them. I kept meticulous plan books that he graded and wrote really ugly comments in red. I tried not to let it interfere, but it was bound to affect the classroom climate. I tried to put up a front for my children. I didn't want to destroy my reputation, but I had an attitude. He influenced my patience in the classroom. I was tense and would get short tempered. I had reached the end of my rope. I felt horrible inside. My lessons suffered. If I had not feared him, I would have done more creative things and the children would have benefited. Lecture just goes in one ear and out the other.

I didn't feel as effective with the kids. I was sort of a split-personality. The kids would come up and hug me, but they knew that something wasn't right. I just wasn't as kind and patient. I was not as creative with lesson planning. I made lesson plans simple and basic so as to avoid having a lot of interaction with the kids. It would have allowed them to see more of how I wasn't myself. Everything was mechanical in the classroom.

I always had good rapport with my students. I was friendly, we would joke around. When the bell rang we would get serious, but we could have fun. I had really good communication. I would rewrite worksheets so that they had all kinds of funny situations to work on. They could apply their physics to analyze cartoons and those sorts of things. But, I went almost strictly to lecture that year; they would just get out their books and read. I saw students as something that I had to deal with during the day. I didn't have as much tolerance for their uniqueness. I had always prided myself that when a student was different, I would build on that difference and make him feel good. I quit doing that. I became much more of an authoritarian. I took over. I had total control.

I had to spend my time following the structured, traditional, 1940s method that she demanded. She didn't want any talking, she didn't want any centers, she didn't want anything—just sit in your seats and hold your heads down. This is not my method, it hurts everybody. I couldn't spend time on centers or individualized things that would especially promote the slow learners.

The first thing that he did was to withhold art supplies. I was supposed to be doing two- and three-dimensional designs and fiber designs with these children. I could do only the two-dimensional things. He was in violation of the state standards and he knew it. But it didn't make any difference. . . . I no longer wanted to be teaching—period. If a child would cut up, I would just let it go. I certainly wasn't going to call parents. He would not support us in disciplining matters. He put a lot of unnecessary pressure on me.

Special education teachers subjected to mistreatment discussed similar as well as unique problems.

I have abandoned my students completely. I am on the front lines. I am fighting for my livelihood. There will be no further teaching, advocating—nothing. The kids will just have to fend for themselves. I hate that. This principal said he would like it just fine if all the teachers put in their eight hours and left. He doesn't want teachers doing anything innovative. There is no way to fight city hall. No matter what I do, it is wrong; it could have been done sooner, it could have been done faster, it shouldn't been done at all, it could have been done in a better way. Everything I do is wrong. I have lost interest in what I am doing because apparently it doesn't suit anybody. I have become very strict with kids and much less tolerant because if they did something wrong, I would get the heat.

She said, "This is not a life skill," and, "You are not supposed to be doing that kind of thing!" She just didn't understand the program. But, in my program, my students jumped two or three grade levels in their academic subjects. She wanted to keep the worst-behaved students in the world buried somewhere out of her hair.

She said that she saw an alarming trend of special education students being dismissed or having their time decreased. I said, "I thought that was my job." She told me that my role was to teach kids coping strategies, and that she felt that if the kids were once identified as LD [learning disabled], they were probably always LD. She said, "We aren't in the business of curing kids at this school." She controlled all student placement meetings. I was not sleeping well, and I was generally on edge. It affected my energy for teaching, my ability to concentrate, and my planning. I did a lot less preparation.

She was becoming a monster, a dictator. I was being punished in front of the students. I thought that it would be unprofessional to argue with her, to tell her she was wrong in front of the students. I thought that maybe they would see me as no better than she was. These kids have a lot of behavior problems—one-parent families, broken homes; some are mentally handicapped. She undermines everything that I am trying to do to teach these kids appropriate behavior. I couldn't be optimistic or motivated like I used to be.

One teacher-counselor reported that her principal forced her to abandon all meaningful counseling with students and, in effect, to ignore her professional responsibilities:

I was called into the office three or four times last year. Once, I wanted to start a group for kids who were in divorced families. The kids kept coming in to me and talking about their problems. I had mentioned it to the head counselor, but nothing ever happened. So, I got things together, got surveys and passed them out. I got called back to the office and was criticized. I was told, "You are only here to help students with their school stuff!" After the fourth time, I came home devastated and cried all night. . . . Another time, the principal said that he didn't like me airing the school's dirty laundry and that I needed to keep quiet about the gangs. Also, many of our girls get pregnant by 22-, 23-, 24-year-old guys. I am pretty straightforward. I tell these girls, "These guys shouldn't be with you. They need to be with women, not little girls. You need to keep your legs crossed and stay away." As a counselor, I can often see something that is going on with a kid in trouble. Do I keep the kid in my office another 20 minutes and maybe expose something the principal wants hidden or do I send her back to class? If I feel that there is something deeper behind her problems, I need to dig. But, when I did things that I thought were significant, I got into trouble for it. I always did pretty well at everything I did.

But now, every time I turned around, it seemed as if I was doing something wrong. The interesting thing was that the teachers were all coming up to me and telling me what a great job I was doing. . . . Now I don't counsel anymore.

A few teachers indicated that, because of principal mistreatment, teaching was a constant struggle; moderately negative effects on the classroom were evident.

I would be grinding my teeth at the back of my jaw while I was mustering that emotional labor to set a tone in the classroom. I was not nearly as elastic and free, or open. So yes, it has taken a huge effort to try and keep that from affecting my rapport in the classroom.

When she came in the classroom, I thought, "I am going to stand up and act like it doesn't bother me," and that is what she saw. It is not what I was feeling; I was totally preoccupied with the situation, even when I was teaching—totally absorbed. But, I wanted to maintain my professionalism.

Of the 50 teachers we interviewed, only one reported no adverse effects on his or her classroom.

Surprisingly, he didn't seem to have a great impact on my teaching; I would just block it out. I treated my children with kindness and caring. It wasn't the kick the dog syndrome. I didn't have any displaced anger. . . . But, I never invite him to observe or participate with my class. I don't want him near me. I don't talk to him unnecessarily, and I don't share positive or negative things that occur in my classroom. I basically X'd him out of my school day.

Impaired Decision Making. Typically, teachers used words such as "autocrat," "tyrant," "dictator," "authoritarian," "despot," and "control freak" to describe the leadership approach of abusive principals. Our data suggest that, with regard to school governance and decision making, principals were *overtly authoritarian* or *covertly authoritarian*; in both cases, abusive principals were extremely coercive and control-oriented; decisions were made unilaterally and, often, arbitrarily. Further, in both cases, communication was one way and intimidation was used to secure teachers' compliance to decisions and decision-making processes. However, principals who used an overt approach to schoolwide governance frequently employed a direct, "in-your-face," "make-my-day" approach to leadership, whereas those who employed a covert approach often appropriated the rhetoric or the veneer of "shared decision making and collaboration" to obscure its authoritarian nature. Thus, the latter form of authoritarianism is considered more manipulative (i.e., deceptive) as compared with the former. Teachers' comments illustrate how overtly authoritarian and abusive principals approached faculty meetings and schoolwide decision making.

At faculty meetings, he believes only one voice should be heard, his. He thinks that he is a people person because he can make almost 70 people sit there and face him . . . . No one else speaks—he just keeps talking. . . . One or two people . . . will ask questions, and he is brutal with them. He'll say, "I am not going to talk with you about that now." If you ask a question and he doesn't want to deal with it, he just cuts you off. One time, I asked a question at a meeting. He said, "I don't appreciate being questioned and, if you have anything to say during a faculty meeting, don't!" One time . . . he went through almost a hundred pages of "You don't do this . . . don't you ever . . . I mean it."

All she could do was criticize. She ran faculty meetings with a negative edge, like you were going in there to get a spanking. Unless you were one of her cronies, you knew that you better shut up. Everyone feared her wrath. She held grudges. You make a mistake and you are on "the list."

We were always talked at during faculty meetings. The faculty sat there and looked at him. There was never any kind of feedback from the faculty.

He would keep us in faculty meetings forever, way beyond the time permitted. He would read to us—read every detail of meetings that he attended, things that we could care less about. He would just go on and on. It was just a power play to keep teachers there.

At a faculty meeting, she went on and on about what it was that she wanted us to do. I questioned her and I was in trouble. Other faculty were appalled, but they were afraid to speak up. They gave me a look of terror. After the meeting, some teachers secretly came to me and said, "Watch your back. She doesn't like anyone questioning her, especially in a public forum. She is very vindictive." She started very slowly, nitpicking at everything that I did. Teachers felt that they were being bullied every time that she came up with a new directive and a new mandate for us.

Her behavior discouraged any questions or opinions. She would say things like, "Do you want to work here?" If you ever raised your hands and questioned anything she would say, "That won't work here," and then go right on to the next comment. Your input wasn't desired.

We did not go to one faculty meeting where the principal wasn't bad-mouthing the board, or central office, or somebody. To me, that is the worst; it's so unprofessional. . . . If anyone questions anything . . . he'll say, "I'll get back to you". . . . There is no dialogue or communication.

You don't ask the principal anything, because he is just going to yell. If he knows the answer, he is not going to tell you. Faculty meetings were crazy; they didn't accomplish anything. He would read a typed written agenda to us; it was just a joke. If you said something and he didn't agree with it, then he would respond, "Did you understand what I said? Well, we are going to do it this way, because I am the principal." We just sat there and wrote notes like, "Can you believe we are sitting here?"

Teachers also described overtly authoritarian principals' approach to faculty committees:

> There weren't a whole lot of committees because she made all the decisions. The committees were few and far between and generally composed of people who were her little pets. That is how all the decisions were made. There was not a lot of input throughout the school.

> Committee members were appointed by her based on whom she liked and whom she didn't like: favoritism. She ran some of the committees. She just told you what to do; she didn't participate. We knew that you couldn't do anything to the contrary of what she would want, so the meetings went something like, "What do you think she wants us to do? Okay, let's do that." She had her spies. There was no way to discuss anything. There was no professional discussion. Everything was an order, and you just followed it and hoped to dodge criticism.

As mentioned earlier, all abusive principals used thinly veiled manipulative techniques to control teachers, such as negative comments ("We have done that before, it won't work") and pejorative labeling, vetoing faculty decisions, inviting dissenting faculty to private meetings, limiting time, and limiting agendas to particular topics to control faculty. However, as suggested above, covertly authoritarian and abusive principals attempted to maintain a veneer of shared decision making:

> One faculty member said to her, "We already voted on this and it was voted down." She said, "I think that we need to reconsider this." She just wadded the paper up and threw it down on the table and walked out. It all boiled down to: Don't oppose her. She kept forcing us to vote until it passed.

> She said, "I will tell you how much shared governance there will be, what you can do, and the topics you can consider." She is an absolute dictator. She has displayed, many times, that she didn't care for people to express their feelings. Anybody who dared to speak up was not chosen to be on the committee to talk to the accreditation team. She put the wealthy whites on committees, but she put blacks, the sucker-uppers, who do what she says, on committees as chairs. At one of those prep meetings, she said, "This is what you are going to say" and if we spoke up about anything negative, that was grounds for dismissal. We had shared leadership supposedly, but the principal was head of the leadership team. She made all the decisions.

> She decided to have this big "democratic" procedure but decisions were predetermined, you know. We were supposed to come to a consensus, but everybody was afraid to voice their opinions. They would just give up. The principal would call a meeting, and sometimes it would start at 2:45 and not be over until 5:30 or 6:00. There was never any warning that we were

going to have a meeting or how long it might last. She would stand up in front of the whole cafeteria full of people and read "her" agenda. You would be quiet and then you would leave. When the accreditation team came, I signed up to be on the communication committee. Low and behold, guess who was chairman of that committee? The principal. She came to the meeting and said, "This isn't going to be long at all. It is going to be a piece of cake. I jotted a few things down on this paper. If you would like to proofread and see if there is anything that you want to change or add, we will be out of here in 10 minutes." What person was going to fight her? So, we all read it, nodded our heads, signed off, and left.

On paper we had shared governance, but it lasted only a week or two. Administrators figured out that it would look good to pretend that we were doing it. They set up this committee with three teachers to represent all the teachers, and they met every three weeks. Everything that got taken to them—all of the issues—were slapped right back down. Finally, everybody just gave up because it didn't matter. "What are we doing this for?"

He was in his office matching up teachers' handwriting on an anonymous questionnaire with their signatures on their insurance forms. I said, "This is confidential." His reaction was, "No big deal." He said, "We have a few faculty members in here who do all the bitching and moaning." In other words, a bunch of bitchy women. He said, "I am going to find out right now what all the complaints are." But he really only wanted to know who was doing the complaining.

In this chapter, we have begun to examine the effects of principal mistreatment on teachers—the wounds of shock and disorientation, humiliation, loneliness, and injured self-confidence and self-esteem. The related effects on schools include damage to relationships among teachers, damage to instruction in classrooms, and damage to educators' collective decision-making processes.

In the next chapter, we will closely examine other seriously destructive and even chronic personal and professional effects of principal mistreatment on teachers.

6 Worlds of Pain

The Undoing of Teachers

[A] boss' abusive disrespect [is] clearly linked to adverse psychological states.

— Hornstein (1996, p. 74)

Workplace bullying can have serious, even devastating, effects on targeted individuals. Psychological effects include stress, depression, mood swings, loss of sleep (and resulting fatigue), and feelings of shame, guilt, embarrassment, and low self-esteem. More serious effects can include Post-Traumatic Stress Disorder, which, left untreated, may cause an individual to react violently against either the bully or anyone else who happens to be in the vicinity. Physical effects include reduced immunity to infection, stress headaches, high blood pressure, and digestive problems.

—Yamada (2000, p. 483)

[E]motion [is] at the center of the cognitive universe . . . the glue of thought . . . the force that engenders creativity.

— Gelernter (1994, p. 149)

It is clear that working in an abusive environment causes considerable harm to teachers, classrooms, and schools as a whole. For mistreated teachers, as for employees in other fields of work, such environments create "fear and mistrust, resentment, hostility, feelings of humiliation, withdrawal, play-it-safe strategies, and hiding mistakes" (Bassman, 1992, p. 141). The bottom-line consequences of mistreatment of teachers by principals are clear. Like the estimated multimillions of abused American employees in a variety of work settings (e.g., Bassman, 1992; Hornstein, 1996; Keashly, 1998; Pearson, 2000), teachers who fell victim to abusive principals responded with decreased commitment and loyalty to their schools, they did the minimum amount of work to get by, and they feared and avoided all interactions with their principals.

In this chapter, we examine another, even more devastating set of effects of principals' mistreatment of teachers. In addition to feeling shocked and disoriented, humiliated, lonely, trapped, and beset by low self-esteem—and beyond the fact of collateral damage abuse has for teachers' relationships in schools, their classroom work, and their participation in decision making—mistreated teachers also experienced a range of very severe and often chronic effects of mistreatment. Such effects on teachers' personal and professional lives appear to "undo" the teacher altogether. They include chronic fear and anxiety, anger, depression, physical problems, and personal life effects including family problems.

WHAT ARE FEAR AND ANXIETY?

Fear, the emotion most studied by neuroscientists and psychologists (Epstein, 1972), is essentially an awareness of psychological distress; it is also considered the most toxic of all human emotions (Tomkins, 1962). Moreover, fear has "a profoundly noxious quality that compels efforts to change the situation that elicited the emotion. Anxiety, on the other hand, involves a cluster or pattern of emotions that may motivate both approach and avoidance" (Izard & Youngstrom, 1996, p. 35).

In contrast to other primary emotions (e.g., joy, anger, and grief), fear "is the emotion of avoidance of a consciously recognized, usually external, imminent danger" (Bartley, 1994, p. 12). Fear is associated with escape and avoidance; however, when such actions are thwarted or blocked (e.g., as in an uncontrollable situation and when one feels constant uncertainty about a potential danger), fear is transformed into anxiety, a state of arousal following the perception of threat (Epstein, 1972). One might compare fear and anxiety in the following way: You may fear a rat that you see, but the feeling of uncertainty, of knowing it is near and may appear at any time, is anxiety. Similarly, teachers in our study felt fear and chronic anxiety because of repeated and unjustified attacks by an abusive principal and because they believed that such attacks could occur in any place at any time.

A poem by Kipling portrays the feelings associated with fear and anxiety quite accurately; note, in particular, the "forward velocity" of a perceived threat and the "acceleration" that is characteristic of anxiety (Riskind, 1997, p. 688).

Very softly down the glade runs a waiting, watching shade
And the whisper spreads and widens far and near
And the sweat is on thy brow, for he passes even now—
He is Fear, O Little Hunter, he is Fear!

On thy knees and draw the bow; bid the shrilling arrow go;

In the empty, mocking thicket plunge the spear;
But the hands are loosed and weak, and the blood has left thy cheek—
It is Fear, O Little Hunter, it is Fear!

Now the spates are banked and deep; now the footless boulders leap—
Now the lightning shows each littlest leaf-rib clear—
But thy throat is shut and dried, and thy heart against thy side
Hammers: Fear, O Little Hunter—this is Fear!

— Kipling (1895/1983, pp. 176-177)

Charles Darwin, best known for developing the theory of evolution, has described the symptoms of fear:

> The frightened man first stands like a statue motionless and breathless . . . the heart beats quickly and violently . . . the skin instantly becomes pale . . . perspiration immediately exudes from the skin and as the surface is then cold [we have what is termed] a cold sweat . . . the hairs on the skin stand erect and superficial muscles shiver . . . in connection with the disturbed action of the heart, the breathing is hurried . . . the mouth becomes dry . . . one of the best marked symptoms is trembling of all the muscles of the body and this is often first seen on the lips. (Darwin, 1872, quoted in Marks, 1978)

Fear, because of its unavoidable links to the body, has particularly injurious effects on our thinking; it subtly invades and pervades our mental work and profoundly degrades human perception, cognition, and action. Fear "reduces working memory, increases superficial cognitive processing, generates cognitive bias, and tends to put indelible traces in memory" (Izard & Youngstrom, 1996, p. 12). Even more serious—a generalized anxiety or fear disorder can evolve into posttraumatic stress disorder, into phobias, and, finally, at the top of the diagnostic hierarchy, into a panic disorder (American Psychological Association, 1987).

Our study revealed that intense and chronic fear and anxiety were teachers' primary long-term responses to principal mistreatment. There were several reasons for this: First, teachers viewed the various forms and patterns of principal mistreatment as extremely threatening and punishing, and they perceived themselves to be particularly vulnerable. Second, teachers tended to internalize their fears and this provoked a chronic state of anxiety, of apprehension, obsessional thinking, and hypervigilance regarding the possibility of further mistreatment. Third, fear of mistreatment provoked an array of powerful secondary fears, for example, fear of losing one's job, losing one's reputation, being ostracized by colleagues, expressing one's opinion, receiving poor evaluations, lack of support from the central office, and failing one's students, instructionally and socially. Fourth, fear was experienced as pervasive: It permeated all aspects of a victimized teacher's work life; for many, it also profoundly and adversely affected the quality of their personal and family lives. Said differently, fear dominated teachers' entire "sense of being" for long periods of time ranging from several months to many years. Some terms that teachers used to denote chronic fear and anxiety states were "fear," "scared," "afraid," "dread," and "paranoid."

> I take it day by day. It is the only way that I can get through it. I am apprehensive, fearful. He is not on my case every day, but he has set the tone. We did a unit on food and fruits, and at one time I would have taught my students the song about sipping cider, but I wouldn't want him to be walking by and not get the connection. I hated to see this happening, and I dreaded going to work. . . . I was always fearful of repercussions . . . the uncertainty of the day. I was in constant fear and would cry because he would accuse me of things. I was worried, and then the anger set in.

> I felt worthless, intimidated. I said to him, "You make me shake." When I knew that I had to meet with him, I became fearful. I knew what the outcome what be. If he came into my room, I would get edgy. I felt I constantly had to explain, to justify. I felt like I couldn't go to him for help because he [didn't] value my concerns. I felt angry with myself because I took this treatment for years. I ate lunch in my room and went to my mailbox once a day. I would try to get there by a quarter 'til 7 to avoid him. I would stutter and stammer. . . . I knew what was coming and what he was going to do to me when I saw him. I felt defeated. I dreaded going to school on faculty meeting days. I hated it. I would sit in the back of the room at faculty meetings.

> He caused me to question my ability, to question myself. It is very scary. It depletes my confidence. It begins every day just driving to work; I can feel myself tense up. I want to stay in my room and not socialize. Keep quiet. I feel subservient on my way to work. I immediately feel the stress in my neck. I feel myself sitting very straight and holding the steering wheel, concentrating intensely on getting where I am going, even though I have taken the same road for ten years. At work I have a feeling of being watched. The first thing that I do in the morning is close my door; I want to know if he comes in my classroom. I want to hear that door open, I don't want him to sneak in on me. I am guarded. I am careful about what I say. I don't go heavy into an issue and get all fired up about anything. . . . Leaving at the end of the day, I immediately feel myself exhaling, I can feel the stress leaving me like, I am out! I am free until tomorrow!

> Sometimes I think that students look at me like, "Is she ok?" I am afraid of being aggressive about my work and having it come back on me. I have a great deal of doubt about my ability. I am paranoid. I am afraid I am going to lose my job and afraid for the next time I am going to be called into his office. Every day I think, "Is today the day I am going to get called into his office?" I have constant fear. A lot of the teachers say, "I never see you anymore. I didn't know that you were still here. I thought that you were sick." When I am unlocking my office door I think, "I am going into my cave now." I have headaches once or so a week. Last year it was two or three days a

week. It is ongoing tension. . . . I have bad dreams like someone is after me.

She was mean and cruel. Everyone feared her. I always felt unsafe. I was always scared. . . . My whole thing was trying to keep her off me. . . .

I have a feeling of always being watched. . . . I am constantly in fear.

On one of the days he chewed me out, I said, "I live in fear every day of what you might do to me, like you have done to others. I don't like this feeling or the way that you treat me." I lived in fear about my evaluations. He would even tell us how to rate fellow teachers. I refused to do that and that is where my journey downhill started. You really didn't want him to be mad at you. I would tell students, "You can't make noise in the halls or you will get me in trouble." I was very uptight, never relaxed. The students had to walk down the hall like soldiers. I am making them act inhuman. I thought, "Look at those little faces. You just can't help but love them. They are looking for me to show them the way. I am their model, and what am I doing, crying in front of them. I am nervous." I was always afraid that I might get into trouble.

[Victim of sexual harassment] I had constant fear that I would be put into a situation that I didn't want to be put into . . . that he would manipulate a situation where he had me where he wanted me. It is not fair as a female to be put into that situation. I felt angry, betrayed, dirty, disgusted. I was cautious in things that I said, about my clothing and about any type of physical contact. I became much more reserved.

His note would say, "See me," and I would spend the whole day with a lot of anxiety. . . . I was constantly looking over my shoulder, always very on edge. There was not one second of down time.

By the second year, after so many surprise attacks, I would go down the opposite hall if I knew that she was on the other one. There was a 50/50 chance of being attacked if you ran into her. I was paranoid, so I stayed away from her, hoping that she wouldn't come into my classroom with something to bawl me out about. At night when I would go to bed, I would rehash the day's events, over and over and over.

The causes or pathways to fear, according to Rachman (1990), include direct exposure to traumatic stimulation, vicarious acquisition (direct or indirect observation of those experiencing or displaying fear), and transmission of information. Mistreated teachers in our study reported that directly observing or learning of a principal's abuse from other teachers (i.e., other targeted teachers) exacerbated their ongoing fears. Regarding the latter, one teacher made the following comments:

When my teammate was seven minutes late, the principal came in and, with kindergarten students in the room, scolded my teammate, telling her that the next time she was late, for whatever reason, she would write her up and a copy would be placed in her personnel file. Two other adults were in the room at the time. I was fearful of being late. I would dream about oversleeping. I rushed around in the morning like a crazy person afraid I would be late.

I was afraid of anything that might draw attention to me because I knew from others that the next step in his harassing you was to attack your classroom.

Many teachers we interviewed indicated that principal abuse was sufficiently extensive among faculty at their schools to create what one described as a "culture of fear." Fear affected entire schools, fostering a situation in which most teachers were afraid to express their opinions and concerns under any circumstances; silence was the pervasive response. Bertrand Russell (1938) stated, "The impulse of submission . . . has its roots in fear" (p. 19). For example,

We were all scared stiff. I was in constant fear of losing my job. I don't know if I ever got far enough in dealing with it to know exactly what I was afraid of. I was just scared to death. The fear was constantly there.

It was hard to even go near her. We were all on eggshells all the time. If you said the wrong thing, you would get nailed. I was afraid of what action she would take if I didn't please her. My son was in intensive care, very badly injured, and I was under strain, because if I lost my job, I lost my insurance. So it was necessary to please that miserable woman. I hope that her days are numbered. She is still there and that's dreadful. I am sure the number of children who have been injured by her is incredibly high. . . . We didn't gossip about her because you never knew who was listening.

There is a very strong culture of fear and caution. You best keep your head down, say as little as possible, and stay away from the front office. A teacher told me, "If you try to make any changes around here you will be her victim. Every year she has at least one and as many as three or four, maybe five or six people, whom she victimizes in order to demonstrate her power and control." I had bad dreams about it. If I was called to the office my heart would absolutely race. I now feel apprehensive about going into administration given how much pollution goes on there. One fear I have is that she may begin to try to infiltrate or pollute or poison my doctoral program. . . . It takes a lot to stick your neck out. Most teachers simply stop championing new creative ideas because the reward is punishment. It is a pretty deep culture of fear. The self is at risk when you are trying to do your thing.

We were threatened by her that we would be "hunted down," so we dared not say anything. I get really riled up about it. Your life can be ripped away from you for no reason. I have tremendous fear. I am always on guard. If she says, "Jump," I would ask, "How high?" A descriptor that she uses for the school is "the caring place." It is ironic, because we are a lot of islands, people do their own thing to survive. People are afraid. You are guarded, you dare not speak up because it will leak back to the principal. It is constant fear.

It was a very depressing, stifling atmosphere. We were all paranoid, insecure, with low self-esteem. I felt mainly anxiety with occasional panic attacks. Can you imagine all of us eating lunch in silence? It was the same group of people who were laughing their heads off, joking and talking, the year before. My integrity and professionalism were under attack and that threatened me. I always felt I would lose my job. I was always afraid. I always felt a lot of distrust.

The teachers were afraid . . . threatened . . . devastated. Morale was horrible. The school was . . . spic and span, but it was so cold, so cold. After three years we had 45 transfer requests.

[P]arents were just as upset as teachers. They too were afraid . . . reluctant to speak out [unless they did it] anonymously. Her negative approach will affect teachers' teaching style for the rest of their lives.

And, as already mentioned, principal mistreatment and teachers' fear significantly and adversely affected most teachers' personal lives. In fact, most of the teachers we studied were so thoroughly traumatized that they generalized their fear of their abusive principals to all school administrators. Some teachers experienced this fear of administrators, sometimes years later, in different schools and with good principals.

It destroyed my self-confidence. I literally drove away from that school and never went back. Later, I would go around the whole town to not go by this school. . . . My new principal said that I was very tentative and just very cautious. I taught and went home. I ate lunch in my room by myself. I didn't say anything that could come back to haunt me. I will probably never truly trust an administrator again.

At that school, I felt like the warden was walking by, looking in my prison cell. . . . At my new school, I didn't even look at the administrators. The principal would go out of his way to say, "Hello," and I would just kind of go, "Hello," and keep going. I am not used to a person caring.

I had lost my motivation as a teacher. I always felt that she was coming to my room to nitpick. I never trusted her, never. I was truly scared. I didn't get much support from the other people; they were afraid of being seen with someone like me. I vowed that I would never work under another woman and I never have.

Finally, as professionals, teachers naturally prized their good reputations. When teachers were mistreated, they feared that their reputations would be damaged. This concern was reflected in teachers' comments about a wide variety of issues:

I felt my reputation was really hurt. I had applied for several assistant principalships, and I didn't get any interviews.

A central office administrator said to me, "Let me find you another school." I said, "Absolutely not. I am not going to leave." She said, "I don't want you to have to spend another terrible year there." I said, "Let me tell you, it had better not be terrible, because I haven't done anything wrong. I am planning to move up in this county and if I go to another school, I will be remembered as the person who he got rid of. I want to be remembered as the person who chose to leave." This came out of nowhere. I thought that I had a super reputation. I had been asked to consult with other teachers. Then all of a sudden I am incompetent and unprofessional.

Once I traveled to New York with a group of administrators from the district and heard them discussing teachers. I realized maybe other people in the district are listening to my principal, and I was very concerned about my reputation in the county.

ANGER

Also considered a primary human emotion, anger is a more or less primitive response to "being either physically or psychologically restrained from doing what one intensely desires to do" (Izard, 1977, pp. 329-330). Hence, anger motivates us and gives us the means to prepare our bodies for real or imagined battles and to defend ourselves with vigor and strength. Ekman and Friesen (1975) stated that the major provocation to anger is "frustration resulting from interference with [one's] activity or the pursuit of [one's] goals" (p. 78). They noted that "your anger will be more likely and more intense if you believe that the agent of interference acted arbitrarily, unfairly, or spitefully" (p. 78). Indeed, Averill (1982) asserted (as did Aristotle) that anger involves an appraisal that one has been intentionally and unjustifiably wronged by another person. Such were the thoughts and feelings of the teachers in our study, many of whom described intense feelings of anger or outrage and indignation (and sometimes a desire for revenge) toward their abusive principals; in addition, they also felt angry with themselves for their inability to confront or successfully curb their principal's mistreatment. Regarding the latter, Martin (1986a), after an extensive review of the relevant literature, concluded that individuals tend to accept unjust treatment from authority figures without responding.

As a fundamental human emotion with significant survival functions, anger can be seen even in infants; it is characterized by a consistent pattern of bodily changes, such as increases in heart rate, blood pressure, and skin surface temperatures (Levenson, 1992). Thus, insult exists in concert with injury, as mistreated teachers suffer psychological–emotional and eventual physical–physiological harm from long-term feelings of anger.

All the teachers we interviewed expressed strong feelings of anger, both explicitly and implicitly. For most teachers, anger was chronic; it was a dominant emotion throughout their mistreatment experiences and, for many, continued long after mistreatment ended. As mentioned, teachers' anger always included strong feelings of indignation, a form of anger due to the unjust and unfair nature of their victimization by principals. Teachers used many strong words such as "bitter," "hate," "furious," "angry," "enraged," "outraged," "appalled," "disgusted," "despise," "resent," and "hot" to convey the intensity of their anger.

> Principals would call me up and say, "Would you go down and open the school?" or do a tournament or some chaperoning? I built up a great reputation in the district. Who is this guy to come in and treat me like dirt? You give your sweat, blood, and tears, and what you get back is, "Thank you, but get out of our way!" Some administrators just don't appreciate the sacrifices the individual makes for the system. I get incensed about injustice!

> It is awful to say, but I hate this person. I have never felt that way before. It bothers me that I feel such a strong dislike for another human being.

> I couldn't believe it. I said, "This is not professional, this is a confidential document!" I was so mad. His reaction was, "No big deal," [indicating that] I was overreacting. He said, "Are you going to a new church or something?" implying that I was a goody two-shoes.

> It is hard to take punishment when you feel like you are innocent and you don't deserve the reprimands that you are getting.

> The whole experience was painful, devastating. I felt sad, betrayed, angry, indignant, outraged, and very "hard done by."

> I was angry and humiliated. I thought that he was incredibly unprofessional.

> I was outraged. It was so unjust. Every day was awful.

> Anger and distrust were the biggest problems that I had with him.

A handful of teachers also expressed strong feelings of revenge, another form of anger rooted in the emotion of "moral outrage" or a "sense of injustice" (Bies, 1987, p. 293). Bies (1987), after carefully studying the phenomenon of moral outrage in organizational life, wrote, "When people feel harmed wrongfully, or witness others enduring such an injustice, they are likely to become morally outraged" (p. 290) and this often leads to "the sympathetic reaction of outrage, horror, shock, resentment, and anger, those affections of the viscera and abnormal secretions of the adrenals that prepare the human animal to resist attack" (Cahn, 1949, p. 24):

> I would wake up in the night and try to figure out how I was going to get even.

> He could have been on the show, *In the Heat of the Night*. He was a com-

plete redneck idiot. I hated him. I was extremely angry. I was just as hateful toward him as he was toward me. I hated his guts. . . . If they were to do a buyout tomorrow I would take it. I wouldn't teach again. I am disgusted that he thought I would respond positively to sexual harassment. I am angry that he knew he had the power to get away with it. This is a sick puppy. . . . I would have sabotaged him if I could for what he had done. I was extremely furious!

He attacked my students and made them cry. From then on, he and I were at war. I was really mad. I wanted to get back at him. I didn't speak to him for months. I couldn't make eye contact with him.

I felt anger brewing inside. I wanted to get her. But I didn't want to do anything to disrupt the school year, so I just ignored her.

Most of the teachers we interviewed expressed disdain and cynicism toward school district administrators and boards of education for not intervening to protect them and their colleagues from abusive principals.

The parent who spoke out about our principal did it anonymously. But, the board didn't investigate him, and no one from central office ever came to the schools to talk to the teachers about what was going on.

This is the thing that I want to write a book on one day: Nobody ever evaluates a principal. How dare they get in that position and they are never challenged! It bothers me a lot. They [the district] allowed her to terrorize the school for four years.

Our former principal used control, favoritism, betrayal, and other types of abuse. Control remains dominant as a way of proving your stripes as an administrator in this district. You need to be able to kick butt, to be one of the clones. It is pretty dominant. There are lots more women now in administrative positions and they are becoming little male creatures. The inner group seems to be the ones prepared to use whatever control tactics it takes. You know, "In your face," and "Try this and make my day" kind of stuff.

My understanding is that any deficiency in my performance needs to be documented, we need to set up a plan for improvement, and I need to have some resources and due process. He didn't do anything like that! It was unethical. When I found out he had a history of this [abusing others], I was even angrier. Somebody at the county office had to know, but nobody stood up to him.

We always wondered how people up there [district office] let it go on. Surely, they were aware. I was angry and embarrassed.

How can the powers-that-be hire a person like that and let it go on for so long?

The school board applauds what she does as long as they don't hear anything and parents are satisfied. They don't care. She knows how to play the game.

As with fear, many teachers admitted that because of their victimization by principals, they harbored feelings of anger toward school administrators in general.

I just loathe and despise him. I would wake up with terrible nightmares, enraged, unhappy, and exhausted. I thought, "This is not what I came on board for." Literally, I despised every one of them [all administrators]. I was enraged.

I have to honestly say that over the past two years my opinion of the principalship has gone down. I have even questioned if this [teaching] is something that I really what to do. I have become disillusioned.

I lost a great deal of respect for administrators in public schools.

I wonder about people in administration; there is so much pollution that goes on. Kids and teachers suffer tremendously.

Several teachers discussed the anger they directed toward themselves:

My anger came from the fact that I wanted to be an effective teacher in a minority, lower-income school that really needs effective teachers. By the end of three years, I was pretty temperamental in my classroom and it was hard to be positive. That made me angry. I had allowed myself to be changed by a person like him.

I feel angry with myself because I had dealt with this treatment for all these years. I tried to be compassionate, but I just wanted to scream.

There was a child I cared about and I understood. But I had to stand there and watch the principal tear him down and hurt him and demean him. I was standing there not doing anything about it. I felt morally compromised. I still hate that memory. Like a lot of [other] young women, you turn anger into depression and sadness.

Predictably, given the power differences between themselves and principals; the principals' inclination to use power in abusive ways; and the failure of school district offices, boards of education, and unions to provide help, teachers felt compelled to suppress their anger.

She is a conniving, stupid, ill-educated, low-class witch. She took great pleasure in torturing people. I would just try to deal with my own problems at school without showing it. I wasn't going to let her see me crumble.

It was absolutely horrendous having this forced down our throats, but we had to go through the motions. I didn't let any of the anger show.

He was constantly on me, but I just put up with it. The union told me that there was nothing they could do. I dreaded going to work. I hated to walk into the building.

The union representative said that you don't have a legal right not to be harassed, and the courts are very sympathetic to employers: If they are paying you, they can harass you. What could I do?

Our data show that teachers tended to internalize intense feelings of anger and this, in turn, led to depression for many.

DEPRESSION

Depressive states refer to pervasive, absorbing, and chronic feelings of being out of control. As described above, anxiety is a kind of *mobilization* response to a future threat that may be developing and that, one hopes, can be avoided. On the other hand, depression is a *demobilization* response to a loss, a "static or unlikely-to-vary situation that can no longer (with any hope) be avoided because it has already developed or come to pass" (Riskind, 1997, p. 687).

Most of the teachers who participated in our study reported being chronically depressed throughout their mistreatment experience. In describing feelings of depression, teachers used terms such as "depressed," "futile," "helpless," "hope-less," "devastated," "beaten down," "paralyzed," "broken," "worn out," "defeated," "disoriented," "distraught," "trapped," "isolated," "sad," "down," "humiliated," and "despair." Clearly, for most victimized teachers, going to work as well as being at work was a "constant struggle to survive each day."

I would go home every day and soak in the tub. I probably soaked my skin off those last four years. At home, I would lose my temper over nothing. I lost the joy of teaching and I wasn't enjoying the journey. I didn't sleep. I tossed and turned in bed. I didn't eat. I was depressed and tried not to show it at school. That is probably what affected my marriage. I have been married for 23 years, but for four years things were very rocky. I don't know if we would have stayed together if we didn't have a son. I was totally wiped out every day. My sex life was nil. Other teachers were depressed too. If it had not been for having a child and loving my husband to death, I would have split; I was at that point. To tell you the honest truth, there was a time I would go to the grocery store at night and sit in the parking lot. I remember sitting one time in the parking lot wondering if I had enough money and could leave and not come back. It took me a year to recover from the nervousness after I left that school.

I felt worse than helpless, like I was a crummy teacher. I was depressed. I had no time for myself or to work out. I wasn't doing anything in my home. I was living in a pigpen.

I felt hopeless. I almost wanted to stop trying. I felt powerless, my moti-vation was gone. It is very depressing to realize that you are not accomplishing anything. It is defeating. I developed a pretty cynical attitude.

I felt like dirt everyday, like I was going to spontaneously combust, explode. I was an emotional wreck.

That year I was feeling so upset, depressed, and anxious all the time that I started to use my sick days. I felt nobody really understood what was happening and that even if I told them they wouldn't believe it. I had a feeling of, "What am I going to do?" I would wake up at night with my stomach turning and my head hurting. I felt very cold.

I feel continued sadness over a long period of time.

I can't stand the guy. The feelings dogged me every time I thought about it. It made me half sick. I turned it into depression. You turn it against yourself and you start asking yourself, "What is wrong with me?" I didn't trust my own judgment. I felt beaten down. I don't like conflict. I don't like verbal abuse. I just felt really tired all the time. I really did look ten years older. I was so tired that I couldn't sleep. I would go in tired in the morning and come home tired at night. I dragged around a lot. My energy level became very low.

I was really hurt. I went through six months of pretty heavy depression. I started to resign, but I needed the income. For the rest of the year I had very little emotional ties to my job; I would simply go there and do what I had to do and get out. I would have left if I could, I felt so depressed.

I was tense . . . looked icky . . . felt crappy all the time . . . didn't realize how bad I looked until I saw some photos. [I looked] awful, very lined and drawn in my face and very pale.

Many teachers' depression was so severe that they sought counseling or psychiatric care for therapy and medication.

I would wake up in the middle of the night thinking, going over the same thoughts, over and over again. I went to the doctor and I had blood work-ups. I ended up seeing a psychiatrist and being diagnosed as having clinical depression. I couldn't see the good side of anything anymore. I had diarrhea and I couldn't eat. I haven't had diarrhea now since school got out for the summer.

I would come home just deflated, wiped out. I felt like I could no longer handle my own life. I had to go to someone else [a psychologist] and have them tell me what I needed to do. I couldn't help myself. I became a weak, unorganized, and uncontrolled person. I was depressed.

I was clinically depressed. I ended up taking Prozac and getting professional help. I took the last two weeks of school off. I couldn't function.

I felt emotionally exploited, abused. I would wake up at three in the morning and be nervous and on edge, couldn't sleep. I lost weight. This happened every day. I turned all the anger inward. I was on antidepressants, on Xanax for four years.

One teacher reported that eight teachers at her school were in therapy because of her principal's mistreatment.

For most teachers, depressive symptoms dissipated or disappeared when mistreatment ended or shortly thereafter. However, in a few cases, depression persisted; teachers failed to fully recover until years later. This was true only for teachers who could not obtain new teaching positions because principals had blackballed them.

> I applied to many systems for the next two years, but I wasn't able to get a teaching job. I had to take jobs that were demeaning, jobs far below my skills. It was very, very, very hurtful for me to have to ask my brother and his wife to let me live with them.

> I resigned and went into sales and retail. I retreated, I felt utter despair. Why get up in the morning? I couldn't even lose myself in a book, I was so depressed. That has always been my escape. TV shows that I had watched for years, basically I didn't care to watch. I never felt that I had enough rest, but when you are sleeping a minimum of 12 hours a night you are obviously getting enough rest. Later I went back into teaching, but it took several years for me to be able to stand up for myself and say, "Excuse me, that is wrong."

In addition, feeling isolated, trapped, and unmotivated were strongly associated with feelings of depression.

Feeling Isolated

To avoid further mistreatment, teachers usually withdrew both emotionally and physically (when possible) from social and professional activities (e.g., faculty meetings, committee work, sponsorship of student activities, professional associations). They refused, for example, to volunteer for committee work and sponsorships; when required to attend certain events they did not participate. According to our findings, teachers' protective actions may have inadvertently exacerbated their feelings of isolation and depression. Other factors typically associated with principal mistreatment—showing favoritism, ostracism by other teachers, and lack of viable opportunities for recourse (e.g., from central office, unions)—also contributed to a targeted teacher's sense of isolation.

> I never had lunch with the teachers. I stayed in my room. The only time that I was out of that room was to go to the bathroom. I am pretty sociable and pretty funny, but I just completely withdrew. I felt alone. I was very alone but I had to protect myself. I had to get through the day. I think if I talked about it [the mistreatment] at school, it might have made it

worse.

I dropped every professional organization except two that I had been very active in. These were organizations that helped me to be productive in the classroom, but I didn't feel motivated anymore, so I closed myself down. Then he began to freeze me out. I felt very isolated. I went to as few faculty meetings as I could and I was never chastised, which indicated to me that he didn't mind. I cut my connection to the building.

I felt like an island. We were pretty much left alone to sink or swim, and I couldn't sink. I was withdrawn from everything. I felt powerless and alienated. I just didn't make waves. I have three kids. I would just collect a paycheck.

I kept to myself, I withheld, I didn't say much.

I was defensive, and cold, and hardened by the experience. I resented feeling alone and feeling invisible. I felt like I was doing a great job, but nobody knew it.

An unwed pregnant teacher's mistreatment and resulting feelings of isolation were exacerbated by the treatment she received from the people of a small town.

I felt like I was branded. I was even told by two teachers that it would be best if I had my lunch in my classroom. None of the other teachers who were once friendly to me would even turn and look my way or give me a gracious smile or say, "Have a good day," even though I would wave and smile at them in greeting. . . . They had a baby shower at the school [for another teacher] and everyone got an invitation to the shower except me. . . . When I would go grocery shopping, people would point me out and ask, "Are you that pregnant unwed teacher?" They would pull their children close to them, like I had some kind of plague. It was so extremely humiliating.

Feeling Trapped

Feeling trapped in a classroom or a school, with few or no avenues for escape, according to our data, was associated with teachers' feelings of depression; such feelings were characterized by a lack of control and not knowing where to turn or what to do to resolve a situation. Feelings of being trapped were, as one teacher stated, "like being in prison." These feelings were a direct result of principals' threats of reprisals for requesting transfers, for unsuccessful attempts to transfer, the prospect of negative letters of reference, and lack of support from central offices and unions, among others. It was clear that chronic fear and depression and related responses (e.g., fatigue, self-doubt, and lowered self-esteem) reinforced teachers' feelings of being trapped as did personal life factors (e.g., being a major or the sole breadwinner in the family, having children in the school district).

She said, "Maybe you shouldn't be in this business." That was a direct quote. I had been afraid to ask for a transfer because she tends to blackball people who ask for transfers. She made us turn in transfer requests to her first, before they went to the county office. She belittled one teacher who asked for a transfer and had another teacher's transfer interview canceled.

I didn't think that I was ever going to get out of there. I thought many times about just quitting, but I knew that if I went out in a bad way, I would never get back on full time. I have a house to pay for, so it wasn't possible.

He did everything he could to block my transfer. Then one day he came by and said that I did not get the transfer. I knew that he would make life hell for me if I complained. . . . He also said he didn't want to work with me anymore; now he wanted me to leave his school. . . . He didn't want me to go to the school of my choice. I called the union and they said that teachers have no power [in this matter] whatsoever.

None of the teachers wanted to be there. They tried to get out every year. At least they had the guts to try, but that put them in a worse position with the principal. If I had been forced to stay another year or two, I would have quit, I would have gotten out of education.

My principal had been badmouthing me to other principals. That is why I couldn't get transferred for six years in a row. I tried to transfer out of the building, but I was a prisoner.

I was warned early on that you don't try to transfer out of her school, because then you are on her bad list.

I was constantly trying to think of what I could do to get out of that building. I didn't want her to know that I wanted a transfer, so I mailed my application from my home. Fortunately, I ended up getting a move up, a promotion.

After I told him I wanted to transfer, he said that he had ways to make people regret the choices they made.

Feeling Unmotivated

Low teacher motivation, as it relates to principals' abuse, is discussed thoroughly in Chapter 5. Here we point out that a principal's long-term mistreatment and chronic feelings of depression and fear and anxiety were strongly interrelated with teachers' motivation to teach.

It took the spunk out of me. It was a drain on my attitude and energy. I would rather be at home sleeping or nursing my wounds.

Now, my teaching is lacking the zest and excitement that it used to have with my kids. I used to look forward to making it exciting and wonderful for the kids year after year.

I used to set fairly high standards for myself, but during this ordeal I wouldn't put as much into teaching as I should have. I would pull things out of the files or just do something out of the textbook or show a movie. I considered it slacking off.

My first eight years of teaching, I thrived on the challenge. . . . But I gave up my special vision. By the end of those years with her, I had lost a lot of my motivation. I was going through the motions. It had taken the heart out of me.

Some days were much worse than others but in general I was just down about going to school. I was just not excited about it.

OCEANS OF TEARS

Most female teachers reported that they cried a great deal during their mistreatment experiences. Crying was associated with states of fear, anger, and depression. Occasionally, teachers cried during an episode of mistreatment; more frequently they cried immediately after an episode of mistreatment in their classrooms or in their homes. It was not uncommon for a teacher to cry for hours several evenings a week at home.

She said, "You can always change your school." I was so upset, I got off the phone and started crying. I couldn't stop crying. I cried from the moment that I got to school to the moment I left, for several weeks.

That day I called my husband and told him that I was being transferred. I was crying and I couldn't stop. I felt homeless.

Most female teachers cried throughout their mistreatment experiences whether or not they had been abused recently by their principals:

By the end of the three years, I would sit on the edge of the bed in the mornings and just cry. One morning my husband was rubbing my back and said, "You know what, darling? I don't care if you have to work at Burger King. You don't have to go back there next year, no matter what." Twenty-two people left the school that year. All the stress had accumulated; I almost had a breakdown. I broke down at least once a week the third year.

I cried probably once a week, if not twice a week, for four years.

I went through a period of several months when I cried almost daily. . . . Sometimes it was even at school, sometimes at home.

By the time I left the school, I was usually in tears. One time I cried for four hours, an hour before my husband came home and then when he got home I cried for a couple hours more. I always cried after I would come out of a meeting with the principal.

All three years I cried. I cried a lot, all three years that I worked for her.

I lost weight and I cried a lot.

REVIVIFICATION: EXPERIENCING IT ALL OVER AGAIN

About one-fourth of the teachers in our study had revivification experiences; in describing their mistreatment during the interviews we conducted, they became upset and many cried, even though, for some, mistreatment had terminated as much as several years earlier.

I left that first meeting very shaken. I broke down in the car. [crying] I am so sorry, this is so hard to talk about.

I was teaching and I couldn't keep my composure. Tears just started coming down my face. I said to the students, "I have just had a rough morning." Every night I lay in bed and cried. I get tears in my eyes thinking about it now.

It just brings me to tears, what she did that affects others' lives, not only the children in our classes but also our own families. I'm sorry . . . [teacher apologizes for crying during the interview].

[Crying] Every time I think about this I get upset. It just comes right back.

I am enraged by his treatment. My bristles are up whenever I come close to this person. I can feel myself getting angrier as I describe what happened.

I saved my anger for when I was safely away from school. I get angry now and I still get upset. Just talking to you, I get nervous again.

PHYSICAL AND PHYSIOLOGICAL PROBLEMS

Drs. Gary and Ruth Namie, psychologists who have extensively studied workplace bullying, have reported that the physical and physiological effects of mistreatment include reduced immunity to infection, stress headaches, high blood pressure, and digestive problems (Namie & Namie, 2000a). We found that teachers, suffering at the hands of abusive principals, experienced these and a number of other physical and psychological problems discussed by Namie and Namie. Like psychological and emotional problems, such problems were typically chronic; they began with the onset of mistreatment and usually ended when mistreatment terminated. In a few cases, problems persisted for several months and even several years later. The seriousness of these problems appears to be related to the longevity of teachers' mistreatment, at least in part. Roughly two-thirds of the teachers we studied sought medical treatment for their problems. The most frequently identified physical and physiological problems were chronic sleep disorders (e.g., insomnia, nightmares, obsessive thinking), chronic fatigue, stomachaches, nausea, weight gain or loss, neck and back pain, and headaches or migraines.

> I gained 50 pounds. The final year was the worst year. I would come home with my neck and back in knots. It would lead to a headache. I had headaches all the time. It affected my sleep. I would toss and turn, and I would scream in the middle of the night. I had bad dreams about fear, like someone was after me. I was always exhausted. Now I have a new life and my health is great. . . .

> I didn't sleep. I felt exhausted. I couldn't sleep. I had terrible nightmares. I was in a rage and I was unhappy. I was exhausted every day. I was tense. I looked yucky. I was really tired, so tired that I couldn't sleep. I dragged around. My energy level became very low. I lost weight; I didn't feel like eating.

> Many nights I would play through my head what had happened that day. If my brain were a tape recorder it would have been worn out.

> I was in a constant state of exhaustion. I would just lay awake at night and not be able to get to sleep for hours. This went on for five years. I never had any trouble sleeping before. I always had knots in my stomach.

> When I would go to bed, I would rehash the day's events. I often only got about four hours of sleep. It would start to show on my complexion and in my eyes. I would wake up with my stomach churning and my head hurting. I had the physical symptoms of being sick. But I knew that I wasn't sick, so I would go to work. I thought if I could just get to the room without breaking down, I knew that I could make it through half the day. At night, I would think about what I could do tomorrow so as to not incur her wrath and be jumped on.

> These are not the kinds of headaches that you take a couple Tylenol for. It is stress, pressure, anxiety from the principal. I have neck pain almost every morning, four out of five days. I am thinking, "What am I going to do today that is going to cause him to erupt?"

> I lost 50% of my sleep and my stomach hurt. I always had diarrhea. I was eating too much of course. When I get upset, I overeat. I constantly over-ate. If something happened, I would go get some M&M's. I would wake up in the middle of the night thinking, going over the same thoughts, over and over again. I was nauseous. My body just shut down and everything I ate just came up. My sleep was really disturbed. I would wake up in a panic. The last time that I ever experienced anything that was close to this

emotion was when I was going through a divorce. That was how intense it was for me. I was beyond tired.

I would go home with headaches and tense upper back muscles. I would get colds, headaches, stomachaches, and anxiety. I had headaches to the point that I went to my gynecologist, who put me on medication, saying that it was stress. I would take medication quite often. The headaches would last for days. I would come home and turn off the lights and stick my head underneath a pillow just to get still.

I started getting migraines; they were documented by my neurologist. I was working with a therapist closely about my migraines and the constant harassment from this man [the principal]. My usual symptoms were fatigue, sleeplessness, depression. I dreaded going to that little hellhole. I was waking up every hour or two hours. I had constant fatigue.

Examples of other severe physical and physiological problems teachers experienced included diarrhea, high blood pressure, blurred vision, nausea or vomiting, respiratory infections, hives, vertigo, heart palpitations, gum disease, auditory impairment, panic attacks, chest pains, and frequent colds and allergies.

My doctor put me on a combination of a beta-blocker to correct my heartbeat and Valium. I went in once a week so that he could help me with the stress. He was my counselor, too. Every evening I had an upset stomach, every single night. I had lost a bunch of weight. I was down to 91 pounds, which for me is pretty skinny. I still have the erratic heartbeat. Every time I get upset now it comes right back, I have had it while we have been talking. As soon as the principal left, my heart problems stopped.

My physical reaction included blurred vision. The nurse said get to the emergency room immediately. My blood pressure was 180 over 120, which is stroke level. My body was suffering tremendously because of the stress. I am now on blood pressure medicine and I can't sleep well. I don't sleep more than two or three hours. I gained probably 25 pounds; I am much bigger than I was before. I have many more headaches than I used to.

The maintenance man told me that the trailer floor was rotted through and [the carpet] harbored fungal mold . . . [but] the principal refused to remove [it]. My doctor said my respiratory problems were a direct result of [that] 20-year-old carpet.

I had heart racing, dizzy spells, my auditory processing was reduced. I had a hard time processing what people were saying. It was all diagnosed and documented. It was pretty debilitating. I also had sleep disruption, bad dreams, and panic attacks.

I would wake up at night thinking, "Man, what am I going to do?" I had chest pains. It was a constant ache. Doctors said that it was a hiatal hernia, but it continued. During the summer it would go away, and then when I got back to school, it would start all over again. I also overate. This sounds crazy, but since I resigned, knowing that I am not going to have to face her, I have slept like a baby. . . . The chest pains stopped.

Only three teachers indicated that they started smoking or drank excessively in response to principal mistreatment.

I started smoking during that time period. Maybe a half pack a day. I also had awful backaches. My shoulders were tensed and stressed. I remember days when I would be in pain all day. I also had insomnia. I would worry all night, "What will go wrong tomorrow?" I would get up during the middle of the night and write down a list of things and put it by my bed.

I hardly drink at all now, but I drank a lot then. I knew that didn't solve anything. I can also eat a lot under stress. I gained a lot of weight that year.

I had hives almost every day. Every time I would get a little cold it just wouldn't go away because I felt stressed all the time. I had migraine headaches. One that lasted for 15 days. I was taking so much medicine. I was given shots. I overate and I probably drank more that year.

According to teachers' reports, principal mistreatment also exacerbated pre-existing medical conditions.

It got to the point where it was physical. It was tearing me apart. I lost weight and I got sick. I spent my days and nights crying and feeling nauseated. I got bronchitis and laryngitis. I was getting really run down. I had back surgery 10 years ago and I had to begin wearing my back brace again.

Nothing, not anything, was wrong with me, but I would come home and drop. I went to bed early that year, often at 8:00 p.m. I was really wiped out—totally drained and exhausted. I ended up with a lot of medical problems . . . and surgery. I went to a lot of specialists that year. I had never been sick before. I thought that something big was wrong. I had chronic pain in my abdomen. I ended up with a hysterectomy. I had a breast tumor. My doctor would tell me, "You know, all this stress affects your health. The headaches and nervousness are a result of the job stress."

I have never had problems with my blood sugar dropping. Suddenly I am losing control. I am in a situation where my nutritional habits, which truly went downhill, could have a severe effect. I am diabetic.

My parents were real concerned about my health. I had asthma and I didn't sleep or eat the first year that I was there. I was so stressed that I dropped two sizes in clothes, from size eight to a four. I had a knot in my stomach all the time and a feeling that I can't describe. At night I lay in bed and cried.

Our data indicate that in addition to the psychological and emotional problems discussed earlier, individual teachers simultaneously experienced, on average, at least four of the physical and physiological problems previously described throughout their mistreatment experience.

INTENTION TO LEAVE ONE'S JOB

Many of the teachers we studied had been recognized as exemplary educators throughout their careers, and it was apparent that they loved children. For them, teaching remained a deep and enduring commitment, notwithstanding the chronic feelings of fear, anger, and depression that dominated their lives. Their decisions to leave the children they loved and the schools in which their mistreatment occurred can be viewed as a form of final withdrawal from the profound pain and suffering that permeated their personal and professional lives.

> Every minute of every day I thought, "Please get me out of here."

> If I hadn't gotten out of there, I am not sure I would still be in teaching.

> I had no intention of leaving, but now I am not happy at all. I will leave at the first chance.

> I didn't know what I was going to be doing, but I was sure that I couldn't come back to that building. I packed my belongings.

> I thought of quitting all the time—at least 15 teachers quit that year.

> I struggled with the idea of quitting. A lot of teachers just walked out and didn't return.

Some teachers were prepared to leave teaching altogether if they could not find employment in another school.

> I struggled. If I hadn't loved my classroom so much, I probably would have been out of there and probably out of teaching.

> At one point, I told my husband, "I will never teach again."

> Before the end of the first year there, I thought that I made a horrible mistake. I knew that I couldn't stay in that county. If I hadn't been forced to stay, I would have quit—I would have gotten out of education. I just couldn't do it another year.

> I really began to doubt that I could teach anymore, but I needed the income and I wasn't going to do anything rash. I thought about leaving the profession altogether.

EFFECTS ON A TEACHER'S PERSONAL AND FAMILY LIFE

Some teachers' most poignant stories related to their personal and family lives. With few exceptions, principals' mistreatment of teachers seriously depreciated the quality of their family life. Teachers reported that they could not compartmentalize their experiences of mistreatment. Feelings of fear, frustration, anger, depression, and fatigue, as well as obsessive thinking about their ordeals, created more conflict and greater social distance between themselves and family members.

> Before, I would come home, go out, and throw the ball with my son; my home was a much more relaxed place. After this started, I would come home defeated, wiped out, tired. My kids would come in, and if they were fussing, I just didn't have the strength or patience to handle it. Rather than say, "OK, come and talk about it," I would say, "Go to your room!" I was short-tempered.

> His abuse made me physically sick. It made me emotionally unable to handle my daughter and my husband in a sane and stable way. I couldn't leave it at school. It affected my self-concept, because, after 28 years of teaching, somebody was discrediting me. Physically, it tore me apart. I lost weight, got sick, spent my days and nights crying. I didn't have time for my family. When I was home with my daughter I kept thinking, "I have got to get you in bed, get your bath done, because I have 60 million other things to do," [such as] cleaning my house, or putting away stuff, or doing laundry. Instead, I would read school things or go through the rest of the stuff that the principal put in my mailbox. . . . Every time I am with my husband, I am complaining about school. My husband is to the point where he really wants to slug the guy. He is really upset. He doesn't even like to come in the building. The abuse has affected every aspect of my life.

> I was obsessive. My wife and I would go out to dinner and to do things, and a lot of times she would tell me, "Hey, that is enough." It was all I could think about. Talking was really the only outlet I had.

> I couldn't enjoy doing things with my son because I wanted my lesson plans to be right . . . perfect. It would take away from my family and I would redouble my efforts at work. I guess when you are anxious you are not pleasant to be around. My husband said, "If you are going to be this miserable, just quit." I think he was trying to be supportive. He said that the money is not worth it. But we needed my income. He was able to work only part time because he is a diabetic and has had five heart bypasses.

> It really affected my family. I was just down. I would cry and cry. It upset my husband. We haven't ever fought about it, but it definitely wears on the relationship. My husband is always trying to encourage me, trying to say positive things. He says, "Let's get through this year and look for another

job." That is partly what a husband does, but now he has to do a lot of that.

After talking with other teachers about the abuse, I found how they were also having problems at home, the same kinds of things. They were very depressed, too. I was always exhausted. I was short-tempered, that was the worst part. I could be just fine cooking supper, and the least little thing . . . I might throw the pan in the sink, or push the chair up against the table hard and say something. It was just not like me. I didn't want to be like that. I couldn't believe what was happening to me and my family. . . . It was so much stress on my marriage.

I was sick. I would go home with headaches, a tense back. My husband said, "I wish we had a cat so that you could kick the cat instead of me." I would come home drained and just cry. I became short-tempered and stressed. It got to the point where my family didn't want to hear it anymore. They would say, "We are tired of this, we don't want to hear it, do something about it." I didn't know what to do. The kids were sympathetic; it hurt them to see me hurting, but they wanted their mom back. They would say, "You are ill all the time, and you are snapping at us, and you are short-tempered."

I would think about the principal all the time, even when with my significant other, to the point where I was becoming dysfunctional in my personal life. I have had bad dreams. A call from the office would make my heart absolutely race.

In several cases, a spouse's inability to provide the kind of support needed by a targeted teacher increased the frustration and depression that resulted directly from their mistreatment at work.

My wife would suggest things for me to try; she would say, "Just march into his office and tell him," or "Call this person and tell them, and that will get the ball rolling." I would ask people to meet with me but they wouldn't. I felt very frustrated, but my wife said, "Just go. Just show up. They will have to talk to you." I felt like there were times when I was very angry and I needed support from my wife and I got challenged by her instead. Instead of saying, "I am sorry, and I understand," she said, "You need to go do this or that." . . . My daughter used to tell me that she wanted to be a teacher. She said that on a camping trip. But then she said, "I am not sure I want to be a teacher anymore, if this is the way that they treat people." It made me realize that I had done a lot to undercut what I had spent a lot of time building up.

My husband couldn't understand why I wasn't more aggressive. He is a lawyer. It wasn't my nature, though. It was hard to come home and explain all this to him. He would get tired of hearing it, and tired of me being sick every night. He just wanted me to handle it the way he would handle it, which probably would have been a lot better for me. The strain was serious enough that we went through a period where we weren't happy, but not serious enough to cause any long-term effects. There was very little communication. He would just do his thing, and I would do mine. When I was sick at night because of this abuse, I would not tell him because if I did, he would get angry. The problem would be there when we would go out, so I didn't want to go anywhere or I would want to come home early.

Clearly, for a number of reasons, family members were frequently unable to provide an abused teacher with adequate social support. This, of course, played right into the principals' hands, often causing the abused teacher to be isolated both at school and at home. Many abused teachers received social support from their colleagues, but it was usually offset by other teachers' fear of associating with a mistreated teacher. Indeed, although colleagues almost always disagreed with the injustice meted out by a principal, they were simultaneously intimidated. Meanwhile, family members frequently justified their lack of support by pointing to the abused teacher's persistent crying and negative behaviors toward them. Conflictive interactions with family members created guilt and additional stress for many teachers, and this further reduced the possibility of relief at home from their ongoing ordeals. In many cases, such factors pushed many mistreated teachers into deeper isolation. Terms such as feeling "caged" or "in a box" and having "nowhere to turn" revealed the despair many teachers experienced because of conflict at home derived from principals' mistreatment at school.

7 Overcoming The Problem of Principal Mistreatment of Teachers

What Can We Do?

We now have an already ample and still growing body of research demonstrating the very harmful effects of workplace bullying on targets and employers alike. They sometimes are called "bullies," "tyrants," or "jerks." However, regardless of how they are described (usually out of earshot), bosses and others who inflict psychological abuse on their coworkers constitute one of the most common and serious problems facing employees in today's workplace.

— Yamada (2000, pp. 477, 536)

[Bullying is] offensive behavior through vindictive, cruel, malicious, or humiliating attempts to undermine an individual or groups of employees. These persistently negative attacks on their personal and professional performance are typically unpredictable, irrational, and unfair.

—Chappell and DiMartino (1998, p. 11)

The toxin of bosses' cruel disrespect is causing harm to employees just as other toxic products cause harm. The fact that this particular toxin is human rather than chemical is of little consequence to those who suffer its effects and should not absolve organizations of their responsibility to eliminate it from workplaces.

— Hornstein (1996, p. 7)

LOOKING BACK ON OUR STUDY

Throughout this book we have referred to the principals' destructive behaviors described by teachers as workplace *mistreatment*; in other instances, we have used the term workplace *abuse* to be consistent with the terms used by other scholars. Likewise, the terms workplace *mistreatment*, workplace *abuse*, workplace *bullying*, workplace *mobbing*, and workplace *harassment*, among others, are essentially defined synonymously in all the related research and theoretical literature. In this instance, the answer to the question "What's in a name?" is simply "It's all the same." The reader may refer to Boxes 7.1 and 7.2 for a summary of some definitions and descriptions as found in the primary literature.

A review of our findings points out that abusive principals, like abusive bosses in general, engage in similar behaviors, and like many thousands of workers represented in the extant literature—a number that has been extrapolated to be multimillions of workers—abused teachers experienced the same devastating effects. Level 1 principal mistreatment behaviors (indirect and moderate aggression) include discounting teachers' thoughts, needs, and feelings and isolating and abandoning them; withholding or denying opportunities, resources, or credit; showing favoritism toward other teachers; and offensive personal conduct. Level 2 principal mistreatment behaviors (direct and escalating aggression) include spying, sabotaging, stealing, destroying teacher instructional aids, making unreasonable work demands, and both public and private criticism of teachers. Level 3 principal mistreatment behaviors (direct and severe aggression) include lying, being explosive and nasty, threats, unwarranted reprimands, unfair evaluations, mistreating students, forcing teachers out of their jobs, preventing teachers from leaving or advancing, sexual harassment, and racism. Generally speaking, these types and related patterns of conduct reveal an "I am the boss" attitude, that is, an authoritarian, coercive, and mean-spirited principal who uses his or her formal and informal power against teachers.

The effects of such mistreatment are extremely harmful to teachers' professional and personal lives. Beyond the initial wounds of shock and disorientation, humiliation, loneliness, and injured self-esteem, principal mistreatment seriously damaged in-school relationships, damaged classrooms, and frequently impaired all school decision making. Even more appalling, principals' abuse of teachers resulted in severe, chronic fear and anxiety, anger, depression, a range of physical and psychological problems, and adverse personal and family outcomes. In some cases, the injury caused by principals led to the virtual undoing of dedicated and caring professional educators, all of whom viewed teaching as a special calling.

Box 7.1 Definitions and Descriptions of Mistreatment, Abuse, Bullying, Mobbing, and Victimization

Workplace bullying . . . includes all types of mistreatment at work.

(Namie & Namie, 1999, p. 17)

Workplace bullying can be described as the intentional infliction of a hostile work environment upon an employee by a coworker or coworkers, typically through a combination of verbal and nonverbal behaviors.

(Yamada, 2000, p. 481)

Emotional abuse is . . . hostile verbal and nonverbal, nonphysical behaviors directed at a person(s) such that the target's sense of him/herself as a competent person and worker is negatively affected.

(Keashly, 1998, p. 87)

Abusive behaviors include aggressive eye contact, either by glaring or meaningful glances; giving the silent treatment; intimidating physical gestures, including finger pointing and slamming or throwing objects; yelling, screaming, and/or cursing at the target; angry outbursts or temper tantrums; nasty, rude, and hostile behavior toward the target; accusations of wrongdoing; insulting or belittling the target, often in front of other workers; excessive or harsh criticism of the target's work performance; spreading false rumors about the target; breaching the target's confidentiality; making unreasonable work demands of the target; withholding needed information; and taking credit for the target's work.

(Keashly, 1998, pp. 97-98)

Aggressive or abusive behavior includes expressions of hostility (e.g., interrupting, being condescending, leaving the area), obstructionism (e.g., failure to return calls or respond, arriving late for target's meetings), and overt aggression (e.g., physical violence, destruction, theft, or sabotage of work materials).

(Baron & Neumann, 1998, paraphrased)

Psychical terror or mobbing in working life means hostile and unethical communication that is directed in a systematic way by one or a number of persons mainly toward one individual. [Its] frequency and duration result in considerable psychic, psychosomatic and social misery.

(Leymann, 1990, p. 120)

Mobbing is an emotional assault. It begins when an individual becomes the target of disrespectful and harmful behavior. Through innuendo, rumors, and public discrediting, a hostile environment is created in which one individual gathers others to willingly, or unwillingly, participate in continuous malevolent actions to force a person out of the workplace.

(Davenport, Distler-Schwartz, & Pursell-Elliott, 1999, p. 10)

(Continued)

Box 7.1 (Continued)

Victimization is recurrent and reprehensible and includes distinctly negative actions that are directed against employees in an offensive manner and can result in those employees being placed outside the workplace community. [It includes] abusive power or any other unacceptable behavior or response, such as deliberate insults, hypercritical attitudes, ridicule, unfriendliness, or supervision of the employee without his/her knowledge and with harmful intent.

(Swedish National Board of Occupational Safety and Health, 1993)

Box 7.2   The Mobbing Syndrome

1. The mobbing syndrome is a malicious attempt to force a person out of the workplace through unjustified accusations, humiliation, general harassment, emotional abuse, and/or terror.

2. It is a "ganging up" by the leader(s)—organization, superior, co-worker, or subordinate—who rallies others into systematic and frequent "mob-like" behavior.

3. Because the organization ignores, condones or even instigates the behavior, it can be said that the victim, seemingly helpless against the powerful and many, is indeed "mobbed." The result is always injury—physical or mental distress or illness and social misery and, most often, expulsion from the workplace.

4. Perpetrated by one or more staff members—"vulturing."

5. Occurring in a continual, multiple, and systematic fashion, over some time.

6. Portraying the victimized person as being at fault.

7. Engineered to discredit, confuse, intimidate, isolate, and force the person into submission.

8. Committed with the intent to force the person out.

9. Representing the removal from the workplace as the victim's choice.

10. Not recognized, misinterpreted, ignored, tolerated, encouraged, or even instigated by the management of the organization.

SOURCE: Davenport, N., Distler-Schwartz, R., & Pursell-Elliott, G. (1999). *Mobbing: Emotional abuse in the American workplace* (pp. 40-41). Ames, IA: Civil Society. Reprinted by permission.

In addition, further analysis of our data suggests that most of the teachers in our study fit all three of Namie and Namie's (1999) profiles of bullies' targets: "nice people," targeted because bullies consider them unlikely to confront the matter; "vulnerable people," targeted because they are nonthreatening; and the "bold, best, and brightest," targeted because bullies, perhaps haunted by feelings of inferiority, strike at and try to undermine those whom they perceive to threaten their presumed authority. *Stated differently, abusive principals may destroy many of our very best veteran and beginning teachers; teachers who are not only highly respected, skilled professionals, but teachers who have also dedicated themselves to providing the compassion and caring frequently needed by America's schoolchildren.*

WHAT CAN WE DO?

The only thing necessary for the triumph of evil is for good men to do nothing. (Edmund Burke, *Webster's Book of Quotations*, 1992, p. 89)

It is not our part to master all the tides of the world, but to do what is in us for the succour of those years wherein we are set, uprooting the evil in the fields that we know, so that those who live after may have clean earth to till. What weather they may have is not ours to rule. (J. R. R. Tolkien, 2001, p. 861)

We are not the first to face moral problems such as those of deception . . . lies. . . . The justifications they invoke are unsubstantial, and . . . they can disguise and fuel all other wrongs. Trust and integrity are precious resources, easily squandered, hard to regain. They can thrive only on a foundation of respect for veracity. (Bok, 1978, pp. 248-249)

Fortunately, there are numerous ways that individuals, school districts, university preparation programs, principals, and researchers can overcome the problem of principal abuse of teachers and prevent the devastating effects it has on teachers, teaching, and schools. Here, we discuss the importance of becoming familiar with the legal and reasonable standards associated with workplace mistreatment, ways to become informed, and how to take individual action in cases of mistreatment.

What Can We Do?

- Become familiar with legal precedents and reasonable standards about workplace mistreatment; lobby for legal recourse
- Become informed about workplace mistreatment
- Take action
- If you witness mistreatment, be a responsible colleague
- Discover what school district offices can do
- Discover what professors in programs of educational leadership and teacher preparation programs can do
- Ascertain what principals can do
- Ascertain what researchers can do

Become Familiar With Legal Precedents and Reasonable Standards About Workplace Mistreatment

In the United States, workplace abuse is not explicitly defined as discrimination; although it has identical consequences, it is not considered illegal. Hornstein (1996) writes,

> Proscribing abusive behavior in workplaces and holding organizations accountable for its occurrence is hardly without precedent. Title VII of the Civil Rights Act signed into law in 1964 bans all discrimination based on race, religion, or national origin in workplaces. That rule was extended to discrimination based on age in 1967, gender in 1972, and pregnancy in 1978. In 1986 the United States Supreme Court ruled that *sexual harassment* [italics added] is a form of discrimination. The Equal Employment Opportunity Commission, created by the 1964 Civil Rights Act, defined behavior in workplaces as harassment if it produces a *hostile or intimidating* [italics added] work environment, hinders individuals' work, or adversely affects employment opportunity. In fact, regardless of the target person's ethnicity, age, gender, or physical condition, abusive disrespect of subordinates by bosses does exactly what the law prohibits: It creates a hostile, intimidating work environment that hinders subordinates' performance and adversely affects their future employment opportunity.
>
> Admittedly, harassment of others due to their membership in these designated social groups is prohibited because it would perpetuate a preexisting pattern of civil rights abuse. For this reason alone, the forms of behavior proscribed under Title VII deserve the special legislative and judicial attention they have received. Nonetheless, from the perspective of human experience and well-being, abuse is abuse. Many of the most insidious consequences of the abuse suffered by . . . millions . . . are no different from those suffered by victims of mistreatment declared illegal more than thirty years ago. (pp. 7-8)

Clearly, our book demonstrates that workplace abuse of teachers continues and legal protections against such abuse remain woefully weak:

> Unfortunately, the growing body of statutory and common-law protections for workers . . . have not been effective against workplace bullying. Consistent with the law's historic reluctance to regulate the everyday employment arena, workplace bullying has yet to be fully recognized and addressed by the American legal system. . . . Claims for intentional infliction of emotional distress (IIED) arising out of the workplace are seldom successful. . . . Existing legal doctrines such as IIED and statutory schemes do not adequately prevent workplace bullying or compensate bullied employees who

suffer emotional, physical, and economic damage at the hands (or words) of a bully. (Yamada, 2000, pp. 478-479)

Are you or others in your school or district being mistreated, abused, and bullied? Yamada (2000) suggests that a reasonable standard of an employer's liability for workplace bullying, whether or not legally actionable, should include the following, all of which we found in our study:

- Behaviors such as yelling and screaming, insults and put-downs, and continuous, unreasonable work demands and unfair accusations
- Behaviors of these types that endure or recur over a period of time
- Evidence of both overt and covert actions intended to sabotage the victim's work or reputation, or frustrate the victim's ability to work
- A power imbalance between the bully and the victim (superior and subordinate) in which the aggressor has direct control over the victim's work and job security
- (Especially objectionable) The aggressor exploiting the victim's emotional vulnerability, thus demonstrating mean-spirited, superfluous behavior to inflict emotional distress
- Assistance to the aggressor by others in the organization (e.g., coworkers, even subordinates who are "agents" of the bully) (pp. 525-526, paraphrased)

Harvey Hornstein (1996) suggests that adult relationships include the assumption of *mutual respect*, and disrespectful behavior violates rules of decency and damages the core of a work community. From his research, Hornstein learned that employees "expect bosses not to commit any of the Eight Daily Sins [i.e., deceit, constraint, coercion, selfishness, inequity, cruelty, disregard, and deification; see Box 7.3] regardless of their . . . personal attributes—status, ability, wealth, education, or performance—and regardless of any organizational condition or crisis" (p. 14).

Once again, and without exception, our findings about principal abuse of teachers are consistent with Hornstein's findings (and those of others) regarding the general population. To assess your experience of abuse by your principal and its possible consequences for your health and productivity, take the "Brutal Boss Questionnaire" found in Hornstein's book, *Brutal Bosses and Their Prey* (1996, pp. 152-154).

Lobby for Legal Recourse. We suggest that all educators work to support a statutory cause of action to give bullied employees legal recourse against abusive administrators as well as their employers. For example, educators can provide teachers' associations, boards of education, and state legislators with information about workplace mistreatment and, as educational activists, lobby as a group for antiharassment legislation.

Box 7.3   The Eight Daily Sins

Deceit	Lying; giving false or misleading information through acts of omission or commission.
Constraint	Restricting subordinates' activities in domains outside of work, e.g., where they live, the people with whom they live, friendships, and civic activity.
Coercion	Threatening excessive or inappropriate harm for non-compliance with a boss's wishes.
Selfishness	Protecting themselves by blaming subordinates and making them the scapegoats for any problems that occur.
Inequity	Providing unequal benefit or punishment to subordinates due to favoritism or non-working-related criteria.
Cruelty	Harming subordinates in normally illegitimate ways, such as public humiliation, personal attack, or name-calling.
Disregard	Behaving in ways that violate ordinary standards of politeness and fairness, as well as displaying a flagrant lack of concern for subordinates' lives (e.g., "I don't give a damn about your family's problems").
Deification	Implying a master-servant status in which bosses can do or say whatever they please to subordinates because they feel themselves to be superior people.

SOURCE: Hornstein, H. A. (1996). *Brutal bosses and their prey* (pp. 15-16). New York: Riverhead Books. Reprinted by permission.

Become Informed About Workplace Mistreatment (Popular Media, Articles, Books, Websites)

Read the rapidly expanding published material in the popular media. Begin, for example, with any of the following:

Bing, S. (1992). *Crazy bosses: Spotting them, serving them, surviving them*. New York: Morrow.

Chaleff, I. (1995). *The courageous follower. Standing up to and for our leaders*. San Francisco: Berrett-Koehler.

Field, T. (1996). *Bully in sight: How to predict, resist, challenge, and combat workplace bullying*. Wantage, Oxfordshire, UK: Wessex.

Fromm, E. (1964). *The heart of man: Its genius for good and evil*. New York: Harper & Row.

Hornstein, H. A. (1996). *Brutal bosses and their prey*. New York: Riverhead Books.

Lundin, W., & Lundin, K. (1995). *Working with difficult people*. New York: AMACOM.

Namie, G., & Namie, R. (2000a). *The bully at work: What you can do to stop the hurt and reclaim your dignity on the job*. Naperville, IL: Sourcebooks.

Peck, M. S. (1983). *People of the lie: The hope for healing human evil.* New York: Simon & Shuster.

Ryan, K. D., Oestreich, D. K., & Orr III, G. A. (1996). *The courageous messenger. How to successfully speak up at work.* San Francisco: Jossey-Bass.

Wyatt, J., & Hare, C. (1997). *Work abuse: How to recognize and survive it.* Rochester, VT: Schenkman Books.

Whyte, D. (1994). *The heart aroused: Poetry and the preservation of the soul in corporate America.* New York: Currency Doubleday.

Also read informative scholarly articles and books on the topic of workplace politics and abuse:

Adams, A. (1992). Holding out against workplace harassment and bullying. *Personnel Management, 24*(10), 48-53.

Adams, G. B., & Balfour, D. L. (1988). *Unmasking administrative evil.* Thousand Oaks, CA: Sage.

Baron, R. A., & Neumann, J. H. (1998). Workplace aggression—The iceberg beneath the tip of workplace violence: Evidence on its forms, frequency, and targets. *Public Administration, 21*(4), 446-464.

Bassman, E., & London, M. (1993). Abusive managerial behavior. *Leadership & Organizational Development Journal, 14*(2), 18-24.

Bolman, L. G., & Deal, T. E. (2000). *Escape from cluelessness: A guide for the organizationally challenged.* New York: AMACOM.

Cropanzano, R. (1993). *Justice in the workplace: Approaching fairness in human resource management.* Hillsdale, NJ: Lawrence Erlbaum.

Enomoto, E. K. (1997). Negotiating the ethics of care and justice. *Educational Administration Quarterly, 33*(3), 351-370.

Keashly, L. (1998). Emotional abuse in the workplace: Conceptual and empirical issues. *Journal of Emotional Abuse, 1*(1), 85-117.

Kets de Vries, M. F. R. (1989). *Prisoners of leadership.* New York: Wiley.

Leymann, H. (1990). Mobbing and psychological terror at workplaces. *Violence and Victims, 5*(2), 119-126.

Yamada, D. C. (2000). The phenomenon of "workplace bullying" and the need for status-blind hostile work environment protection. *The Georgetown Law Journal, 88*(3), 477-536.

Websites can also help those in search of information and assistance in cases of workplace mistreatment. For example, visit the Workplace Trauma website, which offers resources for employers, counselors, and victims dealing with bullying, abuse, and harassment in the workplace (www.worktrauma.org). Another website that is rich in links, resources, and news is the Workplace Bullying website (www.workplacebullying.com); its goals are to reveal the secrecy and denial surrounding workplace bullying and to encourage the targets of abuse to reclaim their lives. In addition, we have found the Success Unlimited website (www.successunlimited.co.uk/bully) and the Campaign Against Workplace Bullying (CAWB) website (www.bullybusters.org) especially informative and helpful. The latter website was founded by Drs. Gary and Ruth Namie, and its mission is twofold:

- To raise public awareness of bullying and initiate a national dialogue
- To create and promote solutions for individuals and workplaces

The focus areas for the Campaign are:

- Public awareness education (the U.S. national conference, public town hall meetings, promotion of Freedom From Bullies At Work Week, BullyBuster Awards, a book series, and the website)
- Support for bullied individuals (telephone coaching, grassroots peer support network)
- Research (online surveys, presentations at professional conferences)
- Guidance for employers (design of integrated solutions to address bullying)
- Social change (support for reform of public policy and law)
- Alliances with organizations and individuals
- The Work Trauma Institute (continuing professional education for attorneys, physicians, and mental health professionals)

You can also read teachers' stories of mistreatment at the website of the American Society for Ethics in Education (ASEE) at www.edethics.org.

Humor, "the ability to be playful and laugh at oneself" (Ford, 1996, p. 43), is considered an effective ego-defense mechanism. Watch your newspaper for the *Dilbert* cartoon, in which incompetent and abusive bosses wielding the latest management fads make life intolerable for innocent employees. You may be interested in reading books that take a humorous perspective on the topic of boss abuse:

Frankel, V., & Tien, E. (1996). *The I hate my job handbook: How to deal with hell at work.* New York: Fawcett Columbine.
King, P. (1987). *Never work for a jerk!* New York: F. Watts.
Sartwell, M. (1994). *Bosses from hell: True tales from the trenches.* New York: Plume.

Finally, if you are interested in the issue of child bullying in schools, and if you want to support children and their parents in ending the secrecy and denial that accompanies bullying in all its forms, we suggest the following books:

Fried, S., & Fried, P. (1996). *Bullies and victims: Helping your child survive the school-yard battlefield.* New York: M. Evans.
Ladson-Billings, G. (2001). *Crossing over to Canaan: The journey of new teachers in diverse classrooms.* San Francisco: Jossey-Bass.
Olweus, D. (1993). *Bullying at school: What we know and what we can do.* Oxford: Blackwell.

The book by Ladson-Billings describes ways to teach children to critique cultural norms and social inequalities.

Take Action

When Namie and Namie (2000b) placed surveys at their national Campaign Against Workplace Bullying website, they received responses from targets (bullied persons including a janitor, nurse, bank teller, teacher, machinist, engineer, and child care worker) and witnesses of bullying; they also received responses to a second questionnaire from targets regarding the aftermath of their bullying experiences. Namie and Namie (2000a) defined *bullying* as "the hurtful, repeated mistreatment of a target (recipient) by a bully (the perpetrator) whose actions are characterized as controlling" (p. 269). The major survey findings were as follows:

- Bullying is different from the more recognizable issues that plague the workplace—sexual harassment, racial discrimination, and violence. Both women and men are victimized as targets and serve as perpetrators. (Verbal assaults and sabotage characterize bullying.)
- Falling prey to a bully's destructive tactics is a career hazard; it is not gamesmanship or fair competition among equals. Bullies commonly adopt surprise and secrecy to gain leverage over targets. Precipitating factors include refusal to be subservient, envy, and the culture of the organization, among others.
- Targets are a diverse group of normal, talented people.
- Bullying devastates the target's emotional stability and can last a long time.
- The employer, as an organization, bears partial responsibility for the systematic disassembly of once productive employees by a mean-spirited, one-person wrecking crew. (2000a, pp. 270-276)

Clearly, when a bullied person is being seriously harmed, he or she must take action. Taking action includes overcoming your fear, "bullyproofing" yourself at work, employing survival skills, and, finally, fighting back—"bullybusting."

Controlling Your Fear. Fear often prevents targeted individuals from taking action; this was true of teachers in our study. Consider this:

Imagine that you came across a wooden board that measured twelve feet long, twelve inches wide, and four inches thick. You would have little difficulty walking from one end of the board to the other. But what would happen if that same board were stretched between two buildings two hundred feet tall—with nothing but the hustle and bustle of the city traffic below—could you summon the courage to walk the same board? Just think, same board, same distance, but a new element is introduced—one that alters your mental attitude considerably—that element is fear. The fear of what could happen. The fear of what might happen holds us back and keeps us in check. We permit ourselves to fail by default rather than run the risk of failing as a result of having made the effort to succeed. It is all a mental image that is depicted in our brains, our actions, and our thoughts. However, it is in here, in our minds—not in the actual practice—where we win or lose. Greatness does not depend upon where you are now—greatness depends upon where you are going. Success does not depend upon what you are now—success depends upon what you are becoming. (Anonymous)

How, then, can you overcome feelings of fear? Here are a few simple ideas that can help. Izard and Youngstrom (1996) note that situations that elicit fear are remarkably void of anger or joy; thus, fear and anger or joy are incompatible. By eliciting either joy or anger, then, one can activate emotions antagonistic to fear. Remarkably, these feelings can be elicited simply by using facial feedback data (i.e., making happy or angry faces). Further, one can learn to become aware of fear-related expressions in the face and body. Moreover, visualization, muscle-relaxation, and deep breathing techniques, combined with such awareness, can ultimately help diminish feelings of fear. It may also be helpful to remember the words of Eleanor Roosevelt:

> There is no experience from which you can't learn something. . . . And the purpose of life, after all, is to live it, to taste experience to the utmost, to reach out eagerly and without fear for newer and richer experience. You can do that only if you have curiosity, an unquenchable spirit of adventure. The experience can have meaning only if you understand it. You can understand it only if you have arrived at some knowledge of yourself, a knowledge based on a deliberately and usually painfully acquired self-discipline, which teaches you to cast out fear and frees you for the fullest experience of the adventure of life. (Eleanor Roosevelt quoted in Cook, *Eleanor Roosevelt, Vol. 1: 1884-1932*, 1993)

Bullyproofing Yourself at Work

In a professional and assertive way, one can "bullyproof" oneself; this involves considerable inner work for a victim, as well as a new approach to interaction with a bully. Namie and Namie (2000a, pp. 127-203) suggest the following actions for bullyproofing yourself at work:

1. Assess the bully's impact (consider your strengths and weaknesses, how others see you, your work performance, your ability to solve problems, your perspective on the treatment)

2. Establish and protect boundaries (know your boundaries and limits, consider your susceptibility to attacks)

3. Avoid unattainable standards (avoid self-defeating "shoulds")

4. Counter your inner critic (be realistic, avoid invalidating your own hard work)

5. Control destructive mind games (avoid catastrophizing, mind reading, overgeneralization)

6. Escape the trap of self-blame (take credit for success, let failure roll off your back)

7. Satisfy your needs and wants (clarify your needs and wants, make assertive requests)

8. Deal with your anger and shame: emotions elicited by bullying (express anger assertively, ignore what is untrue about you)

Namie and Namie (2000a, pp. 189-190) also identify the following *rules* for making requests (for what you need or what you want a bully to do):

1. Try to get the other person to agree on a convenient time and place for your discussion.

2. Keep your requests small to avoid resistance from the bully.

3. Keep your request simple, one or two items will be harder for the bully to claim forgetfulness.

4. Don't attack the other person. Use firm "I messages" so you can stick to your thoughts and feelings. Remember to be objective and stick to the facts. Keep your tone of voice moderate.

5. Be specific. Don't hedge when you give exact times and figures for what you want. Focus on asking for behaviors, not a change in feelings or attitude.

6. Use assertive words and high-esteem body language. Maintain eye contact, sit or stand straight, uncross your legs and arms, and make sure you speak clearly, audibly, and firmly.

7. Practice, practice, practice! Stand in front of the mirror to observe how you look when you request what you need. This will allow you to correct poor posture and to practice confident facial expressions. Remember, you are practicing the truth. The poor bully has to rehearse lying. Your job is ethical, thus easier.

Six Survival Skills

Hornstein (1996) argues that workplace abuse will be seriously challenged only when such abuse is outlawed. In lieu of protective laws, Hornstein offers six survival skills derived from years of research to prevent bosses from brutalizing workers. In short, he suggests that one must learn the eight "sins" (Box 7.3) and recognize when they are being committed, recognize bosses for who they are, be aware of "gotcha" goals, look around and reach out, focus on the accountability of bosses who abuse, and watch yourself (see Box 7.4 for Hornstein's explanation of these skills).

Fighting Back: Bullybusting

Finally, Namie and Namie (2000a) detail eight steps to bullybusting, for use when one has decided to *fight back*:

Box 7.4 Six Survival Skills

1. *Know the Eight Daily Sins and when they're being committed.*
   Do not accept Deceit, Constraint, Coercion, Selfishness, Inequity, Cruelty, Disregard, and Deification as natural ingredients of relationships at the workplace.

2. *Recognize bosses for who and what they are.*
   Know your Dehumanizers, Blamers, and Rationalizers and their motives. Identify Conquerors, Performers, Manipulators, and the roots of their abuse. Note when and why they band together to protect one another at the expense of subordinates.

3. *Be aware of gotcha goals.*
   Be alert to schemes and setups wherein discipline, rather than development, is the objective of employee supervision and monitoring.

4. *Look around and reach out.*
   The "change the victims" approach [the victim blames himself or herself and thinks he or she must change, as opposed to realizing that the abuser need to change] is fundamentally wrong, and will not remedy the misbehavior of abusers; however, it is instructive in its emphasis on workers' self-reliance and on the importance of peer support. Employees who are oppressed from above can move sideways to establish healthy and empowering bonds with fellow sufferers. Isolation is debilitating and is one of the causes and effects of abuse that can be overcome by reaching out.

5. *Focus on the accountability of bosses who abuse.*
   The talking, training, and grading cures that the "change the abusers" approach advocates are unlikely to transform bosses and their habits, but they are worthwhile endeavors and serve to make an important point: Bosses are uniquely responsible for the brutality that's poisoned our work environments.

6. *Watch yourself.*
   Workers of all levels who act abusively toward subordinates are not justified or excused by their own mistreatment at the hands of their bosses. Apply the same categories and criticisms to yourself that you have administered to your boss. Look for yourself in the Brutal Boss Questionnaire. Uphold fairness, even in the face of unfairness. We all have the potential to be brutal bosses.

SOURCE: Hornstein, H. A. (1996). *Brutal bosses and their prey* (pp. 144-145). New York: Riverhead Books. Reprinted by permission.

1. Solicit support from family and friends

2. Consult an outside physician or therapist

3. Solicit witness statements

4. Confront the bully

5. File an internal complaint

6. Prepare the case against the bully

7. Present your case

8. Take your case public

Victims of abusive bosses should consider Eleanor Roosevelt's words that link mastery of fear to courage, "You gain strength, courage, and confidence by every experience in which you really stop to look fear in the face. . . . You must do the thing you think you cannot do." In addition, we believe that the relationship between inappropriate boss behavior and stress, fear, and emotional damage warrants attention to mind, body, and spiritual awareness; support; and solutions. Recent research at Harvard University, the University of California, and the International Center for Integration of Health and Spirituality demonstrates that calmness, gratitude, caring, comforting, and focus can be developed in people and that such approaches can reduce stress, diminish depression, and delay aging; such work can be found, in part, in the following books:

Emmons, R. A. (1999). *The psychology of ultimate concerns: Motivation and spirituality in personality.* New York: Guilford.

Ornstein, R. E., & Swencionis, C. (Eds.). (1990). *Healing brain: A scientific reader.* New York: Guilford.

If You Witness Mistreatment, Be a Responsible Colleague

Virtue is not to be considered in the light of mere innocence, or abstaining from harm; but in the exertion of our faculties in doing good. (Joseph Butler, *Webster's Book of Quotations*, 1992, p. 230)

Each time a man stands up for an ideal, or acts to improve the lot of others, or strikes out against injustice, he sends forth a tiny ripple of hope, and crossing each other from a million different centers of energy and daring those ripples build a current which can sweep down the mightiest walls of oppression and injustice. (Robert F. Kennedy quoted in The Campaign Against Workplace Bullying, www.bullybusters.org)

In *The Courageous Follower*, Chaleff (1995) discussed the dynamics of the leader-follower relationship including the importance of courage—the courage to assume responsibility, to serve, to challenge, to participate in transformation, and even to leave one's job if necessary. Specifically, Chaleff wrote that "followers who provide robust support for leaders are in a strong position to challenge them when their activities threaten the common purpose (p. 79). In such cases, colleagues of teachers victimized by a principal's mistreatment may be able to

- Listen to principals and empathize with their challenges (One ten-year [1988-1998] national study of elementary principals (Doud & Keller, 1998) showed that 42% left their jobs due to stress.)
- Challenge abuse by a principal early
- Discuss appropriate behavior with the principal
- Prepare principals for feedback (i.e., remind them of the value of honesty)
- Give principals feedback
- Invite creative challenges by modeling and advocating
- Challenge indirectly by helping the principal gain another perspective
- Avoid knee-jerk reactions to principal behaviors
- Help overcome groupthink
- Remind others of their duty to implement policies
- Demonstrate the duty to disobey destructive policies
- Challenge a principal's use of pejorative language
- Challenge a principal's arrogance or manipulation
- Challenge principals who scream
- Discuss personal issues that undermine trust, purpose, or values
- Engage newly appointed principals in dialogue
- Challenge leaders who have other (hidden, inappropriate) agendas
- Challenge yourselves to have courage and honesty in relationships

Chaleff's "Meditation on Followship" may be helpful to those who witness principal mistreatment of colleague-teachers (see Box 7.5).

Discover What School District Offices Can Do

School district office personnel and boards of education throughout the United States are legally, professionally, and ethically responsible for the general welfare and safety of teachers and the conduct of school administrators. In addition, proponents of school restructuring—shared leadership, teacher empowerment, learning community—argue that schools must be caring and just communities (Beck, 1994; Cropanzano, 1993; Enomoto, 1997; Glickman, Gordon, & Ross-Gordon, 2001; Noddings, 1992; Sizer, 1996). To overcome the problem of principal mistreatment of teachers we strongly suggest addressing the problem at both the individual and the organizational levels.

First, school district office personnel and boards of education can develop understanding of the principal mistreatment problem and their role with respect to this problem. The roles of school district office personnel and boards of education are especially important in light of research on workplace abuse indicating that

---

Box 7.5 Meditation on Followship

FOR ME, BECOMING A COURAGEOUS FOLLOWER, like becoming a good human being, is both a daily and a lifelong task. Visualizing a desired state helps to realize it. I share this meditation as one visualization of the state I aspire to. You may want to refer to it from time to time.

I am a steward of this group and share responsibility for its success.

I am responsible for adhering to the highest values I can envision.

I am responsible for my successes and failures and for continuing to learn from them.

I am responsible for the attractive and unattractive parts of who I am.

I can empathize with others who are also imperfect.

As an adult, I can relate on a peer basis to other adults who are the group's formal leaders.

I can support leaders and counsel them, and receive support and counsel from them.

Our common purpose is our best guide.

I have the power to help leaders use their power wisely and effectively.

If leaders abuse power, I can help them change their behavior.

If I abuse power, I can learn from others and change my behavior.

If abusive leaders do not change their behavior, I can and will withdraw my support.

By staying true to my values, I can serve others well and fulfill my potential.

Thousands of courageous acts by followers can, one by one, improve the world.

Courage always exists in the present. What can I do today?

---

upper-level management in organizations usually ignores or colludes with abusive bosses when victims make formal complaints; these actors also contribute to the mistreatment problem through the attitudes they convey about employees and the expectations they have for administrators (Davenport et al., 1999; Keashly et al., 1994; Namie & Namie, 2000b). School district office personnel and boards of education should model and encourage a respectful and supportive climate in the school and create staff development programs that address the mistreatment problem for both administrators and teachers.

Further, it is assumed that although some principals may engage in abusive conduct toward teachers because of personality flaws (anger disorder, narcissistic personality, authoritarian personality), others may do so in part because of their inability to handle stress, faulty assumptions about power and its use, faulty assumptions about teachers, gender issues, threatened ego (especially when one's ego is based on inflated or ill-founded self-estimates), lack of awareness of the effects of their behavior, and a host of external-organizational conditions (e.g., central office mandates, administrative performance evaluations, insufficient resources). Such matters may be addressed in administrators' professional development plans and with the assistance of colleagues and specialists.

Second, school district office personnel and boards of education can help each principal improve awareness and understanding of his or her conduct and its impact on others. This can be accomplished, for example, through the use of 360° feedback mechanisms, the use of surveys, and awareness techniques and exercises.

Third, school district office personnel and boards of education can develop enlightened employment procedures and policies. Our study has implications for the recruitment, hiring, professional development, and termination of school-level administrators. Well-publicized procedures and policies for recruitment, hiring (e.g., hiring people who are emotionally intelligent, who are capable of working with diverse people in teams, and who are adept at managing conflict), and termination, and sophisticated professional development programs (e.g., training in interpersonal skills) can go a long way toward eradicating the mistreatment of teachers. Most important, district office personnel and boards of education must ensure that teacher evaluations and continuing employment are contingent solely on job performance and not used by principals to punish competent teachers. In the case of incompetent teachers, appropriate documentation, procedures (including opportunities and assistance to improve), and policies must be applied; such teachers must be afforded due process as well as respectful treatment.

Fourth, school district office personnel and boards of education can develop viable, comprehensive antiabuse policies to protect employees from and provide relief for mistreatment. Without protective policies and procedures, teachers subjected to mistreatment by school principals have little recourse (Davenport et al., 1999; Keashly et al., 1994; Namie & Namie, 2000b; Yamada, 2000). Conflict resolution and mediation, grievance, and employee assistance mechanisms as well as antiabuse, harassment, and mobbing policies (for example, see Box 7.6) and procedures should be unequivocal, broadly publicized, and fully resourced. A zero-tolerance approach to the mistreatment of teachers must be taken.

Discover What Professors of Programs in Educational Leadership and Teacher Preparation Can Do

Yes, we all know this kind of thing [principal mistreatment of teachers] goes on in schools, but I would not want my students to be exposed to this topic. I'm trying to encourage them to go into school administration. (Professor of Educational Administration, reviewer of proposal for *Breaking the Silence*)

Box 7.6   Antimobbing Policy

As an employee of this Organization, you are expected to adhere to acceptable conduct at all times. This involves respecting the rights and feelings of others and refraining from any behavior that might be harmful to your co-workers.

The Organization strongly supports the rights of all employees to work in an environment free from mobbing.

Mobbing is verbal or physical conduct that, over a period of time, continuously and systematically

1. **intimidates, shows hostility, threatens, and offends any coworker;**
2. **interferes with a coworker's performance;**
3. **otherwise adversely affects a coworker.**

   Mobbing conduct includes, but is not limited to

   - threatening, intimidating, or hostile acts directed at a coworker;
   - generally abrasive behavior;
   - using obscene, abusive, or threatening language or gestures;
   - discrediting a coworker;
   - prohibiting due process;
   - slander;
   - withholding information vital to the co-workers job-performance;
   - acts of physical isolation.

These guidelines are fundamental in nature and are matters of judgment and common sense.

The Organization prohibits mobbing. Any violation of the Organization's anti-mobbing policy should be reported immediately to either your supervisor, the office manager, Human Resources, or the President.

All complaints will be treated confidentially to the maximum extent possible and will be promptly investigated.

The Organization prohibits any form of retaliation against an employee filing a bona fide complaint under this policy or for assisting in a complaint investigation. If the result of the investigation indicates that corrective action is called for, such action may include disciplinary measures up to and including immediate termination of the employment of the offender(s), when the Organization believes, in its sole discretion, such action is warranted.

SOURCE: Davenport, N., Distler-Schwartz, R., & Pursell-Elliott, G. (1999). *Mobbing: Emotional abuse in the American workplace* (pp. 144-145). Ames, IA: Civil Society. Reprinted by permission.

Virtually all prospective administrators have been teachers and, as such, undoubtedly have experienced or observed abusive conduct with regard to colleagues. Clearly, many are aware of its effects on victimized teachers and on schools as a whole. Nevertheless, university-based programs in educational leadership and teacher preparation programs typically address only the positive aspects of and approaches to school leadership; they seldom directly address the "dark side" of school life and, as such, fail to equip students to understand or deal with this incredibly destructive problem. Indeed, the professor quoted earlier preferred to ignore the topic of principal mistreatment.

Interestingly, however, our survey of over 300 school administrators and teachers about the practical value of studying the mistreatment problem (discussed in Chapter 1) demonstrates the critical importance of this topic to prospective and practicing administrators' and teachers' development as school "leaders." Adult learning theory and common sense point out that people often derive their most profound learning from a reflective understanding of negative modeling and negative life experiences. This, of course, further supports the importance of studying such experiences in both leadership and teacher preparation programs. To this end, preparation programs for prospective teachers and administrators can examine the phenomenon of principal mistreatment of teachers and consider the following questions:

- What conduct by school principals do teachers define as abusive?
- What is it about the principal's role and those who occupy this role that can result in abusive conduct?
- What effect does such conduct have on teachers (e.g., what are the emotional and physical consequences for teachers, and how does such conduct affect teachers' classroom instruction and student learning?)?
- What are the consequences of abusive conduct by principals on school climate and school culture?
- What coping strategies are efficacious for mistreated teachers?
- What actions can mistreated teachers take (see the first four sections after box 7.6)?
- What actions can administrators, school district office personnel, and school boards take (see section on school district offices above)?
- At what point should district office personnel move beyond counseling, guiding, and providing performance reviews of a principal who mistreats others and move to disciplinary action or discharge?

University preparation programs can also work to create awareness of factors potentially related to the problem of abuse through study of topics such as

- Gender
- Power
- Work stress
- Crisis management
- Conflict resolution
- Labor laws

- Development of positive psychological and social work environments
- Effective orientation programs for teachers and principals (including clear descriptions of codes of conduct as well as support and encouragement)
- Development of mission, vision, and values statements including how employees should be treated
- Development of norms conducive to respect and caring in the workplace[1]
- Setting the example of friendly and respectful interaction
- Standards of professional ethics

With respect to the last issue, we stress that prospective administrators need awareness and understanding of standards of professional ethics. In light of this book's subject, The American Association of School Administrators (AASA) Statement of Ethics for School Administrators and Procedural Guidelines (1976), adopted as a standard of professional ethics by most national school administrators' associations (e.g., the National Association of Secondary School Principals [NASSP], the National Association of Elementary School Principals [NAESP]), warrants reiteration here, including its strong preamble and the first five of ten standards (AASA, 1976, pp. 12-13):

> An educational administrator's professional behavior must conform to an ethical code. The code must be idealistic and at the same time practical, so that it can apply reasonably to all educational administrators. The administrator acknowledges that the schools belong to the public they serve for the purpose of providing educational opportunities to all. However, the administrator assumes responsibility for providing professional leadership in the school and community. This responsibility requires the administrator to maintain standards of exemplary professional conduct. It must be recognized that the administrators' actions will be viewed and appraised by the community, professional associates, and students. To these ends, the administrator subscribes to the following statements of standards. The educational administrator
>
> 1. Makes the well-being of students the fundamental value of all decision making and actions.
> 2. Fulfills professional responsibilities with honesty and integrity.
> 3. Supports the principle of due process and protects the civil and human rights of all individuals.
> 4. Obeys local, state, and national laws. . . .
> 5. Implements the governing board of education's policies and administrative rules and regulations.

Ascertain What Principals Can Do: A Reflective Exercise

We have acknowledged elsewhere in this book that the job of a principal is challenging and stressful. With it comes enormous responsibility, often assumed in an environment replete with economic, social, and political pressures. Such pressures, internal and external to the school (e.g., related to accountability), as well as a principal's personality (e.g., tolerance for ambiguity, need for control, ability to withstand stress) may provoke one to mistreat teachers, good intentions notwithstanding. Practicing principals may find the following reflective questions helpful in preventing mistreatment of teachers:

- In what ways do I encourage or discourage a respectful and supportive climate in the school?
- How can I improve my (and others') awareness and understanding about the issue of teacher mistreatment?
- Am I informed about legal precedents and standards about workplace mistreatment (i.e., what behaviors comprise mistreatment) as well as the district's policies and procedures with respect to mistreatment of teachers?
- Do I understand factors potentially related to the problem of teacher mistreatment (e.g., gender, diversity, and power issues; work stress; conflict)?
- How can I become more aware of the impact of my behavior toward teachers (e.g., the use of confidential feedback, written or oral, from trusted teachers or other administrators; performance reviews)?
- To what extent is my behavior toward teachers driven by a tendency to be authoritarian, by feelings of anger, or by the stress I am experiencing, and how well equipped am I to deal with such feelings?
- Have I unfairly withheld resources, blocked a teacher's professional growth, or done other damaging or hurtful things to teachers?
- Have I been guilty of using teacher evaluation or renewal procedures in ways other than intended (e.g., to punish a teacher for matters unrelated to the school's mission but annoying to me)?
- Can I, in an emotionally mature and responsible way, deal with a teacher's concerns about being mistreated by me? In such a situation, am I prepared to support the principle of due process and protect the civil and human rights of teachers?
- What avenues exist for my personal development and for counseling and guidance with respect to the issue of teacher mistreatment?

Finally, principals may want to check themselves by reading the Arbinger Institute's book, *Leadership and Self-deception: Getting Out of the Box.*

Ascertain What Researchers Can Do

Our study of principal mistreatment has generated new descriptive, conceptual, and theoretical knowledge in the area of workplace mistreatment. It also contributes to the well-established micropolitical and leadership literature, for example, by describing in detail and for the first time the behaviors associated with abusive and authoritarian forms of school leadership as well as the serious adverse effects of such leadership on teachers and their work with students. Our study also contributes directly to the teacher stress literature by providing detailed descriptions of the effects of mistreatment on teachers.

In addition, knowledge of the principal mistreatment problem has special significance for the school reform and restructuring efforts. Recent studies have found that principals' use of manipulative and coercive types of power in school restructuring initiatives (designed along collegial and democratic lines) has drastically undermined such efforts (e.g., Blase & Blase, 2001; Malen & Ogawa, 1988; Murphy & Louis, 1994a, 1994b; Reitzug & Cross, 1994). More research is necessary to fully understand how and under what circumstances school principals both consciously and unwittingly subvert school reform outcomes. Finally, our study is timely and useful in the field of education given recent research interest in schools as "caring" and "just" communities (Beck, 1994; Bolman & Deal, 1995; Katz, Noddings, & Strike, 1999; Noddings, 1992) and the recent emergence of themes such as "organizational justice" in the general organizational literature (Bies, 1987; Cropanzano, 1993; Enomoto, 1997). Educational researchers need to consider studies of schools grounded in such perspectives.

Breaking the Silence is the first empirical report of the actual experiences of abused teachers; that is, what constitutes principal mistreatment and its common effects on teachers' work. Yet, although we have begun to illuminate this problem, it nevertheless requires much more investigation. For example, we have suggested that principals' mistreatment of teachers is contingent on a multitude of internal and external, individual, and political factors (e.g., motivations, courage, patience, district and state regulations, and resources). We would argue that as the call for educational reform and accountability becomes even more deliberate, the job of principal will become more complex, challenging, political, and stressful; this, in turn, may provide an even more fertile ground for the emergence of abusive conduct on the part of principals. (In fact, we have already heard numerous stories of principal mistreatment of teachers linked to new accountability measures.) Useful research could focus on the relationships among abusive principals' personalities, preparation, and school contexts. Studies of school district office personnel and boards of educations' perspectives of the mistreatment problem would also be valuable.

In addition, studies of victimized teachers' coping skills would be helpful. Quantitative studies using random samples of teachers are critical to understanding the pervasiveness of the principal mistreatment problem in our nation's schools and elsewhere. Qualitative studies can provide descriptions beyond those noted here (i.e., beyond forms of abuse, effects, and how abuse is perceived by victims) to include the extent to which abusive principals recognize the effects of abuse, abusive principals' intentions, how and under what conditions abusive relationships evolve, victims' interpretations of abusive principals' behaviors, the degree to which victims may contribute to the abuse, when and how victims are willing to challenge abuse, and the effectiveness of district policies to stop abuse.

Finally, we believe that research and educator-preparation professors have a responsibility to bring the results of research on mistreatment to all educators and the public at large, to publish their findings in professional journals and books, to present their findings at professional organizations (e.g., National Education Association, Association for Supervision and Curriculum Development, National Association of Elementary School Principals, National Association of Secondary

School Principals, University Council for Educational Administration, American Association of School Administrators, American Educational Research Association), and to support legislation, policy, and professional education that will help overcome this problem.

A FINAL COMMENT

Earlier we mentioned that conducting the study discussed in this book was a huge challenge, both from a research perspective and a personal perspective. Further, while conducting the study, carefully analyzing our data, and writing this book, we gained a sense of urgency about overcoming the mistreatment problem. Thus, our continued work in this area will be driven by the following assumptions:

- There is no justification for abusing any teacher, nor for causing fear and intimidation in those who witness such abuse.
- Mistreatment of teachers, that is, demeaning, intimidating, harassing, humiliating treatment, is not a trivial matter; in fact, it is a form of violence that may be commonplace in many schools.
- Mistreatment that is cloaked in organizational norms, habits, and customs will result in a hostile work environment. (Although most often applied in sexual harassment and other Title VII cases, the Supreme Court considers the following factors in determining a hostile work environment: frequency, severity, threat, humiliation, and work interference [Bennett, Polden, & Rubin, 1998].)
- Mistreatment of teachers must not be tacitly permitted by employers; such behavior should be considered to be in direct violation of a school and district's core values; it should also be recognized as a severe form of misconduct toward which the school and district take a zero-tolerance approach.
- We must all take responsibility for eliminating mistreatment in schools. This will require courage.
- Dignity, civility, and mutual respect among coworkers must be demanded for all educators.

In closing, we welcome your comments and participation in this ongoing, vitally important work, and we share this final comment about school leadership:

Schools run on love—of the kids, the subject, the work, the hope, the possibilities, the smiles of satisfaction, the looks of appreciation, the little things that keep teachers and students and leaders going. The principal whose interactions with staff undermine this all-important source of energy by creating a dissociation between teachers' self-confidence and their professional self-image is like the captain drilling a hole in her/his own ship. No matter how hard you bail, it's always sinking. Leaders who cause teachers emotional damage would be wise to reconsider the cost effectiveness, if nothing else, of dis-integrating a teacher's self, a precariously balanced entity that is already overtaxed. Leaders who are sensitive to teachers' needs for congruity and emotional understanding in their professional relationships with their leaders can provide invaluable support and catalyze creativity, which can benefit exponentially, the whole school community. (Beatty, 2000, p. 36)

NOTE

1 As Starratt (1991) noted,

The administrator who is concerned with nurturing the growth of teachers will have to ensure that teachers experience the relationship with the administrator as one of regard, mutual respect, and honest contact between two persons. Even though their traditional organizational roles have conditioned administrators and teachers to an antagonistic relationship, in a school intentionally restructuring itself and concerned about issues of empowerment, it is possible to move toward a relationship based on caring. For relationships of caring to develop, administrators will initially [need to] explore with their teachers those conditions necessary to initiate and maintain trust, honesty, and open communication. (p. 196)

Research Method and Procedures

This book focuses on school principal conduct that teachers themselves define as abusive, and it describes the effects of such conduct on teachers, teaching, and learning. For readers interested in examining the research method and procedures employed to produce the database for this book, we provide the following description.

Clearly, the study that serves as the foundation for this book is extremely sensitive and even incendiary in nature. To actually conduct our study in a variety of school settings, we would normally be required to identify principals responsible for long-standing abusive conduct as well as the teachers they have targeted. However, we assumed that school districts would neither grant permission to conduct on-site interviews with teachers victimized by principals, nor would teachers volunteer to participate in a research project of this nature (even if it were authorized) given the potential risks of doing so. In fact, we consulted with over 100 full-time teachers in our university classes about these matters, which confirmed our assumptions. Therefore, we proceeded in a way in which we could be successful, given the special set of considerations surrounding our study topic (Silverman, 2000).

We employed a snowball sampling technique that requires others—in our case, teachers and professors throughout the United States—to recommend individuals who they believe have experienced significant long-term abuse by a school principal. Snowball sampling techniques are especially useful in grounded theory research that attempts to draw samples from a variety of settings to maximize variation in the database (Bogdan & Biklen, 1982; Glaser, 1978, 1998; Strauss & Corbin, 1998; Taylor & Bogdan, 1998). In this way, we identified over 50 teachers in the United States and Canada who had experienced significant long-term principal abuse, as it turned out, for a duration of six months to nine years. We explained the nature of our study to such individuals and asked them to discuss participation in our study with a victimized teacher.

At this point, we contacted (by telephone) teachers who had expressed an interest in discussing participation, explained our study, addressed questions and concerns, discussed our backgrounds, and generally got to know the teacher. Only teachers who had experienced long-term and significant abuse by their school principal were included in our study. As expected, teachers were very fearful of possible disclosure; therefore, several safeguards seemed to alleviate their fears and promote trust and rapport. We explained to teachers that their identities would remain anonymous. Teachers were informed, per our agreement with the Human Subjects Committee at our university, that our entire database (i.e., audiotapes, typed transcripts, official and personal documents, and other related materials) would be destroyed upon completion of our analysis. We also indicated that all identifiers would be redacted from any materials used in any presentation of our findings. This, of course, required using pseudonyms for the names of people and places. Finally, we shared our general research questions and asked teachers to think about their abuse experience in preparation for the next interview.

As noted, trust and rapport are essential to conducting successful interviews with research participants (Bogdan & Biklen, 1982; Fontana & Frey, 2000; Taylor & Bogdan, 1998). Because we were primarily using telephone interviews, we expected that achieving both rapport and trust would be particularly challenging. Surprisingly, this was not the case; in fact, teachers spoke quite freely and in detail about their abuse experiences, despite the deeply disturbing nature of their experiences. (In about 25% of our interviews, teachers were so emotionally overcome during the retelling of their experiences that the interview had to be stopped briefly or rescheduled.)

Discussions with participants indicate that several factors account for the rapport and trust developed. These factors extend beyond our promises of anonymity and destruction of raw data: By asking meaningful questions, listening attentively, expressing our deep-felt empathy for their suffering, and, in general, treating participants respectfully, we were able to gain their trust and thus their openness about their experiences. Indeed, we found that "to learn about people, we must remember to treat them as people, and they will uncover their lives to us" (Fontana & Frey, 1994, p. 374).

Three additional factors enhanced teachers' trust and willingness to share their experiences. First, our initial contact occurred through a trusted friend or colleague. Second, and perhaps most important, our study held special significance for teachers who participated; as painful as the interviews were, teachers strongly believed that the problem of principal mistreatment should be made public and, as one put it, "This study might crack open the door of hope and eventually change the world of education." Third, teachers indicated that telephone interviews, conducted in the safety of their homes over an extended period of time, added to their sense of comfort, security, and trust in the researchers.

In total, 50 ($n = 50$) teachers participated in our study over a period of a year and a half. The sample consisted of male ($n = 5$) and female ($n = 45$) teachers from rural ($n = 14$), suburban ($n = 25$), and urban ($n = 11$) school locations. Elementary ($n = 26$), middle or junior high ($n = 10$), and high school ($n = 14$) teachers participated. The average age of teachers was 42 years; the average number of years in teaching was 16. The sample included tenured ($n = 44$) and nontenured ($n = 6$), married ($n = 34$) and single ($n = 16$) teachers. Degrees earned by these teachers included B.A./B.S. (n = 7), M.Ed./M.A. (n = 31), Ed.S. (n = 11), and Ph.D. (n = 1). The mean number of years working with the abusive principal was four. Forty-nine (n = 49) teachers resided in the United States and one (n = 1) resided in Canada. Fifteen (n = 15) of the teachers we studied were with an abusive principal at the time of this study; most others had experienced abuse in recent years. Teachers described both male (n = 28) and female (n = 22) principals. On a personal note, examination of the personal and official documents submitted to us and reports from those who had worked with and referred us to the veteran teachers we studied suggests that they were highly accomplished, creative, and dedicated individuals. In most cases, such teachers had been consistently, formally recognized by their school and district not simply as effective teachers but as superior teachers; in many cases, such recognition for their exceptional achievements as public educators extended to state levels.

The research question, interview guide, data collection, and analyses were based on the Blumer-Mead (1969 and 1934, respectively) approach to symbolic interaction theory. In contrast to some approaches, this methodological perspective emphasizes the examination of human subjectivity; that is, it examines perceptions and meanings that people construct in their social settings (Bogdan & Biklen, 1982; Lofland, 1971; Morse, 1991; Schwandt, 1994; Taylor & Bogdan, 1998; Tesch, 1988). According to Meltzer, Petras, and Reynolds (1975), symbolic interactionists who employ this approach study "what goes on inside the heads of humans" (p. 55). They state,

> human beings are defined as self-reflective beings. . . . The behavior of men and women is "caused" not so much by forces within themselves [e.g., instincts] . . . or by external forces impinging upon them . . . but what lies in between, a reflective and socially derived interpretation of the internal and external stimuli that are present . . . (p. 2). Perception functions as a meditative experience for the individual in the relationship between himself/herself and the social environment. (p. 52)

Consistent with symbolic interaction theory, a priori concepts from the literature were not used to control data collection. In addition, we did not examine the literature on workplace abuse until all data were analyzed and written in descriptive form. Instead, we used only a few sensitizing concepts such as principal abuse to focus our study. Sensitizing concepts provide "a general sense of reference and guidance . . . [and] merely suggest directions along which to look" (Blumer, 1969, p. 148). Teachers ascribed meanings to these concepts and these meanings represent the core of our findings, as presented in this book. Thus, teachers are less likely to be influenced by researchers' preconceived ideas about a topic of study (Bogdan & Biklen, 1982; Glaser, 1978, 1992, 1998; Glaser & Strauss, 1967; Taylor & Bogdan, 1998).

Specifically, we used an open-ended format to investigate the broad question: How do teachers experience significant long-term abuse by school principals? Interviews are required in qualitative research that focuses on the determination of meanings from the participant's perspective (Bogdan & Biklen, 1982;

Glaser, 1978, 1992, 1998; Glaser & Strauss, 1967). Accordingly, we developed an interview guide rather than a predetermined schedule, consisting of a set of topics to be explored, a checklist of sorts relevant to the topic at hand (Lofland, 1971, p. 85; Taylor & Bogdan, 1998).

Between two and four interviews were conducted with each of our research participants; these interviews consisted of unstructured and semistructured questions. To avoid premature theoretical analyses and to produce full descriptions of each teacher's experience of abuse, we used the same initial set of questions with all 50 teachers who participated in this study (Lofland, 1971; Noblit & Hare, 1983). Our initial set of questions included the broad question identified above, followed by additional questions designed to explore basic dimensions of the abuse experience including (1) types of principal behavior and conduct teachers defined as abusive, and (2) the effects of such behavior and conduct on teachers' psychological and emotional well-being, physical and physiological well-being, involvement and performance in the classroom, and involvement and performance in the school. We spent about 135 hours interviewing teachers; this procedure generated about 4000 pages of transcription for analysis.

We discovered that, in conducting in-depth telephone interviews with each participant, we could efficiently and unobtrusively make notes and draw diagrams that identified emergent categories and relationships among categories; we were also able to probe categories in great depth during each interview (Fontana & Frey, 2000). This generated a level of descriptive detail beyond what we had ever achieved in other studies using face-to-face interviews (Fontana & Frey, 2000). Put differently, emergent categories saturated quickly and efficiently.

Given the limitations of using computer software for grounded theory research, especially for conceptual and theoretical work (Charmaz, 2000; Glaser, 1998; Taylor & Bogdan, 1998), we analyzed all of our data line-by-line and by hand. This is consistent with a Blumerian emphasis on meaning in symbolic interaction studies (Charmaz, 2000). This procedure, although very time-consuming, allowed us to keep teachers' perspectives on abuse at the center of our research and to generate robust descriptions of each participant's experience of abuse (Fontana & Frey, 2000). Subsequent interviews with our participants were used to "fill out" emergent categories, clarify areas of ambiguity, and explore relationships between and among emergent categories (Bogdan & Biklen, 1982; Glaser, 1978, 1992, 1998; Strauss & Corbin, 1998; Taylor & Bogdan, 1998).

We also requested personal documents from teachers (e.g., letters, diaries, journal entries) and official documents (e.g., administrators' letters, law briefs, faculty meeting minutes) relevant to their abuse experiences. Personal documents were especially useful in deepening our understanding of the meaning of teachers' abuse experiences (Bogdan & Biklen, 1982; Glaser, 1978, 1992, 1998; Glaser & Strauss, 1967; Taylor & Bogdan, 1998).

As noted above, our primary interest in conducting this study was to describe and conceptualize the teachers' perspectives on reality, that is, the "meanings" teachers associated with being abused by school principals. Thus, the present study conformed to general guidelines for inductive exploratory research that emphasizes meanings as well as descriptive and conceptual results. Constant comparative analysis was used to analyze our data. This approach to analysis requires a comparison of each new incident found in the data to those coded previously for emergent categories and subcategories (Bogdan & Biklen, 1982; Charmaz, 2000; Glaser, 1978, 1992, 1998; Glaser & Strauss, 1967; Lofland, 1971; Strauss & Corbin, 1998; Taylor & Bogdan, 1998).

Specifically, data gathered from each teacher involved in our study were analyzed in terms of five primary codes: (1) abusive principal behavior and conduct, and effects of this conduct on teachers (2) psychologically and emotionally, (3) physically and physiologically, (4) involvement and performance in the classroom, and (5) involvement and performance in the school. We used constant comparative analysis to produce descriptive categories and conceptual and thematic analyses from our data. One of us analyzed the entire data set independently, and the other examined the results of this analysis independently. Both researchers met to resolve questions that arose. Upon completion of numerous cycles of analysis, we also made comparisons with the extant empirical and theoretical literature on workplace abuse as a check on the viability of our descriptive and conceptual findings. However, we made no changes in our analysis at any level as a result of this last procedure. To be sure, careful collection and line-by-line comparative analyses of the data reduce the probability of inappropriate borrowing of concepts from the literature (Charmaz, 2000).

Although interview-based protocols are essential to qualitative studies that focus on meanings (Bogdan & Biklen, 1982; Glaser, 1978, 1992, 1998; Glaser & Strauss, 1967; Strauss & Corbin, 1998; Taylor & Bogdan, 1998), interviewees may present idealized versions of themselves and their situations. To address this and other issues related to trustworthiness and reliability of our findings, we used an inductive-generative approach to data collection and analysis; we used no a priori concepts to control data collection, developed rapport and trust with our participants, conducted multiple interviews with each participant, audiotape recorded and transcribed all interviews, probed for detailed responses, examined data for inconsistencies and contradictions within and between interviews for each participant as well as across participants, compared interview data with available personal and official documents, searched for negative or disconfirming evidence, generated low-inference descriptors, and checked for researcher effects. Finally, as a supplemental validation of our findings, we made comparisons with the existing literature on workplace abuse (Bogdan & Biklen, 1982; Glaser, 1978, 1992, 1998; Glaser & Strauss, 1967; Strauss & Corbin, 1998; Taylor & Bogdan, 1998).

In accordance with guidelines for inductive analyses, all of the categories of findings discussed herein were derived directly from our data. This book focuses on teachers' perspectives of principal abuse and, in particular, principal behavior and conduct and its adverse effects on teachers, teaching, and learning. By and large, our database consists of victimized teachers' experience of abuse. However, at times teachers also discussed the abuse experiences of others in their schools. Occasionally, these data are presented as well. Relevant theoretical and empirical literature are presented throughout this book for interpretive and comparative purposes and for supplemental validation of emergent findings (Bogdan & Biklen, 1982; Charmaz , 2000; Glaser, 1978, 1992, 1998; Strauss & Corbin, 1998; Taylor &

Bogdan, 1998). Additional conceptual and theoretical findings drawn from our database will be presented elsewhere. Due to space limitations, excerpts from the database are presented to illustrate selected ideas.

References

Acton, J. E. E. Dahlberg (Lord). (1948). *Essays on freedom and power*. Boston: Beacon Press.

Adams, A. (1992). Holding out against workplace harassment and bullying. *Personnel Management, 24*(10), 48-53.

Adams, B. P. (1988). *Leader behavior of principals and its effect on teacher burnout*. Unpublished dissertation, University of Wisconsin-Madison.

Adams, G. B., & Balfour, D. L. (1998). *Unmasking administrative evil*. Thousand Oaks, CA: Sage.

Albrecht, J. (1988). Educational leadership: A focus on teacher-student interaction. *NASSP Bulletin, 72*(510), 28-33.

Allcorn, S. (1994). *Anger in the workplace: Understanding the causes of aggression and violence*. Westport, CT: Quorum Books.

American Association of School Administrators. (1976). *AASA Statement of ethics for school administrators and procedural guidelines*. Arlington, VA: Author.

American Psychological Association. (1987). *Diagnostic and statistical manual of mental disorders* (3rd ed.). Washington, DC: Author.

Anderson, L. M., & Pearson, C. M. (1999). Tit for tat? The spiraling effect of incivility in the workforce. *Academy of Management Review, 24*(3), 452-471.

Arbinger Institute. (2000). *Leadership and self-deception: Getting out of the box*. San Francisco: Berrett-Koehler.

Argyris, C. (1982). *Reasoning, learning, and action: Individual and organization*. San Francisco: Jossey-Bass.

Argyris, C. (1990). *Overcoming organizational defenses: Facilitating organizational learning*. Boston: Allyn & Bacon.

Argyris, C. (1994). *On organizational learning*. Malden, MA: Blackwell.

Arthur, W. J. (1992). *The morality of leadership: More than ethics*. New York: Vantage.

Ashforth, B. (1994). Petty tyranny in organizations. *Human Relations, 47*(7), 755-778.

Averill, J. R. (1982). *Anger and aggression: An essay on emotion*. New York: Springer.

Ball, S. J. (1987). *The micropolitics of the school: Towards a theory of school organization*. London: Methuen.

Bandura, A. (1977). Self-efficacy: Toward a theory of behavioral change. *Psychological Review, 84*(2), 191-215.

Bandura, A. (1982). Self-efficacy mechanism in human agency. *American Psychologist, 37*(2), 122-147.

Barnette, J. E. (1990). *The relationship between leadership styles of school principals and teacher stress as perceived by teachers*. Unpublished dissertation, West Virginia University, Morgantown.

Baron, R. A., & Neumann, J. H. (1996). Workplace violence and workplace aggression: Evidence on their relative frequency and potential causes. *Aggressive Behavior, 22*, 161-173.

Baron, R. A., & Neumann, J. H. (1998). Workplace aggression—The iceberg beneath the tip of workplace violence: Evidence on its forms, frequency, and targets. *Public Administration, 21*(4), 446-464.

Barreca, R. (1995). *Sweet revenge*. New York: Harmony Books.

Bartlett, J. (1968). *Familiar quotations* (14th ed.). Boston: Little, Brown.

Bartley, S. H. (1994). Fear. In R. J. Corsini (Ed.), *Encyclopedia of psychology* (Vol. 2, pp. 12-14). New York: Wiley.

Bass, B. M. (1981). *Stogdill's handbook of leadership: A survey of theory and research*. New York: Free Press.

Bassman, E., & London, M. (1993). Abusive managerial behavior. *Leadership & Organizational Development Journal, 14*(2), 18-24.

Bassman, E. S. (1992). *Abuse in the workplace: Management remedies and bottom line impact*. New York: Quorum.

Beale, H. K. (1936). *Are American teachers free? An analysis of restraints upon the freedom of teaching in American schools*. New York: Scribners.

Beatty, B. R. (2000). The emotions of educational leadership: Breaking the silence. *International Journal of Educational Leadership, 3*(4), 331-357.

Beck, L. G. (1994). *Reclaiming educational administration as a caring profession*. New York: Teachers College Press.

Becker, H. S. (1980). *Role and career problems of the Chicago public school teacher*. New York: Arno.

Bennett, M. W., Polden, D. J., & Rubin, H. J. (1998). *Employment relationships: Law and practice*. New York: Aspen Law and Business.

Bies, R. J. (1987). The predicament of injustice: The management of social outrage. In L. L. Cummings & B. M. Staw (Eds.), *Research in organizational behavior* (Vol. 9, pp. 289-320). Greenwich, CT: JAI Press.

Bing, S. (1992). *Crazy bosses: Spotting them, serving them, surviving them*. New York: Morrow.

Björkvist, K., Österman, K., & Hjelt-Bäck, M. (1994). Aggression among university employees. *Aggressive Behavior, 20*, 173-184.

Blase, J. (1984). School principals and teacher stress: A qualitative analysis. *National Forum of Educational Administration and Supervision, 1*(32), 35-43.

Blase, J. (1986). A qualitative analysis of sources of teacher stress: Consequences for performance. *American Educational Research Journal, 23*(1), 13-40.

Blase, J. (1990). Some negative effects of principals' control-oriented and protective political behavior. *American Educational Research Journal, 27*(4), 725-753.

Blase, J. (1991a). The micropolitical orientation of teachers toward closed school principals. *Education and Urban Society, 23*(4), 356-378.

Blase, J. (1991b). *The politics of life in schools: Power, conflict, and cooperation*. Newbury Park, CA: Sage.

Blase, J. (1997). The micropolitics of teaching. In B. J. Biddle et al. (Eds.), *The International handbook of teachers and teaching* (Vol. 2, pp. 939-970). Dordrecht, The Netherlands: Kluwer.

Blase, J., & Anderson, G. L. (1995). *The micropolitics of educational leadership: From control to empowerment*. London: Cassell.

Blase, J., & Blase, J. (1996). Facilitative school leadership and teacher empowerment: Teachers' perspectives. *Social Psychology of Education, 1*(2), 117-145.

Blase, J., & Blase, J. (1998). *Handbook of instructional leadership: How really good principals promote teaching and learning*. Thousand Oaks, CA: Corwin Press.

Blase, J., & Blase, J. (2001). *Empowering teachers* (2nd ed.). Thousand Oaks, CA: Corwin Press.

Blase, J., & Kirby, P. C. (2000). *Bringing out the best in teachers: What effective principals do* (2nd ed.). Thousand Oaks, CA: Corwin Press.

Blase, J., Strathe, M., & Dedrick, C. (1986). Leadership behavior of school principals in relation to teacher stress, satisfaction, and performance. *Journal of Humanistic Education and Development, 24*(4), 159-171.

Blase, J. J. (1988a). The politics of favoritism: A qualitative analysis of the teacher's perspective. *Educational Administration Quarterly, 24*(2), 152-177.

Blase, J. J. (1988b). The teacher's political orientation vis-à-vis the principal: The micropolitics of the school. *Journal of Education Policy,* 3(5), 113-126.

Blase, J. R., & Blase, J. (1995). The micropolitics of successful supervisor-teacher interaction in instructional conferences. In D. Corson (Ed.), *Discourse and power in educational organizations* (pp. 55-70). Cresskill, NJ: Hampton Press.

Blumer, H. (1969). *Symbolic interactionism: Perspective and method*. Englewood Cliffs, NJ: Prentice Hall.

Bogdan, R. C., & Biklen, S. K. (1982). *Qualitative research for education: An introduction to theory and methods* (2nd ed.). Boston: Allyn & Bacon.

Bok, S. (1978). *Lying: Moral choice in public and private life*. New York: Vintage.

Bok, S. (1989). *Secrets: On the ethics of concealment and revelation*. New York: Vintage Books.

Bolman, L., & Deal, T. (1995). *Leading with soul: An uncommon journey of spirit*. San Francisco: Jossey-Bass.

Bolman, L. G., & Deal, T. E. (2000). *Escape from cluelessness: A guide for the organizationally challenged*. New York: AMACOM.

Burns, J. M. (1978). *Leadership*. New York: Harper & Row.

Bush, J. (June 29-July 5, 2000). Is Dan Barton a take change reformer or a boss from hell? Or both? Retrieved June 5, 2002 from http://www.seattleweekly.com/features/0026/news-bush.shtml.

Butler, J. (1996). Professional development: Practice as text, reflection as process, and self as locus. *Australian Journal of Education, 40*(3), 265-283.

Cahn, E. (1949). *The sense of injustice*. New York: New York University Press.

Chaleff, I. (1995). *The courageous follower: Standing up to and for our leaders*. San Francisco: Berrett-Koehler.

Chappell, D., & DiMartino, V. (1998). *Violence at work*. Geneva, Switzerland: International Labor Office.

Charmaz, K. (2000). Grounded theory: Objectivist and constructivist methods. In N. Denzin & Y. Lincoln (Eds.), *Handbook of qualitative research* (2nd ed., pp. 509-535). Thousand Oaks, CA: Sage.

Clarke, E. A., & Kiselica, M. S. (1997). A systematic counseling approach to the problem of bullying. *Elementary School Guidance and Counseling, 31*(4), 310-325.

Cleveland, J. N., & Kerst, M. E. (1993). Sexual harassment and perceptions of power: An under-articulated relationship. *Journal of Vocational Behavior, 42*, 49-67.

Cook, B.W. (1993). *Eleanor Roosevelt, Vol. 1: 1884-1932*. New York: Viking Penguin.

Cropanzano, R. (1993). *Justice in the workplace: Approaching fairness in human resource management*. Hillsdale, NJ: Lawrence Erlbaum.

Davenport, N., Distler-Schwartz, R., & Pursell-Elliott, G. (1999). *Mobbing: Emotional abuse in the American workplace*. Ames, IA: Civil Society.

Davis, S. (1998). Taking aim at effective leadership. *Thrust for Educational Leadership*, *28*(2), 6.

De la Boétie, É. (1975). The politics of obedience: The discourse of voluntary servitude. New York: Free Life Editions.

Dewey, J. (1916). *Democracy and education*. New York: Free Press.

Diehl, D. B. (1993). *The relationship between teachers' coping resources, feelings of stress, and perceptions of the power tactics employed by the administrators.* Unpublished dissertation, Georgia State University, Atlanta.

Doud, J. L., & Keller, E. P. (1998). *A 10-year study of the National Association of Elementary School Principals.* Alexandria, VA: National Association of Elementary School Principals.

Dreeben, R. (1968). *On what is learned in school.* Reading, MA: Addison-Wesley.

Dunham, J. (1984). *Stress in teaching.* London: Croom Helm.

Dworkin, A. G., Haney, C. A., Dworkin, R. J., & Telschow, R. L. (1990). Stress and illness behavior among urban public school teachers. *Education Administration Quarterly, 26*(1), 60-72.

Einarsen, S., & Skogstad, A. (1996). Bullying at work: Epidemiological findings in public and private organizations. *European Journal of Work and Organizational Psychology, 5*(2), 185-201.

Ekman, P., & Friesen, W. V. (1975). *Unmasking the face: A guide to recognizing emotions from facial cues.* Englewood Cliffs, NJ: Prentice Hall.

Emmons, R. A. (1999). *The psychology of ultimate concerns: Motivation and spirituality in personality.* New York: Guilford.

Enomoto, E. K. (1997). Negotiating the ethics of care and justice. *Educational Administration Quarterly, 33*(3), 351-370.

Epstein, S. (1972). The nature of anxiety with emphasis upon its relationship to expectancy. In C. D. Spielberger (Ed.), *Anxiety: Current trends in theory and research* (Vol. 2). New York: Academic Press.

Evans, R. (1996). *The human side of school change.* San Francisco: Jossey-Bass.

Farber, B. A. (1991). *Crisis in education: Stress and burnout in the American teacher.* San Francisco: Jossey-Bass.

Field, T. (1996). *Bully in sight: How to predict, resist, challenge, and combat workplace bullying.* Wantage, Oxfordshire: Wessex.

Fitzgerald, L. F., & Shullman, S. L. (1993). Sexual harassment: A research analysis and agenda for the 1990s. *Journal of Vocational Behavior, 42*, 5-27.

Folger, R. (1993). Reactions to mistreatment at work. In J. K. Murningham (Ed.), *Social psychology in organizations: Advances in theory and research* (pp. 161-183). Englewood Cliffs, NJ: Prentice Hall.

Fontana, A., & Frey, J. H. (1994). Interviewing: The art of science. In N. Denzin & Y. Lincoln (Eds.), *Handbook of qualitative research* (pp. 361-376). Thousand Oaks, CA: Sage.

Fontana, A., & Frey, J. H. (2000). The interview: From structured questions to negotiated text. In N. Denzin & Y. Lincoln (Eds.), *Handbook of qualitative research* (2nd ed., pp. 645-672). Thousand Oaks, CA: Sage.

Ford, C. V. (1996). *Lies! Lies!! Lies!!!: The psychology of deceit.* Washington, DC: American Psychiatric Press.

Foster, W. (1986). *Paradigms and promises: New approaches to educational administration.* Buffalo, NY: Prometheus.

Frankel, V., & Tien, E. (1996). *The I hate my job handbook: How to deal with hell at work.* New York: Fawcett Columbine.

Fried, S., & Fried, P. (1996). *Bullies and victims: Helping your child survive the schoolyard battlefield.* New York: M. Evans.

Friedkin, N. E., & Slater, M. R. (1994, April). School leadership and performance: A social network approach. *Sociology of Education, 67,* 139-157.

Fromm, E. (1947). *Man for himself: An inquiry into the psychology of ethics.* New York: Holt, Rinehart & Winston.

Fromm, E. (1964). *The heart of man: Its genius for good and evil.* New York: Harper & Row.

Fromm, E. (1973). *The anatomy of human destructiveness.* New York: Holt, Rinehart & Winston.

Gardner, J. W. (1990). *On leadership.* New York: Free Press.

Geery, D. (2001). How the Idaho and National Education Associations behave when you need them most: A true horror story from an elementary teacher. Retrieved from http://www.users.qwest.net/~gdaniel6587/neasite.html.

Gelernter, D. H. (1994). *The muse in the machine: Computerizing the poetry of human thought.* New York: Free Press.

Gibb, C. (1954). Leadership. In G. Lindzey (Ed.), *Handbook of social psychology* (Vol. 1, pp. 877-920). Worchester, MA: University Press.

Gibb, C. A. (1968). Leadership. In G. Lindzey & E. Aronson (Eds.), *Handbook of social psychology* (2nd ed., Vol. 4, pp. 205-282). Reading, MA: Addison-Wesley.

Ginsberg, R., & Davies, T. (2001, April). *The emotional side of leadership.* Paper presented at the annual meeting of the American Educational Research Association, Seattle.

Glaser, B. G., & Strauss, A. L. (1967). *The discovery of grounded theory: Strategies for qualitative research.* Chicago: Aldine.

Glaser, B. G. (1978). *Theoretical sensitivity: Advances in the methodology of grounded theory.* Mill Valley, CA: Sociology Press.

Glaser, B. G. (1992). *Emergence vs. forcing: Basics of grounded theory.* Mill Valley, CA: Sociology Press.

Glaser, B. G. (1998). *Doing grounded theory: Issues and discussions.* Mill Valley, CA: Sociology Press.

Glazer, M. P., & Glazer, P. M. (1989). *The whistleblowers: Exposing corruption in government and industry.* New York: Basic Books.

Glickman, C. D., Gordon, S. P., & Ross-Gordon, J. M. (2001). *Supervision and instructional leadership: A developmental approach.* Needham Heights, MA: Allyn & Bacon.

Greiner, L. E., & Schein, V. E. (1988). *Power and organizational development: Mobilizing power to implement change.* Reading, MA: Addison-Wesley.

Gunn, J. A., & Holdaway, E. A. (1986). Perceptions of effectiveness, influence, and satisfaction of senior high school principals. *Education Administration Quarterly, 22*(2), 43-62.

Heck, R., & Hallinger, P. (1999). Next generation methods for the study of leadership and school improvement. In J. Murphy & K. Seashore Louis (Eds.), *Handbook of research on educational administration.* San Francisco: Jossey-Bass.

High, R., & Achilles, C. (1986). An analysis of influence-gaining behaviors of principals in schools of varying levels of instructional effectiveness. *Education Administration Quarterly, 22*(1), 111-119.

Hodgkinson, C. (1991). *Educational leadership: The moral art.* Albany: State University of New York Press.

Hornstein, H. A. (1996). *Brutal bosses and their prey.* New York: Riverhead Books.

Izard, C. (1977). *Human emotions.* New York: Plenum.

Izard, C. E., & Youngstrom, E. A. (1996). The activation and regulation of fear and anxiety. In R. A. Dienstbier & D. A. Hope (Eds.), *Perspectives on anxiety, panic, and fear* (pp. 1-59). Lincoln: University of Nebraska Press.

Katz, F. E. (1993). *Ordinary people and extraordinary evil: A report on the beguilings of evil*. Albany: State University of New York.

Katz, M. S., Noddings, N., & Strike, K. A. (Eds.). (1999). *Justice and caring: The search for common ground in education*. New York: Teachers College Press.

Keashly, L. (1998). Emotional abuse in the workplace: Conceptual and empirical issues. *Journal of Emotional Abuse, 1*(1), 85-117.

Keashly, L., Trott, V., & MacLean, L. M. (1994). Abusive behavior in the workplace: A preliminary investigation. *Violence and Victims, 9*(4), 341-357.

Kelley, R. E. (1992). *The power of followership: How to create leaders people want to follow and followers who lead themselves*. New York: Doubleday Currency.

Kets de Vries, M. F. R. (1989). *Prisoners of leadership*. New York: Wiley.

Kiger, P. J. (2001, May). Truth and consequences. *Working Woman*, pp. 57-64.

King, P. (1987). *Never work for a jerk!* New York: F. Watts.

Kipling, R. (1895/1983). *The second jungle book*. London: Macmillan.

Kipnis, D. (1972). Does power corrupt? *Journal of Personality and Social Psychology, 24*(1), 33-41.

Knights, D., & Willmott, H. (Eds.). (1985). *Job redesign: Critical perspectives on the labor process*. Brookfield, VT: Gower.

Kreisberg, S. (1992). *Transforming power: Domination, empowerment, and education*. Albany: State University of New York Press.

Krug, S. E., Ahadi, S. A., & Scott, S. K. (1991). Current issues and research findings in the study of school leadership. In P. Thurston & P. Zodhiates (Eds.), *Advances in educational administration: Vol. 2. School leadership* (pp. 241-260). Greenwich, CT: JAI Press.

Ladson-Billings, G. (2001). *Crossing over to Canaan: The journey of new teachers in diverse classrooms*. San Francisco: Jossey-Bass.

Lee, B. (1997). *The power principle*. New York: Simon & Schuster.

Leithwood, K., Jantzi, D., Ryan, S., & Steinbach, R. (1997, March). *Distributed leadership in secondary schools*. Paper presented at the annual meeting of the American Educational Research Association, Chicago.

Leithwood, K., Thomlinson, D., & Genge, M. (1996). Transformational school leadership. In K. Leithwood, J. Chapman, D. Corson, P. Hallinger, & A. Hart (Eds.), *International handbook of educational leadership and administration* (pp. 785-840). Dordrecht, The Netherlands: Kluwer.

Levenson, R. W. (1992). Autonomic nervous system differences among emotions. *Psychological Science, 3*, 23-27.

Levinson, H. (1968). *The exceptional executive: A psychological conception*. Cambridge, MA: Harvard University Press.

Lewis, M., & Saarni, C. (Eds.). (1993). *Lying and deception in everyday life*. New York: Guilford Press.

Leymann, H. (1990). Mobbing and psychological terror at workplaces. *Violence and Victims, 5*(2), 119-126.

Leymann, H. (1993). *Mobbing* (N. Davenport, Trans.). Hamburg: Rowohlt Taschenbuch Verlag GmbH.

Lofland, J. (1971). *Analyzing social settings*. Belmont, CA: Wadsworth.

Lombardo, M. M., & McCall, Jr., M. W. (1984, January). Dealing with the intolerable boss. *Psychology Today, 9*(1), 44-48.

Lundin, W., & Lundin, K. (1995). *Working with difficult people*. New York: AMACOM.

Ma, Xin (2001). Bullying and being bullied: To what extent are bullies also victims? *American Education Research Journal, 38*(2), 351-370.

Malen, B., & Ogawa, R. (1988). Professional-patron influence on site-based governance councils: A confounding case study. *Educational Evaluation and Policy Analysis, 10*(4), 251-270.

Marks, I. M. (1978). *Living with fear: Understanding and coping with anxiety*. New York: McGraw-Hill.

Martin, J. (1986a). The tolerance of injustice. In J. M. Olsen, C. P. Herman, & M. P. Zanna (Eds.), *Relative deprivation and social comparison: The Ontario symposium* (Vol. 4, pp. 217-242). Hillsdale, NJ: Lawrence Erlbaum.

Martin, J. (1986b). When expectations and justice do not collide: Blue-collar visions of a just world. In H. W. Bierhoff, R. L. Cohen, & J. Greenberg (Eds.), *Justice in social relations* (pp. 317-335). New York: Plenum.

May, R. (1972). *Power and innocence*. New York: Norton.

McNeil, L. M. (1986). *Contradictions of control: School structure and school knowledge*. London: Routledge.

Mead, G. H. (1934). *Mind, self, and society*. Chicago: University of Chicago Press.

Meltzer, B. N., Petras, J. W., & Reynolds, L. T. (1975). *Symbolic interactionism: Genesis, varieties and criticism*. London: Routledge and Kegan Paul.

Morse, J. M. (1991). *Qualitative nursing research: A contemporary dialogue*. Newbury Park, CA: Sage.

Murphy, J., & Louis, K. S. (1994a). *Reshaping the principalship: Insights from transformational reform efforts*. Thousand Oaks, CA: Corwin Press.

Murphy, J., & Louis, K. S. (1994b). Transformational change and the evolving role of the principal: Early empirical evidence. In J. Murphy & L. G. Beck (Eds.), *Reshaping the principalship: Insights from transformational reform efforts* (pp. 20-53). Thousand Oaks, CA: Corwin Press.

Muth, R. (1989). Toward an integrative theory of power and educational organizations. *Educational Administration Quarterly, 20*(2), 25-42.

Namie, G. (2000). *U.S. hostile workplace survey 2000*. Benicia, CA: Campaign Against Workplace Bullying.

Namie, G., & Namie, R. (1999). *Bully proof yourself at work!* Benicia, CA: Campaign Against Workplace Bullying.

Namie, G., & Namie, R. (2000a). *The bully at work: What you can do to stop the hurt and reclaim your dignity on the job*. Naperville, IL: Sourcebooks.

Namie, G., & Namie, R. (2000b). *Domestic violence—Part 1: Employers' discovery*. Benicia, CA: Campaign Against Workplace Bullying.

Namie, G., & Namie, R. (2001). *The bullybusters: Advice from veterans of the bullying wars*. Retrieved from http://www.bullybusters.org.

Neuman, J. H., & Baron, R. A. (1998). Workplace violence and workplace aggression: Evidence concerning specific forms, potential causes, and preferred targets. *Journal of Management, 24*(3), 391-419.

Newman, J. (1999, July). The worst boss I ever had, *Mademoiselle, 7*, 98.

Northwestern National Life Insurance Company. (1993). *Fear and violence in the workplace*. Minneapolis, MN: Author.

Noblit, G. W., & Hare, R. D. (1983, April). *Meta-ethnography: Issues in the synthesis and replication of qualitative research*. Paper presented at the annual meeting of the American Educational Research Association, Montreal.

Noddings, N. (1992). *The challenge to care in schools: An alternative approach to education*. New York: Teachers College Press.

Nyberg, D. (1981). *Power over power: What power means in ordinary life, how it is related to acting freely, and what it can do to contribute to a renovated ethics of education*. Ithaca, NY: Cornell University Press.

Nyberg, D. (1993). *The varnished truth: Truth telling and deceiving in ordinary life*. Chicago: The University of Chicago Press.

Ogawa, R., & Bossert, S. (1995). Leadership as an organizational quality. *Educational Administration, 31*(2), 224-238.

Olson, L. (1999, March). Demands for principals growing but candidates aren't applying. *Education Week, 18*(20), 20.

Olweus, D. (1993). *Bullying at school: What we know and what we can do*. Oxford, England: Blackwell.

Ornstein, R. E., & Swencionis, C. (Eds.). (1990). *Healing brain: A scientific reader*. New York: Guilford.

Ott, J. S., & Russell, E. W. (2000). *Introduction to public administration: A book of readings*. New York: Longman.

Pearson, C. (2000). *Workplace "incivility" study*. Chapel Hill: University of North Carolina.

Peck, M. S. (1983). *People of the lie: The hope for healing human evil*. New York: Simon & Shuster.

Pfaffenbach, W. L. (2000, November 27). Verdict for workplace "bullying" is upheld: Bias claim falls, but plaintiff gets $730K. *Massachusetts Lawyers Weekly, 29*, 731. Retrieved from http://bullybusters.org/home/twd/bb/legal/masslaw.html.

Pfeffer, J. (1992). *Managing with power: Politics and influence in organizations*. Boston: Harvard Business School Press.

Phillips, B. N. (1993). *Educational and psychological perspectives on stress in students, teachers, and parents*. Brandon, VT: Clinical Psychology.

Price Spratlen, L. (1995). Interpersonal conflict which includes mistreatment in a university workplace. *Violence and Victims, 10*(4), 285-297.

Rachman, S. J. (1990). *Fear and courage* (2nd ed.). New York: W.H. Freeman.

Rayner, C. (1998). *Bullying at work*. Stoke-on-Kent, UK: Staffordshire University Business School.

Reitzug, U. C., & Cross, B. E. (1994, April). *A multi-site study of site-based management in urban schools*. Paper presented at the annual meeting of the American Educational Research Association, New Orleans.

Riehl, C., & Lee, V. E. (1996). Gender, organizations, and leadership. In K. Leithwood, J. Chapman, D. Corson, P. Hallinger, & A. Hart (Eds.), *International handbook of educational leadership and administration* (pp. 873-920). Dordrecht, The Netherlands: Kluwer.

Riskind, J. H. (1997). Looming vulnerability to threat: A cognitive paradigm for anxiety. *Behaviour Research & Therapy, 35*(8), 685-702.

Robinson, S. L., & Bennett, R. J. (1995). A typology of deviant workplace behaviors: A multidimensional scaling study. *Academy of Management Journal, 38*(2), 555-572.

Rokeach, M. (1956). Political and religious dogmatism: An alternative to the authoritarian personality. *Psychological Monographs: General and Applied, 70*(18), 1-43.

Rusch, E. A. (1999). The experience of the piñata: Vexing problems. In F. K. Kochan, B. L. Jackson, & D. L. Duke (Eds.), *A thousand voices from the firing line: A study of educational leaders, their jobs, their preparation, and the problems they face*, (pp. 29-43). Columbia, MO: University Council for Educational Administration.

Russell, B. (1938). *Power: A new social analysis*. New York: Norton.

Ryan, K. D., & Oestreich, D. K. (1991). *Driving fear out of the workplace: How to overcome the invisible barriers to quality, productivity, and innovation*. San Francisco: Jossey-Bass.

Ryan, K. D., Oestreich, D. K, & Orr III, G. A. (1996). *The courageous messenger: How to successfully speak up at work*. San Francisco: Jossey-Bass.

Sampson, R. V. (1965). *The psychology of power*. New York: Pantheon.

Sartwell, M. (1994). *Bosses from hell: True tales from the trenches*. New York: Plume.

Schwandt, T. A. (1994). Constructivist, interpretivist approaches to human inquiry. In N. Denzin & Y. S. Lincoln (Eds.), *Handbook of qualitative research*. Thousand Oaks, CA: Sage.

Scott, J. C. (1990). *Domination and the arts of resistance: Hidden transcripts*. New Haven, CT: Yale University Press.

Scott, M. J., & Strandling, S. G. (1994). Post-traumatic stress disorder without the trauma. *British Journal of Clinical Psychology*, *33*, 71-74.

Shakeshaft, C., & Cohan, A. (1995). Sexual abuse of students by school personnel. *Phi Delta Kappan, 76*(2), 512-520.

Shakeshaft, C., Mandel, L., Johnson, Y. M., Sawyer, J., Hergenrother, M. A., & Barber, E. (1997). Boys call me cow. *Educational Leadership, 55*(2), 22-25.

Sheppard, B. H., & Lewicki, R. J. (1987). Toward general principles of managerial fairness. *Social Justice Research, 1*(2), 161-177.

Silverman, D. (2000). Analyzing talk and text. In N. Denzin & Y. Lincoln (Eds.), *Handbook of qualitative research* (2nd ed., pp. 821-834). Thousand Oaks, CA: Sage.

Sizer, T. R. (1996). *Horace's hope: What works for the American high school*. Boston: Houghton Mifflin.

Sorokin, P., & Lunden, W. (1959). *Power and morality: Who shall guard the guardians?* Boston: Porter Sargent.

Starratt, R. J. (1991). Building an ethical school: A theory for practice in educational leadership. *Educational Administration Quarterly, 27*(2), 185-202.

Steinberg, J. (1999, November 14). Federal funds for teachers reveal surprising hurdles. *New York Times*, p. 18.

Strauss, A. L., & Corbin, J. (1998). *Basics of qualitative research: Techniques and procedures for developing grounded theory* (2nd. ed.). Thousand Oaks, CA: Sage.

Swedish National Board of Occupational Safety and Health. (1993). *Statute book*, Ordinance (AFS 1993: 17), Sections 1 & 6 Stockholm.

Taylor, S. J., & Bogdan, R. (1998). *Introduction to qualitative research methods: A guidebook and resource* (3rd ed.). New York: Wiley.

Tesch, R. (1988, April). *The contribution of a qualitative method: Phenomenological research*. Paper presented at the annual meeting of the American Educational Research Association, New Orleans.

Tharp, R. G., & Gallimore, R. (1988). *Rousing minds to life*. New York: Cambridge University Press.

Toch, H. (1984). *Violent men*. Cambridge, MA: Schenkman.

Tolkien, J. R. R. (2001). *The lord of the rings*. Boston: Houghton Mifflin.

Tomkins, S. S. (1962). *Affect, imagery, consciousness. Volume 2: The negative affects*. New York: Springer.

Tyler, R. (1949). *Basic principles of curriculum and instruction*. Chicago: University of Chicago Press.

Vygotsky, L. S. (1978). *Mind in society: The development of higher psychological processes*. Cambridge, MA: Harvard University Press.

Webster's book of quotations. (1992). New York: PMC.

White, R. K., & Lippitt, R. (1960). *Autocracy and democracy: An experimental inquiry.* New York: Harper & Brothers.

Whyte, D. (1994). *The heart aroused: Poetry and the preservation of the soul in corporate America.* New York: Currency Doubleday.

Winter, D. G. (1973). *The power motive.* New York: Free Press.

Wyatt, J., & Hare, C. (1997). *Work abuse: How to recognize and survive it.* Rochester, VT: Schenkman Books.

Yamada, D. C. (2000). The phenomenon of 'workplace bullying' and the need for status-blind hostile work environment protection. *Georgetown Law Journal, 88*(3), 475-536.

Yukl, G. A. (2001). Leadership in organizations (5th ed.). Upper Saddle River, NJ: Prentice Hall.

Index